I0091110

THE HISTORY AND CONSERVATION OF MAMMALS IN MALAWI

BRIAN MORRIS

To the memory of a friend and a pioneer wildlife conservationist
G.D. Hayes (1904 -1981)

The History and Conservation of Mammals in Malawi
Copyright © Brian Morris 2006

All rights reserved. No part of this publication may be reproduced, stored in a retrieval system, or transmitted in any form or by any means, electronic, mechanical, photocopying, recording or otherwise, without prior permission of the publishers.

ISBN: 99908-76-69-X
ISBN-13: 978-99908-76-69-7

This book is part of Kachere Series which offers a wide range of books on religion, culture and society in Malawi.

Kachere Monographs no. 21

Published by
Kachere Series
P.O. Box 1037, Zomba, Malawi

The Kachere Series is represented outside Africa by:
African Books Collective Oxford (orders@africanbookscollective.com)
Michigan State University Press East Lansing (msupress@msu.edu)

Layout and cover design by:
Davie Sapuwa

CONTENTS

PREFACE

I first came to Malawi in February 1958, sitting with my rucksack on the back of a pick-up truck as it passed through the Fort Manning (Mchinji) customs post. I had spent the previous four months hitch-hiking around Southern and Central Africa, mostly sleeping rough. During that time I encountered no other hitch-hiker, and very few tarred roads, and the only place I met tourists was at the Victoria Falls. I was, however, so attracted to Malawi and its people that I decided to give up my nomadic existence. I was fortunate to find a job working as a tea planter for Blantyre and East Africa Ltd, an old company founded by Hynde and Stark around the turn of the century. I spent over seven years working as a tea planter in the Thyolo (Zoa) and Mulanje (Limbuli) districts, and spent much of my spare time engaged in natural history pursuits - my primary interests being small mammals (especially mice) and epiphytic orchids. The first article I ever published was based on my spare-time activities at Zoa, where I spent many hours with local people digging up mice. It was entitled 'Denizen of the Evergreen Forest' (1962), and recorded the ecology and behaviour of the rather rare pouched mouse *Beamys hindei*.

Since those days I have regularly returned to Malawi to undertake ethno-biological studies. I thus have a life-long interest in Malawi - in its history, in the culture of its people, and in its fauna and flora. Some of my most memorable life experiences have been in Malawi, and many of my closest and cherished friendships have been with Malawians, or with 'expatriates' who have spent their lives in Malawi. Altogether, I have spent over ten years of my life in Malawi, and apart from Chitipa and Karonga, I have visited and spent time in every part of the country, having climbed or explored almost every hill or mountain - usually with a Malawian as a companion, and looking for birds, mammals, medicines, epiphytic orchids or fungi, whichever was my current interest.

The present study is specifically based on ethno-zoological researches undertaken in 1990-1991, which were supported with a grant from the Nuffield Foundation. For this support I am grateful.

I should like to thank, with respect to this present study, many friends and colleagues who have given me valuable data, encouragement, support and hospitality over the past thirty years. In particular I should like to sincerely thank the late Derrick Arnall, Father Claude Boucher, Wyson Bowa,

Carl Bruessow and Gillian Knox, Shaya Bushman, Salimu Chinyangala, Janet and Les Doran, Jafali Dzomba, Efe Ncherawata, Cornell Dudley, the late Cynthia and Eric Emtage, Peter and Suzie Forster, Jillian Hugo, Vera and the late Rev Peter Garland, the late Paul Kotokwa, Frank and Iono Kippax, John and Anne Killick, Heronimo Luke, Useni Lifa, Kitty Kunamano and her daughters, John Kajalwiche and his sister Evenesi Maluwa, Catherine Mandelurnbe, Ganda Makalani, Late Malemia and her family, Bob and Claire Medland, Davison Potani, Kings Phiri, Lackson Ndalama, Hassan Patel and his family, the late Pritam Rattan, Pat Royle, the late Lady Margaret Roseveare, Brian and Anne Sherry, Chenita Suleman and her family, Patrick and Poppit Rogers, Francis and Annabel Shaxson, Chijonjazi 'Muzimu' Shumbe, Lance Tickell, Catherine and Stephen Temple, Samson Waiti, George and Helen Welsh, June and the late Brian Walker, John and Fumiyo Wilson, and the late Jessie Williamson.

I should also like to thank those who generously gave me institutional support: the Centre for Social Research, University of Malawi (the late Wycliffe Chilowa); the National Archives of Malawi (Frances Kachala); Matthew Matemba and many members of the Department of National Parks and Wildlife; and M.G. Kumwenda and George Sembereka of the National Museums of Malawi.

Finally, I much appreciate the support of Dr Martin Ott in kindly seeing the book through to publication. The Wildlife and Environmental Society of Malawi and the Danish Hunters Association generously contributed towards the printing costs.

Brian Morris
1 December 2005

INTRODUCTION

Until comparatively recently neither philosophers, nor anthropologists, nor social historians expressed much interest in mammalian life. Apart from some notable exceptions, human life in Africa was thus discussed with hardly any reference to wild animals. Historians and ethnographers of Malawi tended therefore to bypass the importance of hunting in the social life of Malawians, and to downplay the crucial role that the ivory trade played in the economic life and politics of the pre-colonial period. In contrast, this present study examines, from a historical perspective, the relationship between humans and mammals in Malawi.

It consists of three parts. In the first chapter, I examine the history of Malawi: Batwa hunter-gatherers, the early stone-age culture, and the rise of political chiefdoms in the pre-colonial period - specifically examining the place of mammals during Malawi's early history. I explore the crucial role that elephant hunting and the ivory trade played in the politics of Malawi from the 16th to the 19th century. I conclude the chapter by examining the social impact that rinderpest and tsetse fly had on the relationship between Malawians and their environment during the early colonial period.

In the second chapter, I describe the Malawian landscape, focusing on the five major bioregions, and on the history of the mammals in these locales. I outline specifically the history of the various wildlife sanctuaries that were established in Malawi, and the mammals associated with them.

In chapter three, I give a short history of wildlife conservation in Malawi - the social impact of the colonial game laws, the early measures taken to protect and conserve the larger fauna, the history of the Nyasaland Fauna Preservation Society (NFPS) and the development of wildlife conservation programmes and environmental education during the post-colonial years. I conclude the chapter by discussing contemporary issues and perspectives on wildlife conservation.

This present book complements my other studies, *The Power of Animals* (1998) and *Animals and Ancestors* (2000) which take an anthropological perspective, and examine the role of mammals in Malawi cultural life.

CHAPTER ONE

HISTORICAL PERSPECTIVES

THE AKAFULA:
THE ORIGINAL INHABITANTS OF MALAWI

The earliest inhabitants of Malawi were not Bantu people. In oral traditions they are usually described as Batwa or Akafula. The stem -twa,
Alan Barnard suggests, essentially means small or diminutive (person),
and it is widely used by people in Southern Africa, such as the Zulu, to
describe the Bushmen - Khoisan people. The term used by the Tswana
and Sotho to describe the Bushman is Masarwa, the suffix -rwa having the
same meaning: small (Barnard 1992: 85). The term *akafula* probably
derives from the root *ku-fula*, one of its meanings being 'to dig'; thus, with
ka- also indicating the diminutive, the word essentially denotes a 'small
digger', i.e. someone who forages for roots. The activity of bushpig in digging up roots is commonly described by the verb *ku-fula* (see Nurse 1967
on the term *akafula*).

Throughout Malawi there are legends and oral traditions relating to
these earliest inhabitants. At the end of the 19th century Harry Johnston
recorded an 'ancient tradition' which suggested that until recently
Bushmen still lived on Mulanje Plateau. The Mang'anja of the district
assert, he writes, that there used to live on the upper part of the mountain
'a dwarf race of light yellow complexion with their hair growing in scattered tufts, and with (the) large development of the buttocks.' They gave
these people the specific name Arungu, which, as the term means 'gods',
i.e. spirits, signified to Johnston that these legends were untrustworthy
(1897: 53).

In his *Mbiri ya Achewa* (1949)/*History of the Chewa* (1973) Samuel
Ntara has an account of the Batwa, based on oral traditions of the Chewa,
although it is worth noting that there are wide variations in the content of
the Chewa text of 1949 (Phunziro 26) and the later English translation of
the 1965 edition. Ntara suggests that the name Batwa is derived from the

3

habit of these people of hiding (*tabisala*) like head lice (*nsabwe*), and that they were called Akafula because they dug their houses (*nyumba*) in the ground like a cave (*phanga*), although they also used leaves (*masamba*). But their other name was Amwandionerapati, which literally translates as the question 'from which distance did you see me?' When you met these people, Ntara writes, they would ask you, 'Where did you see me?'. If you replied that you had seen them from afar, they would be happy, as it was considered insulting (*chipongwe*) to refer to their small stature (*afupi misinkhu*). This name Amwandionerapati (or Kuti) and the above dialogue is commonly recalled in conversations throughout Malawi, and some people I knew well suggested to me that they knew people who had actually seen the Batwa when out hunting in the hill forests of Mulanje and Michesi,

Akafula
Chamare Museum, KuNgoni Art Craft Centre, Mua by Fr Claude Boucher Chisale

which are particularly associated with the legendary hunter-gatherers. Other oral traditions confirm Ntara's writings, with the implication that if you gave the wrong answer then you would be speared by these people, who had a reputation of being very fierce and quick-tempered (Stannus 1922: 318, Sanderson 1954: 194, under the synonym Namlukuwewe, Department of Antiquities: Oral Records 1971/zB 3/1, MJ 6/3).

The habits (*makhalidwe*) of the Batwa, as recorded by Ntara, suggest that they had their own language and customs, and were very keen hunters. Their main food was meat (*nyama*) which they cooked in a pit (*dzenje*), but some ate the meat raw (*mwinanso akadya nyama yaiwisi*). They also ate roots, and had smelters to forge iron, (*analindi Ng'anjo ndipo akasula zitsulo*) which was used to make arrows (*mibvi*) and spears (*mikhondo*) used to kill elephants (*akaphera njobvu*). They also ate many fruits such as bananas (*nthochi*) and *mteme* (*Strychnous spinosa*). Ntara records that the Batwa were greatly feared by the Chewa, for they were accurate in shooting arrows, and they possessed arrow poison (*inali yaulembe*). There was much conflict between the Batwa and the early Kalonga kingdom (Ntara 1949: 92-93, 1973: 99).

Oral traditions associate the Batwa with forested mountains like Mulanje, and they are usually regarded as spirits that live on the mountains (*mizimu yokhala m'mapiri*), and as being particularly linked to hunting pursuits. While out hunting game with a dog you may well hear the Batwa, one woman in Zomba recalled, call out, 'You, leave our animals alone' ('*inu, siyani nyama zathu'zo*'). But you will not see the Batwa, and if you do not heed their words, you will not get any game, or you may even get lost completely on the mountain.

On Michesi or Machemba Hill near Phalombe, people often talk about the Batwa, although it is often difficult to distinguish in conversation whether they are speaking of the Batwa themselves, or the spirits of the Batwa, or whether it is the spirits of the dead (*mizimu*) taking the form of these primal hunter-gatherers. Voices may be heard, but woe betide anyone who looks around - an act that is reputed to be fatal. The Batwa are particularly associated with the wild plantains that grow in the riparian gullies, and on Mulanje and neighbouring hills they are said to leave food for people. It is not recommended to ignore these offerings. The small beings or 'hobgoblins' referred to as *chiruwe* and *chitowe* which are associated with hill forests, and indicate to people the whereabouts of game or medicinal plants, are possibly synonyms of Batwa (Stannus 1922: 318, Scott 1929: 82, Sanderson 1954: 61).

In the early 1950s the amateur cultural historian W.H.J. Rangeley travelled widely in Malawi collecting oral traditions relating to the early inhabitants of the country, as well as searching out painted rock shelters in the Mzimba district. His article relating to the Akafula was published posthumously (1963). What emerged from Rangeley's researches was the following:

The Akafula/Batwa were a hunting and gathering people who practised no agriculture, and used spears and poisoned arrows to obtain game. This poison was extremely virulent, and Bantu peoples were said to have learnt the use of these poisons from the Akafula. Although essentially nomadic, these foraging people built circular beehive huts, which were plastered with wet clay and then burnt. Thus the hut itself was like a kiln. All the traditions suggest that the Akafula were skilled iron-workers making spears, arrows and a long broad-bladed knife (*mkalamanja*: sits in the hand). Short in stature, the Akafula were said to have long beards, and to have a fierce disposition. Rangeley suggests that the Akafula were distinct from the Amwandionerapati (Kuti), the latter being no more than the gnomes and pixies of popular legend throughout the world. He also emphasizes his feeling that the Akafula were not Khoisan people - for they were an 'iron-age' people; nor were they associated with the schematic paintings found on rock shelters throughout Malawi. Rangeley held that such rock paintings were made by 'stone-age' people who possessed a microlithic culture. He wrote to the archaeologist J. Desmond Clarke, 'There is absolutely no evidence that the Akafula painted in Nyasaland' (28 March 1950). Thus he suggested that the Akafula, a 'skilled iron-age people', had supplanted the earlier 'stone-age' people who had painted the rock shelters. From my own experiences in visiting painted rock shelters in the Mulanje, Blantyre, Zomba and Dedza districts, not only do local people have little interest in these paintings, and often do not know their whereabouts (even when close to their own villages), but they always affirm that they do not know who painted the rock shelters long ago. Yet the same people are very forthcoming about the Akafula or Batwa. There seems, then, to be no direct link between the traditions of the Akafula hunter-gatherers and the painted rock shelters.

This was earlier confirmed by Margaret Metcalfe, who under the penname Geraldine Elliot wrote the famous animal stories, who wrote a pioneering article on the rock paintings of Malawi (1956). She wrote to Rangeley (24 May 1952) that the people considered the rock paintings to be very old, that they were made by 'spirits', and that they were there when the Chewa arrived in the country. No 'connection' was ever made between the rock paintings and the Akafula, the "little people". The suggestion in a recent film on Malawian art that the Batwa lived in these rock shelters and painted on their walls is certainly invalid. Had they done so, the paintings would soon have been obliterated. The rock shelters were probably ritual sites not places where they lived. Sadly, such rock shelters in the Zomba and Dedza districts that have been used by local hunters have had their paintings badly disfigured by the smoke.

Equally important in the oral traditions is the existence of another legendary people, the Akatanga or Alenda. These were tall people, with a pastoral economy. They lived in villages, and were also celebrated elephant hunters. Tradition held that there was continuous conflict between the Akafula and these pastoral people, as well as between the Akafula and the incoming Maravi people. The Akafula were driven south and eventually exterminated, although Rangeley believes that they may have still survived in the more remote parts of Malawi until the beginning of the 19th century (Rangeley 1963, Rangeley papers, correspondence 1/1/1). Although Rangeley was adamant that the Akafula were not 'bushmen', i.e. Khoisan speakers, and Alan Barnard is skeptical of any accounts of Khoisan people north of the Zambezi - at least in recent times (but there are coexisting Khoisan speakers in Tanzania) - G.T. Nurse has offered evidence, from linguistics, that the Akafula may have been Khoisan-speakers. He points to the linguistic affinities between Nyanja ideophones, the emphatic interjections recorded by Clement Scott (1929) - suffixes such as *ba!* (full) and *cho!* (to stand up) - and words used by the L'auni, the Southern bushmen (see Nurse 1968, Barnard 1992: 88-90).

It is also worth noting that David Phillipson (1976: 186) has suggested that the red schematic 'paintings' found throughout Malawi and Eastern Zambia, were the work of food-producing early iron-age people, who were contemporaries of the 'stone-age' people who painted the naturalistic paintings of the Bushman (Khoisan)-type. I will discuss the significance of the rock paintings elsewhere (Morris 2002), but suffice to say here that oral traditions suggest a pre-Bantu people who were small and bearded, and who, though hunter-gatherers, were also iron-smelters making their own arrow-heads, knives and spears. These Akafula are not explicitly associated with the red schematic rock paintings. The popular writer Oliver Ransford suggests that the Batwa, whom he describes as a 'race of little half-breeds', are the outcome of a 'short-lived truce' between the original Bushmen inhabitants of Malawi, and the invading Bantu people, the Batwa deriving their iron-working skills from the Bantu (1966: 12-18). Malawian historiography, it seems, has been bedevilled with a kind of 'invasion' theory, akin to the early historical accounts of Europe and India, which

7

Waterbucks
Archives of the Society of Malawi

assumes a virtual equation between culture, language and physical type. Thus we have the original inhabitants of the country, the Akafula, the pre-Bantu hunter-gatherers, with a stone-age culture that is invariably identified with the Khoisan people. Then comes the 'invasion' of Bantu-speaking agriculturists, skilled iron-workers, who displace or absorb the early foragers. Then we have the 'invasion' around 1500 of the Phiri clan and the setting up of state institutions. The historical reality, however, as archaeologists like J. Desmond Clark have intimated, is probably far more complex. It is more than likely that some early Bantu speakers were hunter-gatherers, as well as being responsible for the red schematic cave paintings.

EARLY IRON-AGE CULTURE IN MALAWI

The earliest human remains in Malawi - with respect to the published record - are stone artefacts dating from about 60 thousand years ago. They were excavated at Mwanganda, about 5 miles west of Karonga on the lakeshore. At the site were also found the bones and teeth of elephant, hippopotamus and giraffe (Clark and Haynes 1970). This seems to indicate that hunting was an important aspect of their subsistence. Cultural artefacts have also been discovered at other late stone-age (30,000 BC to 200 AD) sites. Fingira cave on the Nyika, for example, which contains red schematic rock paintings, is believed to have been occupied around 1000 BC by short-statured people, who were 'neither employing metal working techniques, nor pottery techniques, nor were they farming'. Among the large amount of faunal remains found were eland, roan, reedbuck, warthog, zebra, monkey as well as smaller mammals and birds - all tentatively identified. Hunter-gatherers were thus flourishing on the Nyika Plateau around 3000 years ago (Sandelowsky and Robinson 1968). Other late stone-age sites have been recorded at the Mwalawolemba rock shelter on Mikolongwe Hill, Hora Mountain north of Mzimba, and at Cape Maclear (Tobias 1972: 8-9). From about 15,000 BC it is thought that there was a marked advance in technology, with the making of microlithic artefacts, and the use of bows and poisoned arrows in hunting (Clark 1959, Crader 1984: 4). Although much evidence of late stone-age people has come from rock shelters, it would be misleading, I think, to view such people as 'cave-dwellers' for, like later hunter-gatherers who sometimes frequent caves, they probably foraged widely and lived in leaf shelters (cf. my study of the Hill Pandaram 1982). But it is probably true to say that around 35,000 years ago in Africa, as elsewhere in the world, human communities entered the final phase of their stone-age - hunter-gathering - existence, and experienced what John Pfeiffer (1982) has called 'The Creative Explosion'. This probably involved the emergence of rock art, beliefs in the after-life (spirits of the dead), and more complex hunting techniques involving poison arrows. It also led, according to Roland Oliver (1991: 27-37) to the gradual adoption of farming as a form of subsistence, which included the domestification of livestock. A discussion of this important transition, whose social implications were far-reaching, is beyond the scope of the present study. But evidence seems to suggest that in Malawi, the 'iron age' began around 200 AD. There may well have been a long period, perhaps stretching over centuries, when hunter-gatherers, and Bantu agriculturists co-existed, but archaeologists seem to be generally agreed that between 50 BC and 300 AD Bantu people moved into South-Central Africa, and that these people are ancestral to modern Malawians. A farming way of life was thus established that has been the basic form of livelihood for Malawian people for almost two millenia.

The people who came to Malawi around 200 AD brought with them what Martin Hall has described, in his excellent study, as 'The Iron Age package'.

This suggests that these 'first farmers' who arrived in Malawi at that period, were people of the same physical type and language - Bantu - and had a knowledge of metallurgy, pottery-making, agriculture and animal husbandry, as well as of advanced hunting techniques. The introduction of this cultural and economic 'package' is thought to have been complete by 500 AD. But Hall suggests that, although there is evidence to suggest that farming techniques, metallurgy and the Bantu language may all have spread gradually through Africa about the same time, coming to Malawi from the north, there is no necessary connection between these various 'components' of the iron-age 'package' - language, pottery-making, metallurgy and farming techniques (1987: 31). The various iron-age cultures in Malawi have been distinguished by their types of pottery, and of these the following are noteworthy, each distinctive pottery style being linked to a specific locality. Nkope ware, first recognized at Nkope on the lakeshore, north of Mangochi, dates back to at least 300 AD. This ware seems to have been replaced around 1000 AD by Kapeni pottery, named after Kapeni Hill in the Ntcheu district. At a later date Mawudzu pottery came to be important, named after a hill on the lakeshore, near Nkope. This type of pottery has been found widely in Malawi - from the South Rukuru area, Hora Mt, Nkhotakota, and the Kasitu Valley - suggesting to Robinson (1982) that there were cultural links between the ancestral Tumbuku people and the early Maravi. Mwabvlambo ware, from a village of this name north of Karonga, was noted from around the same period, to be replaced by the Mwamasapa pottery from the same area around 1100 AD. Evidence from all these sites suggests that iron-smelting was well represented, and from the faunal remains, that hunting and fishing were important economic activities alongside farming. Evidence from iron-age sites north of Michesi Mountain suggests that ancestors of the Lomwe people, with their Nkope, Mawudzu and Longwe pottery ware, may have been living in the area long before the arrival of the Maravi circ. 1500 AD (for discussions of early iron-age cultures in Malawi see Phillipson 1976).

Hunting, as I have intimated, was an important aspect of the early iron-age people in Malawi, and I discuss elsewhere this hunting tradition more fully, with reference to archaeological excavations in the Dedza area (Morris 1998: 75-6).

Hunting in Malawi goes back into prehistory. For both the pre-Bantu hunter-gatherers, the Akafula or late stone-age people, and the early iron-age communities in Malawi, hunting played a significant role in their economic life. Savannah woodland is a fairly rich environment with regard to the larger mammals, and by all accounts the transition to farming was a long and gradual process, as iron-age cultivators gradually replaced the earlier foraging peoples. Evidence suggests that the earliest cultivators reached Malawi at the end of the 2nd century AD, but for many centuries after this, these early iron-age farmers co-existed with the hunter-gatherers. But importantly, hunting remained a very significant part of the economic partern of the early iron-age cultivators. As elsewhere, there may have been a definite shift in the transition to farming, with the increasing exploitation of smaller mammals, and the wider use of traps and snares than at the ealier foraging period (Clark 1972: 23-25, Mgomezulu 1983: 54-55).

There have been two important studies on the zooarchaeology of the early iron-age period in Malawi both focussed on the Dedza highlands. Mgomezulu's excavations were made in the area of Chingoni Mountain, to the east of the Linthipe River, while Crader's study focussed on Chencherere rock shelter, 13 km north of Dedza. Although entitled 'Hunters in Iron Age Malawi' (1984), and although the excavations unearthed pottery and even maize from a later period, the latter study was felt to deal with material culture relating to people whose subsistence base included only hunting and gathering (1984: 174). However, the radiocarbon dates obtained for the Chencherere rock shelter range from 500 BC to 800 AD. The two studies are based on bone fragments collected from rock shelters. Mgomezulu's material relates to six shelters in the vicinity of Chongoni Mountain (dating from 130 BC) while Crader's deals with the Chencherere materials. From their analysis it is evident that ungulates constituted the main animals hunted during the early iron-age period. I list on Table One, page 12, the number of individual mammals that their excavations indicated, as these relate to the more important species.

From their analysis it can be seen that hunting focussed essentially on six mammals - grey duiker, klipspringer, bushpig, zebra, hare, hyrax - and these constituted some 41% of the bones found in the rock shelters. Other mammals that were important include ungulates (sable, hippopotamus, red duiker, impala, waterbuck, Sharpe's grysbok), as well as such animals as antbear, lion, jackal, serval, wild dog, and hyaena. From the evidence it is clear that Burchell's zebra was once plentiful in the Dedza highlands. Other animals noted in these studies which are no longer to be found in the area include the suni (1), wildebeest (2) and cheetah (2), and three species were recorded from this early iron-age period for which there are no contemporary records from Malawi - Thompson's gazelle, steenbok, and springbok. Among the small mammals noted were gerbil (11) mole rat (9) and cane rat (12). The bones of tortoise (19) and monitor lizard (2) were also found in the Dedza rock shelters.

The evidence from the early iron-age period presented above shows a

11

TABLE ONE
Minimum Number of Individual Mammals

Species	Chongoni Mountain	Chencherere	Total	%
Buffalo	-	7	7	1.0
Bushbaby	30	2	32	4.4
Bushbuck	12	3	15	2
Bushpig	44	9	53	7.3
Eland	4	4	8	1.0
Grey Duiker	26	17	43	5.9
Hare	42	8	50	6.8
Hartebeest	2	6	8	1.0
Hyrax	52	14	66	9.0
Klipspringer	14	12	26	3.9
Oribi	2	11	13	1.8
Porcupine	8	2	10	1.4
Reebuck	4	9	13	1.8
Rhinocerus	4	-	4	0.5
Slender mongoose	2	3	5	0.7
Warthog	-	10	10	1.4
Zebra	48	17	65	8.9
Total	294	134	428	59
Other species	192	106	298	41
Total	486	240	726	100

Source: Mgomezulu 1993: 44-45, Crader 1984: 46-47

very similar pattern to that of the present time, although as larger mammals species are now confined to game sanctuaries or hill forests they are less frequently hunted perhaps than they were in the past.

THE MARAVI STATES

The inception of the early iron age into Malawi and to East Central Africa more generally represents a culture that contrasts markedly with the earlier hunter-gathering existence. The evidence suggests that the introduction of metallurgy, pottery-making, and food production techniques had a profound impact on the ecology and culture of the area. But throughout much of the iron-age period it is probable that people lived in small, scattered communities, settled in cleared areas of woodland, and combined shifting agriculture with hunting, fishing, and the gathering of wild vegetables. Chiefdoms may have developed in some areas, but these tended to be fragile and transitory, and a decentralized form of politics seems to have been the norm. From around the 8th century onwards this state of affairs began to slowly change, with the continuing influx of Bantu people into Malawi from Central Africa, and increasing opportunities for trade. As Hall writes, the ability of local rulers to prevent fission of their growing polities, thus holding together their power base, indicated a new political and economic order. Trade and the development of tribute were crucial to this process, and the first early states in Southern Africa based on the control of trade, seem to have emerged on the Limpopo River between about 800 and 1100 AD (Hall 1987: 74-75).

In Malawi the emergence of the Maravi states is often portrayed in a more sudden and dramatic fashion, with the arrival of the Phiri clan from the Luba country in Katanga around the 14th century, and the setting up of a centralized state based at Mankhamba (Malawi) near Ntakataka on the lakeshore. This involved the subjection of the original Banda and Mbewe clans, who continued to have ritual connections with the land, and rain-making powers, and the development of an 'empire' that covered much of Northern Zambezia, stretching as far as the East African coast. Subsequently, through conflict within the Phiri dynasty, the Kalonga kingdom fragmented, and independent or subsidiary states were established at Maano in Northern Mozambique (Undi), at Mbewe-wa-Mitengo near Chikwawa (Lundu), and at Muonda in the Mwanza Valley (Kaphwiti).

The original Maravi 'empire' fragmented even further during the 19th century, with the Ngoni and Yao invasions, and with many Chewa chiefs, Mwase Kasungu, Kanyenda and Mkanda setting up small, but independent chiefdoms. This portrait is somewhat overdrawn, as the analyses of Alpens and Schoffeleers suggest. For one thing the Phiri are a clan, and therefore, as an exogamous kinship group, can hardly be conceived of as a separate, invading people - as it is in some of the oral traditions. Secondly, shifting patterns of trade, rather than personal struggles within the ruling dynasty, or a splinter migration of a section of the ruling clan, are largely responsible for the fact that the respective states emerged at different historical periods, and subsequently declined in political influence. Although

13

the hunter-retainers of these various states may have numbered several hundred, and ranged over a wide area, there appears to have been no centralized civil administration nor a unified military control, so the power of the Kalonga and Undi states was perhaps somewhat limited. These states were political structures in which the centres - the trading depots - lacked autonomous power resources over their subordinates (cf. Mann 1986: 69). Moreover, it is misleading to equate the Maravi states (the plural has to be emphasized), focussed as these were around various Phiri dynasties, with Maravi 'culture', and even more misleading to equate them with the Chewa. Political power, culture, and ethnic identity constitute distinct social networks or phenomena (cf. Pachai 1973: 4-6).

I will discuss briefly, in turn and in chronological order, the three main Maravi chiefdoms (tributary states): Kalonga, Undi and Lundu.

Kalonga

Much of the oral traditions relating to the Phiri clan, and to the formation of the Kalonga chiefdom, essentially serve, as Harry Langworthy points out, as a social charter, justifying the right to rule by various members of the ruling Phiri clan (in Ntara 1973: XI). These traditions suggest that a group of people, the Maravi, led by their paramount chief, the Kalonga, whose name was Chinkhole, left their home in Luba country, and travelling via Choma, the Luangwa Valley and the Dzalanyama Mountains, eventually settled at a place called Malawi, on the South-Western Lakeshore. The Kalonga was a member of the Phiri clan, whose mother/ancestress was called Nyangu, and this clan settled near the Nkadzipulu stream near Ntakataka/Mua. The Banda clan, who traditionally provided the wife, *Mwali*, of the paramount chief Kalonga, established themselves at Mankhamba, nearby. Mankhamba later became an important shrine of the Kalonga kingdom (Ntara 1973: 1-15, K. Phiri 1975: 44-53). Kalonga was the title of the paramount chief (or King), and Malawi (Maravi) has the essential meaning of 'fire flames', and seems to have many associations - with iron-smelting, with the ritual burning of the bush, and with shrines associated with the ruling Phiri clan (Schoffeleers 1972). Its essential meaning seems to have been the *place* where the Kalonga (Phiri) dynasty held political dominion. Maravi was therefore, as Thomas Price suggested, a 'geographical indicator' and initially referred to the south-western corner of Lake Malawi where the first tributary state was established around 1500. Later it referred to Undi and Lundu's political domains.

Early Portuguese writers, however, who came into contact with the Maravi states in the 16th and 17th century, used the term Maravi in a cultural sense to apply to the people who came under the dominion of the Kalonga, Undi and Lundu chiefdoms - which in oral tradition were linked by kinship ties, the paramounts all being members of the Phiri clan. They also spoke of the Maravi as being an 'empire' or 'nation'. This has led many scholars to assume that the unity derived by political domination was reflected at a cultural level, such that the Maravi constituted a 'people' or ethnic group. With the break-up of the Maravi states, the 'Maravi Mother tribe', as Bruwer describes it, (1950: 33) also fragmented into various ethnic communities: Mbo, Chewa, Nsenga, Mang'anja, Sena, Chipeta and Nyungwe. But as Price remarks 'No people are known to have called themselves Maravi' (1952: 75), and it is clear from the writings of the early Europeans visiting the area - both Portuguese and British - that ethnic groupings were recognized by local people with whom they came into contact. As Antonio Gamitto recorded in the early 19th century, the

Tribute to Chief Kalonga

Chamare Museum, KuNgoni Art Craft Centre, Mua by Fr Claude Boucher Chisale

15

Makua, Chewa, Nsenga, Yao and Mang'anja were totally independent of each other 'and each has its own name. Nevertheless it is beyond dispute that all are of the same Maravi race, having the same habits, customs, language, etc.' (Gamitto 1960: 64). Gamitto clearly recognized the cultural unity of the people living in Northern Zambezia, and he referred to Maravi as a 'land', but it would be misleading to infer from this that Maravi was a single ethnic community that fragmented into various 'tribes' on the break-up of the centralized Maravi polities. As we shall later explore, ethnicity in pre-colonial Malawi referred essentially to locality and to people having some linguistic continuity over time - not to a distinct, clearly demarcated ethnic group. Price notes that Maravi was always used in the plural form, unlike tribal (ethnic) designations (1952: 76, see Morris 1998: 7–11).

The Kalonga state was established around the beginning of the 16th century, and its political hegenomy at the height of its power, extended some distance from the lakeshore, and embraced a wide range of people - Nsenga, Chikunda, Chewa, Mbo, Mukua, Zimba, Chipeta, Ntumba, Nyanja and the Mang'anja. Although its hunters - military retainers - undoubtedly ranged over a wide area and exacted tribute from the local chiefs within these regions, as well as having established trade links with Mozambique Island, and later with Tete, it is probable that the Portuguese writers exaggerated the power and influence of the Kalonga state. Recognizing that Maravi was the place where the Kalonga (Muzura) resides, the suggestions of these writers that his dominion not only reached the coast at Quilemane, but extended as far as Mombasa was I think overdrawn (in Manuel Barreto Report {1967} in Theal 1899: 480). Mary Douglas (Tew) long ago hinted that the political unity and internal cohesion of the 'Maravi Empire' was perhaps exaggerated, although this is not to deny the traditions of common identity, and the beliefs relating to the overall leadership and sovereignty of the Kalonga (Tew 1950: 34, K. Phiri 1973: 22).

The history of the Kalonga state has been lucidly portrayed by Kings Phiri who in pioneering studies has fruitfully combined data from both the oral traditions of the Chewa and written sources. Phiri contends that the Kalonga state was established around 1480, and that the area it controlled in a direct manner was initially relatively small, being confined to the eastern fringes of the Dedza and Ntcheu districts. By the late 17th century, however, its power and influence had increased tremendously, such that it was able to establish territorial jurisdiction, i.e. political dominion, over about seven other 'chiefdoms' in what Phiri describes as 'Chewa country' -

Kanyenda at Nkhotakota, Dzoole at Mndolera (both of these chiefs belonged to the Mwale clan) and Mkanda at Mchemani near Mchinji (who was of the Mbewe clan) were among the more important of these chiefdoms. The Kalonga was paramount chief, but he was nominally recognized as owner of all the lands over which he held dominion, not simply those recognised as under Chewa chiefs. Each territorial chief (Mfumu or Mambo) was considered to be *mwini dziko* (owner or guardian of the land), because his predecessors had acquired the title from the Kalonga. Such a chief was in possession of a *muzinda*, a bundle of medicines having mystical powers. He also possessed the symbols of chieftainship: a medicine tail (*mchila*), a knife (*lupanga*) and occasionally an iron stool (*chipapa*). Muzinda was ritually conveyed (*kudzika*) by the Kalonga to his subordinate chiefs, and this entitled them to conduct initiations (*chinamwali*), control and organize *nyau* rituals, and to conduct funeral rites (*maliro*). Each of these services entailed the giving of gifts to the chief, and this enabled him to accrue substantial amounts of local wealth. Each territorial chief had his own court attendants (*ankhoswe*) and several village headmen under his jurisdiction (Phiri 1975: 73-76). This pattern of political authority was common to all the 'Maravi' states, and suggested that the territorial chief possessed both political and ritual authority. But with the Kalonga paramount, ritual power was associated with the Banda clan, to which he was affinally related, his wife (*mwali*) being a member of this clan. Members of the Banda or Mbewe clan were held to be responsible for the well being of the land, and for the provision of rain. I discuss the importance of these rain shrines in another study (see Morris 2000: 175-219).

Also important for the Kalonga dynasty, Phiri records, was the Mlira ceremony, which was held each year during the month of September. The important chiefs were invited to the capital (Malawi or Manthimba) for the ritual veneration of *Mlira*, the spirit of great Kalonga chief (Chinkhole), who took the form of a snake. The calling of the snake was answered by appropriate ritual offerings, and by the ritual burning of the Marimba bush which then stretched along the lakeshore (cf. Schoffeleers 1971, Phiri 1988: 7).

In examining what factors were important in enabling the 'Kalonga and his Phiri kinsmen to create a centralized state', Kings Phiri suggests four basic theories of state formation (1975: 52-53, 1988: 4-5).

The first was that of Melville Herskovits who looked upon states as essentially the 'by product' of an agrarian revolution, involving the emergence of specialist occupations, metallurgists and ritual priests, and the development subsequently of hierarchical structures. This hypothesis is inadequate, Phiri suggests, because it does not explain why states failed to develop in many parts of Africa where the same agrarian revolutions took place.

The second is the 'invader theory' which suggests that the Kalonga and his Phiri followers were already equipped with an 'ideology of dominance' when they entered the country, and as an immigrant group were able to 'impose' themselves over the indigenous inhabitants who have usually been referred to as the 'proto-Chewa'. Unhappy with this theory, Phiri suggests that it neither informs us of what 'ideology' of dominance the Maravi immigrants possessed, nor does it take into account the fact that there are no oral traditions relating to wars between the Phiri invaders (rulers) and the proto-Chewa - although there are plenty of traditions relating to conflict between the incoming Bantu (Maravi) and the Akafula. Phiri tends to downplay the role of coercive power in state formation. But the oral traditions depict the Chewa as coming into Malawi as a group consisting of several clans - and the notion that the Phiri clan are later immigrants is sociologically untenable. In fact the oral traditions seem to suggest that they already had the institution of Kalonga during their travels. The dichotomy

Chief Kalonga receives gifts
Chamare Museum, KuNgoni Art Craft Centre, Mua by Fr Claude Boucher Chisale

between the proto-Chewa and the Phiri invaders (Maravi) is misleading, implying that until their 'arrival' (coinciding with the formation of the state) there were no members of the Phiri clan present in the region. Groups of people belonging to Phiri, Banda and other clans, and not specifically Chewa (which is only one of a number of 'ethnic' communities that came under the dominance of the Malawi {Kalonga} state probably drifted into Malawi for several centuries prior to the establishment of the Kalonga state (cf. Hamilton 1955, which Phiri takes as an exemplar of the 'invasion' theory).

The third theory of state formation is the one that Kings Phiri himself advocates: As a 'conflict' theory, it suggests that Kalonga state had its origins in a 'dialectic' between the Maravi immigrants - the invading Phiri migrants arriving at a later date - and the proto-Chewa inhabitants. In this dialectic the 'Maravi' emerged as rulers, while the proto-Chewa retained prestige as being the ritual 'owners of the soil'. It was the result of the interaction, involving tension and conflict, between seemingly two completely independent groups of people (clans). The rise of the Kalonga state thus involved the 'coalescence' of two systems of authority. In this coalescence neither trade nor coercive power are mentioned. The theory is hardly explanatory.

The fourth theory is the 'trade theory', namely that the Kalonga state was rooted in the need for a centralized authority to control the ivory trade between the shores of Lake Malawi and the East African coast. In discussing Kalonga state formation in his earlier writings (1975: 52-53) Phiri does not mention the ivory trade at all; it is seen as developing only at a later period. In his article on the pre-colonial states of Central Africa, however, he discusses the theory, suggesting that it has to be demonstrated that there was any trade between the Maravi country and the East African coast prior to the Portuguese occupation of the Zambezi Valley in the mid-16th century. (1988: 4-5). Yet there is plenty of evidence to suggest that ivory was being traded down the Zambezi to the coast as early as 1000 AD (Fagan 1965). As Edward Alpers wrote: Malawi country, i.e. East Central Africa, was rich in ivory, and the Muslims at the coast were eager to trade for it. It was, as he put it, the staple of trade in East Central Africa, and the firearms derived from this trade, not only facilitated the further hunting of elephants, but allowed the Kalonga - and later, other chiefs - to assert their political dominance over local communities. As Alpers wrote: 'There is good reason for believing that the Malawi chiefs depended for much of their power on their control of trade. We know that the Malawi chiefs had a monopoly of the ivory trade and that the ground tusk of every elephant which was killed in a particular chief's territory belonged to him, the hunter keeping the other' (1968: 20). When Alpers wrote that 'The keystone of this Malawi empire was trade' (1967: 82), he was indicating an essential truth, and, of course, in the early period, from 1000 AD onwards, the most important trade item was ivory. The impact of elephant hunting, and the ivory trade, on the social life and politics of the North Zambezi region cannot be emphasized enough. The rise and fall of the Kalonga state only makes sense in terms of the dynamics of the ivory trade. In the early centuries East Central Africa was a region where elephants abounded, and it was thus 'rich in ivory'. In the Luangwa valley, the Bua watershed, and the Dzalanyama hills elephants were found in abundance. Before the Portuguese penetration of the Zambezi, with the establishment of Sena and Tete in the 1530s, the main trade route from this region to the East African coast passed - as Alpers indicated - around the southern end of Lake Malawi. Throughout the latter part of the 15th century, with the development of the ivory trade, groups living strategically on this trade-route, specifically some members of the Phiri clan, were able to establish a centralized polity. The trades not only included ivory, but also iron goods, machila (a coarse cloth) and many slaves. Manuel Barreto was to describe this trade in the 17th century as 'very profitable' (Theal 1899: 481). In the mid-17th century, when Muzura was (possibly) the Kalonga, this Maravi state was at the height of its power, and greatly feared by the Portuguese colonists. Tete was described as the 'part of the Maravi', and the dominion of the Kalonga stretched to Quelimane, some 600 km from his capital at Maravi near the Lake. The Lolo (Bororo) and Mukua people of Mozambique both came under the suzerainty of the Kalonga, although at this time the Bororo kingdom was seen as a 'subject' of the Lundu chief, who in turn, was described by the Portuguese writers as 'the second person in the empire of Maravi' (Theal 1899: 480). The 'success' of the Kalonga at this time, as K. Dasgupta records, was to 'a large extent due to his control over the long distance ivory trade along the new overland route from the Zambezi to Mozambique Island. This helped him to get cotton cloth from the coastal traders and then to make gifts to his powerful supporters' (1990: 41). Equally important, of course, was the supply of firearms.

Malawi has been spoken of as the 'cross roads' between the different cultural regions of Central, Eastern and Southern Africa, and Alpers noted that Southern Malawi was as important a 'meeting ground' of regional and international trade as was the coast itself (1975: 27). But not only was the Southern Lakeshore an important trading venue, focussed around the

Maravi Court, it was also from an early period a highly populated region.

By the end of the 17th century the Kalonga kingdom began to decline, due not so much to conflicts within the dynastic group, but because of the changing patterns of trade, particularly the increasing opportunities for the export of ivory. This political decline of the Kalonga state was intrinsically related to the development of two other important chiefdoms, both of which had originally been tributary chiefs of the Kalonga, Undi and Lundu. We can turn now to the first of these.

Undi

During the 17th century the Kalonga had experienced a period of expansion and had established suzerainty over chiefs in the Zambezi/Luangwa valleys, beyond the Dzalanyana range. One of the more important of these chiefs was Undi, who Chewa oral traditions suggest, was sent by the Kalonga to this region, in order to be a tributary chief over the Nsenga and Chewa people. He established himself as chief at Maano, situated at the headwaters of the Kapoche stream in Mozambique, some 260 km from the Maravi capital. Soon the chieftainship built up its power base, and by degrees became an independent kingdom. By the middle of the 18th century its power and influence was on a par with that of the Kalonga, and oral traditions also suggest major conflicts between the two kingdoms, personified in these traditions as conflicts between the two incumbents. The Portuguese having established themselves in the heartland of Central Africa at Tete, which was an important market on the Zambezi, soon proved to be an important outlet for ivory. The Luangwa Valley and the Zambezi escarpment to the west of the Dzalanyana Hills had, as noted earlier, an abundance of elephants, and a close trading relationship in ivory was established between Undi and the Portuguese at Tete. The wealth and political influence of the Undi kingdom was directly based on this ivory trade, and it quickly developed from being a tributary chiefdom, to being an independent kingdom, with an extensive territorial organization, a hierarchical political system with delegated authority, and a degree of centralization of power (Langworthy 1972: 106, Phiri 1979: 15).

The studies of Harry Langworthy on the Undi state are of particular importance, for he has cogently outlined the political sociology of the state. Its essential characteristics were as follows:

As the people of East Central Africa were matrilineal, succession to the Undi chiefdomship, as with Kalonga and Lundu, followed the matrilineal line. This usually implied the chief's sister's son, but any relative of the Nyangu, Kalonga's mother or sister, was eligible. As, Langworthy suggests, the chief's role was often that of simply confirming and installing the choice of local people; there was thus an element of 'decentralization' in the authority structure - although he acknowledges that the decline of Kalonga's central authority may have been due to 'external factors'. All the chiefs in an area, as members of the Phiri clan, were thought to be linked by ties of perpetual kinship with the King. But the paramount chief also established links with non-Phiri chiefs, and often married women from these chiefdoms, thus establishing ties of perpetual cousinship (*chisuwani*). His ties with the important chief Mkanda were of this nature. As with the Kalonga kingdom, the Banda clan had important ritual functions in terms of rain-making, and Undi was closely associated with and custodian of the Msinja shrine near the Diampwe River in the Lilongwe district. Here a member of the Banda clan was in charge of the spirit-shrine, and the female spirit medium Makewana, resided. I discuss this shrine more fully in another study (Morris 2000: 195-201). It implied a separation of political and ritual powers. As with the Kalonga, the Undi had judicial functions, and was served by a group of councillors at the capital, who were mostly of non-Phiri clans. Langworthy suggests that they might be considered as representing the people's interests, as against those of the Phiri dynasty. There was however no organized bureaucracy.

Undi was entitled to tribute from local communities through their chiefs, and while such tribute included subsistence goods, of particular importance were the skins of certain mammals: lion, leopard and serval, the red feathers of *nkulukulu*, the Green Loerie (Tauraco Livingston, T. Schlalowi), the pangolin, and the ground tusk of all elephant killed in the chiefs' territory. All these had symbolic importance, although they were also important trade goods. Ivory seems to have thus been an item of allegiance as well as a form of tribute. Undi's capital at Maano was the focus of the regional trade, and ivory was the most important export commodity in East Central Africa from the 10th to the end of the 19th century. Slaves, though evident, were rarely important in the export trade of the early Maravi rulers. Although Langworthy seems to emphasize the 'succession' problems in the collapse of the Kalonga kingdom, he acknowledges that it was the export of ivory and other tributary goods that was important for paramount chiefs 'in terms of the maintenance of their central authority' (1972: 117). This was because they were able to organize the redistribution of such imported goods as cloth, beads, *mpande* shells, copper wire, and occasionally guns and ammunition - thus ensuring the loyalty and obedience of the subordinate chiefs. Langworthy does not emphasize the coercive power that the import of firearms to the area brought, and the fact that this facilitated the hunting of elephants by armed groups of men.

Access to external trade contracts - for ivory especially - was undoubtedly an important factor in undermining Kalonga's authority at the end of the 17 century. By the end of the following century the power of Undi was also in decline - by the 'tendency towards decentralization' that Langworthy sees as inherent in the Maravi system of political authority, and by the temptations of local chiefs to trade directly with the Portuguese themselves. Thus by the beginning of the 19th century, Mkanda chiefdom had become independent, and had seceded from Undi's kingdom (Langworthy 1972: 106-120). By the mid-19th century, when Livingstone journeyed up the Shire Valley, he was writing that the Mang'anja had formerly been united under a great chief Undi, 'whose empire extended from Lake Shirwa (Chilwa) to the River Luangwa', but that since Undi's death it had 'fell to pieces' (1865: 198). Livingstone saw the 'rise and fall' of African 'empires' - kingdoms/chiefdoms - as being due to the talents of a 'chief of more than ordinary ability', one able to subdue his neighbours. He thus ignored the material conditions of political structures.

Thus by about 1850, Langworthy concludes, Undi's authority in Central Malawi was 'negligible', for he was unable to protect the Makewana Shrine, or to render services to his subordinate chiefs.

When Antonio Gamitto travelled through Northern Zambezia in 1831-32, on an expedition to Kazembe's capital, the Undi state still had some political relevance, although the power of the paramount chief Undi (Unde) was then in decline. Gamitto described the state as 'despotic and hereditary' (1960: 68). The land over which Undi held dominion was described as Maravi, and it comprised an area north of the Zambesi, its western boundary being the Shombwe stream. The Chewa (Chewa), Lolo (Bororo) and Mang'anja (Maganja) are seen as being beyond Unzdi's jurisdiction. Besides the paramount chief Undi, two levels of political authority are recognized, the territorial chiefs Mambo, who are known as *mwini dziko* (*muene-shiko*), owners/guardians of the land or country, and the *fumu*, the *mwini mudzi* (*mwene-muzi*), guardians of the village. Gamitto thought their power to be 'arbitrary', even though there were recognized forms of tribute. No formal military organization was observed, although in times of conflict, the territorial chiefs were able to summon large contingents of men. The Maravi country, in the Zambezi Valley and the foothills to the west of the Dzalanyama range is described as 'fertile' with 'abundant harvests' (80), and as being well populated. Agriculture was the

23

main form of subsistence, but weaving, basket-making and blacksmithing were common pastimes - done mainly for 'amusement' Gamitto records (68). Hunting was important - especially the hunting of elephant for ivory, and the use of medicine was ubiquitous. He also notes the common practice of people keeping in their houses *arungos*, which are believed to be one or more snakes called *nyamezarumbo*, which seem to have embodied the spirits of the dead (76). Oral traditions suggest that the Undi state did not reach the Nsenga people living in the Lungwa Valley itself (Phiri 1988: 11).

Lundu

With the opening up of Sena as a trade entrepot by the Portuguese in the early 16th century, the Lundu chiefdom, which it seems had formerly owed obeissance to the Kalonga, began to assert its political independence. Able to control the important trade, particularly of ivory, passing down the Shire Valley, Lundu came to assert paramountcy over the Shire Valley. In oral traditions Lundu was considered subordinate to the Kaphwiti chiefdom, and was thought to be his sister's son. In the late 16th century, the Kaphwiti chief was described as controlling the whole of the Lower Shire Valley from Wamkurumadzi River south to the Zambezi, his capital probably being situated at Muonda village, near Mikolongo in the Mwanza Valley, west of the present Majete Game Reserve. By 1572 Kaphwiti suffered what Kings Phiri called an 'enigmatic blow' with Lundu taking control of the Sena ivory trade, and thus greatly expanding his sphere of influence at the expense of Kaphwiti (Phiri 1979: 10-11, 1988: 8). Thus between about 1590 and 1630 the Lundu (Rundo) chiefdom became a 'powerful state system', which eventually extended its dominion along the entire north bank of the Zambezi, asserting suzerainty over the Lolo people - the Lolo being a section of the Lomwe people, who are mainly represented in present-day Malawi by the Kokhola in the Mulanje, Chiradzulu and Thyolo districts (Nurse 1972: 123-133). The power of the Lundu chief, as Father Schoffeleers suggests, was partly based on the rich agricultural land of the Lower Shire Valley - such agriculture combining dry-land cultivation (*munda/mphala*) with wetland gardens (*dimba/dambo*) (see Mandala 1990: 5-7) - and partly on the strategic position of the Lower Shire Valley, particularly in relation to Sena and Tete, the principal trading stations on the Zambezi. Muslim traders had been established at Sena from an early period - probably from the 12th century - and had been exchanging beads, Indian cloth, firearms and gunpowder, for iron-ware, local cotton cloth (*chimbwi*), ivory and slaves. Although the Portuguese seem to have been mainly interested in the gold mined in the Zimbabwe region south of the Zambezi, the export of ivory was nevertheless important. The early Maravi states of Kalonga and Lundu also traded with the port of Quelimane, some 240 km south-east of Lundu's capital, which was situated at Mbewe ya Mitengo, near Chikwawa (Schoffeleers 1968: 138-145, 1987: 344).

Two important aspects of the Lundu kingdom are worth noting; both have been explored with considerable scholarship by Father Schoffeleers. The first is that the Lundu dynasty had a close, though complex, relationship with the Mbona rain shrine situated at Khulubvi forest, south of Nsanje. The history and sociology of this shrine has been discussed by Schoffeleers in a number of publications, and is treated at length in a later study (Schoffeleers 1972, 1980, 1992, Morris 2000: 212-16).

The second important aspect of the Lundu chiefdom is that given the crucial importance of the ivory trade in the early 17th century, the chief seems to have had in his service large groups of professional elephant hunters or warriors known as *Azimba* (singular: *Zimba*). These hunter-warriors appear to have played an important role in the court rituals, and were under the command of a man called Tundu. Zimba hunter-warriors seem to have ranged widely, whether or not in the service of the Lundu, and there are records of Zimba not only attacking Sena and Tete, but also the East African coastal towns. Alper refers to the Zimba as wandering 'hordes' (1975: 50-51). The Matundu Hills in the Lower Shire Valley, and the male spirit Chitundu - believed by the Mang'anja of the Lower Shire to be responsible for 'man-eating' lions, whirlwinds and heavy storms - are contemporary reminders of the warrior-chief of the Lundu retainers, the Azimba (Schoffeleers 1968: 140, 1987: 346-349).

The power of the Lundu chief was seemingly curtailed around 1622 when he was defeated by Muzura, assisted by the Portuguese colonists who were heavily implicated in local politics. When Gaspar Bocarro journeyed from Tete to Kilwa in 1616, he visited Muzura at Marauy (Maravi?) and the chief was described as the chief 'lord in the territory of Bororo' (Theal 1899: 416, cf. Rangeley 1954 for interesting reflections on Bocarro's journey). The Portuguese also, it seems, collaborated with the Kalonga dynasty in its own campaigns against the Karanga states south of the Zambezi, and at times also with the Lundu. But by the middle of the 18th century the Maravi political systems were in decline - the power of the Lundu and Undi states being rather short-lived. For a period, put simply, the Kalonga, and his Bororo subordinates were trading ivory largely through Mozambique Island or Quelimane, the Undi through Tete, and the Lundu chief through Sena, and their power was derived from these trading contacts. Although oral traditions portray the era of the Maravi dynasties as one of peace and tranquility, the written records suggest that the three centuries between 1500 and 1800 as being ones of turmoil and conflict. There was conflict between the various Maravi dynasties, and between the Portuguese and Muslim traders (in 1572 the Portuguese murdered the entire Muslim population of Sena fearing that they were being poisoned), and a series of uprisings and rebellions against the Portuguese by the Maravi states and local chiefdoms also occurred (Theal 1899: 220-27, Schoffeleers 1968: 138-143, Phiri 1979 13-15, Newitt 1995 56-59). Equally important was the fact that, local chiefdoms, given increasing access to trade goods through the trading of ivory, began to establish their own power base and to assert their political independence from the Maravi states. The essential thesis of Edward Alpers is that the Maravi kingdoms - specifically that of the Kalonga - came into being from the 14th century, and were largely based on the control of the ivory trade, and that by the middle of the 17th century the Kalonga Muzura, with the help of the Portuguese, who were primarily interested in gold, had dominion over the Northern Zambezia (1975: 46-49). Although I am in general agreement with Alpers' 'ivory thesis', this thesis has been subject to criticism by both Newitt (1982) and Schoffeleers (1987). Malyn Newitt has suggested, what Schoffeleers describes as a 'Volkerwanderung thesis', that the Maravi states were not the outcome of Phiri invaders at an early period, but were rather formed in the period 1580-1640 by a number of different immigrant groups, such as the Mumbos, Zimba and the followers of chief Mongazi, who migrated into North Zambezia and 'conquered the existing population'. Newitt seems to emphasize 'plunder' not trade - although how they got the means to plunder he does not explore - and he argues that the establishment of the 'settled Maravi states' only occurred as a result of the rise of Muzura in the early 17th century. The key figure in Newitt's account is in fact Muzura. According to Antonio Gomes, who as a Jesuit priest travelled in the Zambezi region in the 1640s, Muzura was an ex-slave who had escaped, and who, due to his prowess as a hunter and liberality towards his followers, had built up a large following among people in Northern Zambezia. Thus Newitt concludes that Muzura was 'the man who founded the State north of the Zambezi, which later became known as the empire of the Maravi... and that the paramountcy which he established later assumed the title of Kalonga' (1982: 159-162).

Newitt acknowledges that Muzura attached a lot of importance to trade with the Portuguese, but nevertheless emphasizes that his expansionist policy was based on 'plunder' and on 'conquering' the neighbouring territories. But of course plunder could hardly be achieved without the use of firearms derived from the trade of ivory - for ivory trade and political dominion went hand-in-hand, as Alpers implied. If elephant hunting, trade in ivory, access to firearms coalesced, then even local petty chiefs were soon able to assert their political dominion over local communities, and with local support derived from the redistribution of trade goods, would be able to establish a degree of autonomy from what were at one time centralized kingdoms. Kanyenda was able to do this in relation to the Kalonga, Mkanda in relation to Undi, and, towards the end of the 19th century, the Kololo servants of Livingstone were able to assert their dominion over the local Mang'anja, and the declining Lundu chiefdomship. The distinction between trade-based, and tribute-based political power, however, seems inappropriate in the Malawian context - for both were intrinsic to the Maravi states (cf. Curtin et al 1978: 172). Although Newitt questioned the *early* formation of the Maravi state - Phiri, like Alpers, had dated it from the early half of the 16th century - almost all scholars seem to accept that by about 1640 the two states encountered by the Portuguese, the Kalonga and Lundu, were already well established. They were powerful kingdoms, to whom were attached groups of hunter/warrior retainers, and besides being feared by the Portuguese, who attempted to collaborate with them in their own imperial ventures, they were deeply implicated in the ivory trade. Both Newitt and Schoffeleers, unlike Alpers, tend to play down the importance of the ivory trade, and almost ignore entirely the crucial significance of firearms that were derived from this trade. But while scholars like Alpers, Phiri and Newitt seem to accept the identification of Muzura as the Kalonga incumbent in the early 17th century, Schoffeleers suggests that Muzura was an independent chief, whose dominion centred on the Neno-Mwanza area. He was thus neither a member of the Kalonga (Phiri) dynasty, nor a precursor of the Kalonga state, but rather a successor to Lundu as the most powerful chief in the 'Maravi state system', it being assumed that all the early states - which seem to have emerged and disappeared with remarkable frequency - belonged to the same cultural formation. It is worth noting that the notion of a foreign hunter, like Muzura, who through his hunting prowess and trade links forms an independent kingdom, is common throughout Africa, and has been described as a 'legendary cliché' (Vansina 1985: 139, Schoffeleers 1987: 345). It is an idea that may have historical substance in Malawi, for, as we shall see, both the Chikulamayembe and Mwase Kasungu dynasties or chiefdoms were based on the assumption of political power by a foreign hunter-trader.

Although the Maravi states - Kalonga, Lundu, Kaphwiti, Muzura, Undi - were already in decline by the end of the 18th century, their demise was completed in the 19th century, with the growing expansion of the ivory trade, and emergence of many independent chiefdoms, many of many of which were made up of immigrants to Malawi. The political history of the 19th century in Malawi is largely a history of the ivory, and the later slave trade, and this is the subject of the next section. The ivory trade was largely captured by petty chiefdoms, and this led to the political disintegration of the Maravi states. It was a process which Harry Langworthy describes as 'decentralization', which was generated both by internal dissension within these states, and by the invasion of such immigrants as the Swahili traders, the Ngoni and the Yao.

19th CENTURY CHIEFDOMS AND THE IVORY TRADE

The history of the 19th century in Malawi has been well and cogently described by a number of scholars (e.g. McCracken 1968, Langworthy 1975, Phiri 1984, 1988). It is beyond the scope of the present study to outline this history here: what I wish to do is to briefly discuss the history of several chiefdoms, or incipient states, and to explore the crucial role that elephant hunting, and the trade of ivory played in their formation and in their functioning.

The ivory trade in East Central Africa probably goes back to antiquity, and certainly by around 1000 AD a complex trading network of African hunters, local chiefs, African or Muslim traders and Asian merchant 'capitalists' had been established. A.L. Masudi writing in the 10th century noted that elephants were common in the land of Zinj, and that ivory was taken to Oman, from where it was sent on to India and China. By the 16th century some 66 thousand kg of ivory passed through the port of Sofala annually. African ivory, at least from the eastern part of the continent, was highly valued, for it was white, opaque and soft enough to be easily carved. Though greatly esteemed in the Orient, it was also exported to Europe, and ivory-carving centres sprang up during the late medieval period in such places as Dieppe, Hesse and the Jura mountains (Beachey 1967).

But it was from the end of the 18th century that the great development of the ivory trade took place in East and Central Africa. There was a marked increase in the demand for ivory in both Europe and the United states, the ivory being used for a wide variety of ornaments and household goods: piano and organ keys, snuff boxes, umbrella handles, chess sets, and carved figures, 'not to mention the ivory inlaid butts of six-shooters for the American west' (op. cit. 288). Zanzibar was the main market for the ivory trade on the East African coast, but in relation to Malawi, the main entrepots for ivory were Kilwa, Ibo, Mozambique Island and Quelimane. The demand for ivory coincided with the opening up of East Africa by Arab traders and European explorers during the 19th century, although even by the beginning of the century, there seems to have been a well-established trade route from the region of Katanga, specifically Kazembe's court (the Lunda state) in the Luapula River valley - this kingdom was founded in the early part of the 18th century - to the east coast ports of Kilwa and Mozambique. This trade route crossed the Lake and the Southern Lakeshore, where the Kalonga kingdom had earlier flourished. As Andrew Roberts wrote, by about 1800, Kazembe's capital on the Luapala, like Unyanyembe (Tabara) and Ujiji further to the north - in what is now Tanzania - became a 'meeting point' of trade routes that spanned the continent (Roberts 1970: 729). The Bisa played an important role in this ivory trade.

Although ivory was undoubtedly the 'dominant export' from the region, it would be misleading to suggest that 'the first trade of any dimensions involving Central Africa was the trade in ivory' (Pachai 1971: 37). For the ivory trade was based on, and intrinsically connected with, a pre-colonial pattern of trade which included subsistence goods, and which probably went back to the early iron-age period. Long before the export of slaves, ivory and gold had assumed predominance in the long-distance caravan trade, subsistence-oriented trade undoubtedly took place. This involved the economic exchange of iron tools and weapons, salt, cloth, pottery, dried fish and animal skins, as well as such items as cowrie shells. This internal exchange of largely subsistence goods, 'underpinned' the development of the export trade at a later period. Nevertheless, there is some truth in Fagan's contention that ivory was the 'staple' item in the East Coast trade (Fagan 1970: 36, Roberts 1970: 716). Kings Phiri has shown that in the 19th century a flourishing trading network in Central Malawi was evident, involving salt, locally produced 'Tumbuka' hoes, dried fish, cotton cloth (*chimbwi*), as well as animal skins and ivory. Several types of economic exchanges co-existed (tribute, gift exchange and barter) and the trade network involved both internal and external export aspects. Although the Chewa were deeply implicated in the ivory trade, Phiri suggests that it was such ethnic communities as the Bisa, Chikunda and Yao who largely functioned as the itinerant traders. Significantly, while the importation of muzzle-loading guns was important in the development of ivory trade, there was also an increased demand for iron spears and axes which led to a resurgence of the local iron industry (Roberts 1970: 736, Phiri 1976: 15-20).

It is of interest that Kings Phiri recognized four spheres of economic exchange, outlined in the following schema:

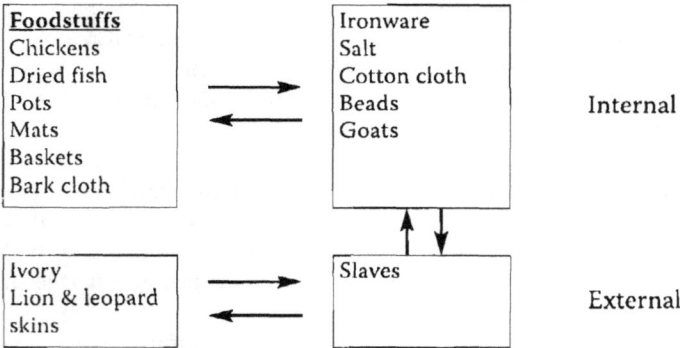

| **Foodstuffs** Chickens Dried fish Pots Mats Baskets Bark cloth | ⟶ ⟵ | Ironware Salt Cotton cloth Beads Goats | Internal |
| Ivory Lion & leopard skins | ⟶ ⟵ | Slaves ↑↓ | External |

Source: Phiri 1975: 115

The ivory trade (hunting) was thus seen as a separate sphere of exchange, though intimately connected with the other exchanges, especially with the subsistence sphere which Phiri does not highlight. By the mid-19th century there were well-established caravan/trade routes from the Luangwa and Zambezi valleys to the coastal towns of Kilwa, Mozambique and Quelimane. Beads, various types of cloth (*merikani, kaniki*), brass or copper wire, and sometimes muskets of the flintlock type were exchanged for the ivory. There was a complex but intimate connection between guns and ivory in the 19th century, and with the development of breech-loading guns and repeating rifles - Snider, Martini-Henry, Mannlicher, Lee-Metford - towards the end of the century, thousands of obsolete muzzle-loading guns were imported into East Africa, in what was inevitably an 'arms trade'. The British consul at Zanzibar, Evan-Smith estimated in the 1880s that around 90 thousand firearms were annually imported into East Africa, and along with many missionaries he called for restrictions on the arms trade (Beachey 1962: 451). The impact of the ivory trade - most of the elephant hunting, but not all, being done by armed groups of men using the imported muzzle-loading guns - was devastating on the elephant population of Central and East Africa.

By the end of the 19th century the ivory trade was all but defunct, even though it has continued to have significance in a limited way until the present decade, although much hunting of elephant in Malawi nowadays is illegal. Nevertheless some 762 kg of ivory was exported from Malawi in 1988, valued at $114,300 (Barbier et al 1990: 7-37). In the heyday of the ivory trade, however, in the last decade of the 19th century, ivory accounted for around 80% of the total exports from Malawi and was valued at £5,500 - although it was suspected that much more was being illegally transported to the coast. During the period 1891 to 1904, Malawi exported 80 tons (80,000 kg) of ivory, which fetched around £50,000 (Baker 1971: 91).

Taking 60 lbs (approx. 27 kg) per pair of tusks as an average (and even this may be on the high side), this amounts to around 3,000 elephants. Livingstone felt that ivory to the British Market meant the death of about 30 thousand African elephants each year (1865: 243). Tusks about 90 lb (approx. 41 kg) in weight were always considered exceptional, and the average weight as ship cargo was around 17 lb (approx. 8 kg) according to Livingstone's sources.

Many writers have suggested that the trade in ivory was more lucrative than slaves, for there was no loss in transit, and its value increased towards the coast. Colin Baker indeed writes that one of the reasons for capturing slaves was to provide human porterage for the ivory that was being conveyed from the interior to the coast (op. cit. 91). But the East Africa slave trade, which became important after about 1840 when the Maravi region became a major source of slaves, had a logic of its own, and was largely under the control of the Swahili Arabs and Yao Muslims. Thus the suggestion has been made that the ivory caravans were largely composed of professional traders and porters, even though the ivory trade and the slave trade were closely enmeshed. There seems to have been a distinction between the chiefs and ruling elites who controlled and benefited from the ivory trade; the professional hunters like the Azimba and Chikumba, who formed armed groups attached to local chiefs; the itinerant traders like Swahili, Bisa and Yao who organized the transportation of ivory and other trade goods; and the Indian merchants at the coastal towns who 'virtually monopolized' the ivory trade. Examining the 18th century trade at Mozambique, Alpers suggests that the ivory trade was exclusively capitalized by Indian merchants, while the trade itself was in the hands of the Yao, whereas the slave trade was mainly the affair of the Makua, and was capitalized by Europeans (Beachey 1967: 276-7, Alpers 1975: 143).

Although Gray and Birmingham (1970: 13) suggest that 'close links' between the formation of states and organized trade has yet to be established, it is my contention that throughout Malawi in the 19th century there was an intrinsic relationship between the hunting of elephant, the ivory trade and the emergence of petty states - most of which were short-lived, given the changing patterns of trade. Moving through the century I will discuss in turn a number of these chiefdoms, emphasizing their connections with the ivory trade.

TABLE TWO
African Ivory Exports 1988

	Volume/kg	Value/US$
Burundi	8655	1,298,250
Cameroon	2538	380,700
Congo	18806	2,820,900
Ivory Coast	988	148,200
Djibouti	10901	1,635,150
Ethopia	2160	324,000
Gabon	13542	2,031,300
Malawi	762	114,300
Mozambique	7302	1,095,300
Nigeria	6000	900,000
South Africa	7557	1,133,550
Tanzania	42581	6,387,150
Uganda	281	42,150
Zaire	11009	1,651,350
Zambia	1622	243,300
Zimbabwe	6983	1,047,450

Source: Barbier et al 1990

The Chikulamayembe Chiefdom

At the end of the 18th century the Nkhamanga Plain and the Henga Valley, south of the Nyika Plateau, were heavily populated with elephants, and

Owen Kalinga suggests that elephants probably outnumbered the human population. The people of the area (Henga, Nkhamanga and Phoka) were largely Tumbuka speakers, and clan membership (Luhanga, Mkandawire, Munthali) was an important source of social identity. Local chiefs, within the communities, had a certain authority and were entitled to tribute - such as the skins of lion or leopard - but the region lacked political central-ization (Vail 1972, Kalinga 1984).

Into this region around 1780 came a group of people who are referred to as the Balowoka. They were traders, and Cullen Young suggests proba-bly elephant hunters, and their leader was known as Mlowoka, meaning 'he who has crossed (the lake)'. Cullen Young and Alpers both suggest that these traders were Yao, probably dressed 'as Arabs', who came looking for ivory among a people for whom ivory had no commercial value, and was used as 'props for pots beside the fire' (Young 1932: 36, Alpers 1975: 161)! It is probable that these Yao traders had contact with Kilwa, and were already engaged in the long-distance trade in ivory, and were seeking new sources of supply. Their arrival in the Nkhamanga region completely changed its 'political configuration', for the Balowaka rose to power by manipulating social ties with local chiefs, using their economic power, and their control of the ivory trade as well as the trade of rhino horn and valu-able animal skins. According to some oral tradition the Balowoka chiefs like Kakalala and Katumbi were of Nyamwezi origin, but equally involved in the ivory trade. Marrying women of the Luhanga clan, and by giving generous gifts to local chiefs, the Mlowoka in pursuit of economic monop-oly were forced, as Kalinga notes, to seek and assert political hegemony (1984: 43). He concludes, 'The assumption of political power by a group of hunter-traders, usually referred to as the Balowoka, occurred as a result of the scramble for ivory which took place in the 18th century, when demand for that product greatly increased'.

But the link between the ivory trade and politics was complex, for 'not every wealthy and successful trader became a King' (op. cit. 49-50). A son of the Mlowoka, Gonapamuhanya, is reputed to have founded the Chikulamayembe dynasty in around 1805, and to have ruled the Nkhamanga region for a time. The dynasty, however, only had a loose con-trol over the subordinate chiefs, and it is doubtful if Chikulamayembe ever became a territorial chief. Leroy Vail suggests that what Mlowoka and his successors ruled over was 'less a state than a trade route for ivory' (1972: 156). Whether the local Tumbuka were actually ignorant of the commer-cial value of ivory is debatable, but for a period the Balowoka gained con-trol of the ivory trade which until then had largely been organized by the

Bisa. Vail notes that Saulos Nyirenda's history of the Tumbuka (1931) is little more than a glorification and justification of the Chikulamayembe chieftainship, which is reputed to have exercised power over a wide area. But although the dynasty exacted tribute in the form of ivory, Vail contends that its power and military strength was limited. It had neither a strong military system nor a unified political structure beyond the Nkhamanga plain. Undermined by the Swahili slave traders, and probably by the continuing presence of Bisa and Chikunda independent ivory hunters/traders, the Chikulamayembe dynasty easily succumbed to the Ngoni invasion in the mid-19th century. Although the British colonial administration re-established the Chikulamayembe chieftainship in 1907, it was already by then a shadow of its former self (Vail 1972: 158-163).

The Chewa Chiefdoms

The power and influence of the original Kalonga state was undoubtedly somewhat exaggerated, and its essential form was probably akin to that of the Chikulamayembe - having limited military power, and a unified political structure only within a fairly circumscribed area around the lakeshore. Thus, as we have earlier noted, access to the ivory trade allowed many Chewa chiefs to assert their political independence from the Maravi kingdoms - Undi and Kalonga - and this long before the Ngoni invasions. The more important of these chiefdoms were Mkanda (Mchinji), Kanyenda (Nkhotakota) and Mwase (Kasungu). Kings Phiri refers to these as 'successor Chewa states', although in fact they were little more than powerful chiefdoms, whose power, though limited and transitory, was based on the ivory trade which facilitated the importation of guns and other valued commodities.

Mkanda, in oral traditions, was originally a tributary chief under Undi, and, belonging to the Mbewe clan, was married to Undi's sister, Chirunje. They were thus linked by perpetual cousinship (*chisuwani*) (Ntara 1973: 74-75). Towards the end of the 18th century, Bisa and Yao traders became extremely active in the Luangwa and Bua watershed, which was then extremely rich in elephant. With new sources of wealth, both in the form of tribute (ivory) and by exacting a toll (*nsonkho*) on traders passing through the area - for Mchinji lay on the route to the coast - Mkanda was able to develop an independent power base. He became more and more independent of Undi, and in the 1830s the chief is described by Portuguese travellers as the most powerful and 'dreaded' Maravi chief of the region.

From the written records, Phiri concludes that 'state-formation' in Mkanda's area, at the headwaters of the Bua River near Chinji, 'was a result of the development of the ivory trade' (1988: 15, Langworthy 1975: 6-7). Equally important in the rise of the Mkanda chiefdom were the groups of Chikunda elephant hunters who roamed the area. Many being ex-slaves, the Chikunda were the armed retainers/hunters of the Pereira family, who in the 19th century were virtually the rulers of the Makanga region. This was situated north of the Zambezi in Mozambique, about 160 km south-west of Dedza and to the east of the Undi kingdom. For some 70 years Makanga was a 'State of slave and ivory hunters ruled by its Pereira chiefs' - these chiefs were from a Portuguese family (Newitt 1973: 234-37). The Chikunda retainers not only undermined the Undi kingdom, but many of them, as elephant hunters, attached themselves to the Mkanda chiefdom, selling their ivory to local chiefs, or to Bisa and Swahili traders (Phiri 1975: 124, Langworthy 1975: 7, see Morris 1998: 114-15 on the Chikunda as a hunting group).

Another Chewa chiefdom that was able to assert its independence in the 18th century, this time from the Kalonga kingdom, was that of Kanyenda. A member of the Mwale clan, and in oral traditions said to be a son of Kalonga, Kanyenda was originally a tributary chief for the Maravi ruler. His capital was in the Nkhotakota district, near the lakeshore on the lower Bua River (Ntara 1973: 90-91). As with Mkanda, at the end of the 18th century, the Kanyenda chiefdom began to assert its political independence, and its power and influence, Phiri writes, was 'predicated on its control of scarce resources like iron and ivory, coupled with its retention of religious authority' (1988: 17). Kanyenda seems to have controlled a trade route that crossed the Lake, ivory being particularly crucial and in the early 19th century the dynasty seems to have established authority over the present districts of Ntchisi and Dowa. As the 19th century progressed with the Ngoni invasions, and the development of the Swahili 'chiefdom' under Jumbe at Nkhotakota, the Kanyenda chiefdom lost much of its power and influence. In fact, the only Chewa chiefdom that was able to maintain substantial political power during the 19th century was Mwase at Kasungu. Able through the ivory trade to obtain a sturdy supply of muzzle-loaders, he was able to hold the Ngoni Impis at bay in the 1860s.

Oral traditions suggest that the senior chief in the Kasungu district was originally Chulu, who travelled with Undi when they left Malawi, on the lakeshore. But the chiefdom that came to establish political dominion in the Kasungu area was that of Mwase. This dynasty is said to have been established at Kasungu around 1740 by an ivory hunter and trader named

Mwase. He is said to have belonged to the Phiri clan, and to have been born at Bunda, near Lilongwe. As a hunter Mwase was able to kill a wild animal *lauzi* (*kauuzi*, the male sentinel baboon) that was said to be terrorizing women who went to collect water. Fulfilling a promise made to him, the local chief Lukwa gave Mwase the chieftainship (Ntara 1973: 67). Thus as a hunter-trader Mwase came to displace the chiefs Chulu and Lukwa, and to establish the Mwase dynasty, which became de facto rulers of the Kasungu area, the local chiefs becoming his vassals. From being an elephant hunter, Mwase had accumulated power through securing the goodwill of local people, and through his military and commercial exploits - the trading of ivory from the lands west of Kasungu being crucial in this transformation. At the height of his powers, around 1850, Mwase was able to control, Phiri suggests, a large area between the Bua River in the East, and the Luangwa in the West.

According to a later Mwase, Samuel Chimzimu his ancestor, the original Mwase, secured the chieftainship because he was able to clear the land of dangerous wild animals, and to protect them from hostile neighbours. Kasungu is thus derived from the verb *ku-sunga*, to keep, or watch over (Phiri 1982: 27-28, 1984: 57, 1988: 16). Because of this power base, particularly the possession of firearms derived from the ivory trade, Mwase was able to successfully repulse the Ngoni invasions towards the latter part of the century. As with Mkanda and Kanyenda, Mwase's rise to power in the early 19th century undermined the political power of Undi and Kalonga, which were already in decline. In fact, the two processes are intrinsically inter-connected, as the writings of Langworthy and Phiri suggest. The process has been described as 'political fragmentation' or as one of 'decentralization'. In fact, the locus of power merely shifted - from the lakeshore and the Kapoche stream to Nkhotakota, Mchinji and Kasungu. The 19th century was no more 'decentralized' or politically 'fragmented' than the previous two centuries: there were simply more established chiefdoms in the 19th century, and axes or foci of centralized coercive authority were merely widespread and intrusive on local communities. Kalonga and Undi in the 17th century and Chikulamayembe and Mwase dynasties in the early 19th century were in their power and influence probably similar polities and only incipient states. The petty states formed by the Swahili immigrants on the lakeshore, referred to by Phiri as 'sultanates', were probably of a similar kind, even though there may have been less cultural links between the ruling elite and the local Chewa communities. The most important of these Swahili chiefdoms was that of Jumbe of Nkhotakota.

The Jumbe of Nkhotakota

Throughout the 19th century Swahili traders together with the Yao moved westwards into the Maravi region, along the Southern Lakeshore. Not only was there an expansion of the ivory trade, with elephant hunters as groups playing an important role in the life of local communities, but there was also a growth in the slave trade. Domestic slavery probably has a long history in East-Central Africa, but during the 19th century slaves (*akapolo*) were increasingly transported to the coast. At the turn of the 19th century around 5,000 slaves were being exported from Mozambique Island annually, and it has been estimated that by the mid-century between 8-10,000 slaves were taken from Central Malawi and Eastern Zambia. Among the Chewa, each slave was valued at 20 yards of cloth, although the Portuguese willingly sold guns for slaves. Yao, Chikunda and Swahili traders tended to act as the 'middlemen' in the trade of both slaves and ivory (Alpers 1975: 186-187, Phiri 1975: 126-29).

Although Arab-Swahili influence was pervasive in Malawi from the beginning of the 19th century, the trading and social relationship between these immigrants and the Chewa took a different turn in the 1840s. For, at that time, a group of Swahili traders from the East Coast settled at Nkhotakota, which was situated on the lakeshore, around 90 km directly east of Kasungu. The leader of this group, and the first Jumbe (meaning 'Prince') was Salim bin 'Abdallah. He was an Arab from Zanzibar and had been actively engaged in the ivory/slave trade at Tabora and Ujiji in Tanzania. He initially traded peacefully with the Kanyenda chiefdom, but he soon established political dominion in the area around Nkhotakota, partly because of his trading contacts - for he built dhows to conduct trade in ivory and slaves across the Lake - and partly because he possessed firearms and was thus able to protect the Chewa, Tonga and Nyanja of the lakeshore against the Ngoni invasion. He assumed the title of 'Sultan of Marimba', expressing an allegiance for the Sultan of Zanzibar, and set up what George Shepperson describes as a system of 'indirect rule' (1966: 255-56, Langworthy 1975: 15-16). By degrees Jumbe and his successors - Salim bin 'Abdallah died in the 1860s - built up a prosperous and thriving trading centre at Nkhotakota, employing local hunters to collect ivory, and utilizing the local chiefs as subordinate headmen. Rice cultivation was expanded along the fertile lakeshore, and the area came to support a high population of people. Elephants were then still plentiful in the hills to the west of Nkhotakota. Towards the end of the century Nkhotokata became a thriving town, with about 6,000 inhabitants, and the first Islamic centre in Malawi. When Harry Johnston visited the third Jumbe, Mwinyi Kisutu, in 1889, he found him to be an astute diplomat, as well as hospitable, and described him as a 'Swahili merchant prince'. By then the slave trade had been partly suppressed, and the Jumbe derived most of his wealth from the ivory trade. His hunters, it appears, ranged all over Central Malawi in all directions (Oliver 1957: 161-2). The power of these Swahili Arab merchants was, therefore, intrinsically linked to the ivory trade.

As Mwase and Jumbe chiefdoms were both situated on the same trade route, between the Luangwa/Bua region and the East African coast, it was inevitable that animosity and conflict developed between them - as well as between Jumbe and the Yao chief Makanjila. This was mentioned by the German traveller, Carl Wiese, who along with the elephant hunter Alfred Sharpe visited the Mwase chief in the late 1880s. Wiese noted that Jumbe and his retainers had raided Mwase's caravans returning from the coast after selling ivory (Wiese 1983: 266). What is also evident from Wiese's account is that Swahili traders were influential in the Chipata and Kasungu regions, and because of the Ngoni, most Chewa villages were moated and fortified (*chemba*, a moat, is the term used for these fortified villages). It also seemed common, at this period, for each territorial chief, as well as paramounts like Mwase and Mkanda, to be a patron for a number of hunters. Such client hunters would not only assist in providing ivory, and thus help the chief to amass wealth, but would also act as a coercive force in the maintenance of the chief's authority (1983: 258). Chikunda and Bisa elephant hunters both served chiefs in this capacity. The Chewa themselves, under Mwase and Mkanda, seem not to have engaged in trading activities - such trade was undertaken by the Chikunda, Bisa, Swahili, and at a later period, the Yao. Although muzzle-loading guns - 'matchlocks' - seem to have been commonly used at the end of the 19th century, the Bisa hunted elephants in groups with large spears (*nthungo*), and with the help of dogs. According to Wiese, the Bisa were enterprising travellers, knew the savanna woodland ('bush') between the Kasai and Lake Bangwenlu and the Mwase chiefdom intimately, and were therefore patronized by both Mwase and the Lunda rulers (op. cit. 267).

The Jumbe chiefdom played a significant role in the politics of Central Malawi for over 50 years. Its influence came to an end in 1895, when, with the advent of Johnston's colonial administration, the fourth Jumbe was deposed and deported to Zanzibar (Shepperson 1966: 261, on the relationship between the Mwase and Jumbe chiefdoms see Langworthy 1975: 28-33).

The Yao Chiefdoms

Four Ngoni groups, three Yao groups, and a Swahili trader, Langworthy wrote (1975: 11), settled in Malawi during the 19th century, and all had a profound impact on the history of the country. We discussed the Swahili trader, Salim bin 'Abdallah in the last section. We turn now to the Yao immigrants who came in three groups but who established a series of small, but powerful chiefdoms on the Southern Lakeshore, and in the Shire Highlands towards the end of the 19th century.

The history of the Yao ivory trade has been superbly described by Alpers in his classic study *Ivory and Slaves in East Central Africa* (1975), and I have no wish to recapitulate this work here. I shall focus instead on the Yao chiefdoms in Malawi. The Yao claim their origins from a hill of the same name in Northern Mozambique, Chao, the plural form of which is Yao. The Yao hill is said to be situated between the Mwembe and the Luchilingo rivers. *Chawe* also means a plateau region or hill and in the Zomba district is widely used in this way, *ku-chawe*, so like the Chewa clan name Phiri, Yao essentially means hill-people (Abdallah 1973: 7). As with other groups like the Mang'anja and Chewa, the Yao were a matrilineal people who, in pre-colonial times, combined hunting and fishing, undertaken mainly by men, with subsistence agriculture focussed round a group of women.

Iron-smelting was important - the making of iron hoes, axes, spears and needles being undertaken by a specific 'clan' called the Wachisi - and internal trade with the Maravi people, involving salt, iron goods, cloth and other subsistence goods, probably goes back many centuries. But the Yao, particularly the blacksmith clan, were great travellers and traders, and Abdallah describes the Yao in 'the old days' as having 'a roving disposition' (1973: 28).

From the beginning of the 18th century, the Yao became actively involved in the international trade in ivory. Hunting thus became increasingly important among the Yao, although elephant hunting was not organized in specialist guilds or hunting fraternities as it was among the Bisa and Makua. It was rather, as Alpers writes, focussed around the political structure of the village and chiefdom. A symbiotic relationship thus emerged between a local territorial chief, or even a headman, and a professional elephant hunter-trader together with his hunting associates. The hunting of elephants was highly ritualized, with a prohibition on sexual relations prior to the hunt, special medicines used and ritual offerings made to the spirits of the dead (see Morris 1998: 97-107) on these hunting rituals. The

39

ground tusk of every elephant was deemed the property of the chief, and a big tusk was said to be worth 30-60 yards of cloth, much more than that of a slave (op. cit. 31). By the 19th century the Yao became implicated in the slave trade, the slaves (*akapolo*) procured being mainly Nyanja (Nyasa), Bisa (Wisa), Nsenga and Chikunda people. Some of the slaves were employed as domestic workers, some were porters carrying the ivory tusks, and some were sold as slaves at the coast - referred to as Mbwani. From the trade of ivory and slaves, the Yao obtained muzzle-loading guns (*mlandawala*, *uti*) and gunpowder (*wonga*), beads, various coloured cloths, sugar and coconut oil. Elephant tusks were referred to as *meno ga ndembo* (teeth of the elephant). Although the Yao men were primarily traders and hunters, the procurement of ivory may have been left to other ethnic communities, and the chief as owner (*mysene*) of the territory or country (*chilambo*) was perhaps not himself a trader, but rather the focus and controller of the trade. In the past only chiefs were allowed to adorn themselves with the skins (*lipende*) of such animals as lion (*simba*), serval (*njusi*) and leopard (*chisuwi*) (Abdallah 1973: 12-13, 29-31, Alpers 1975: 15-22).

The transition from an earlier regional trade of mainly subsistence goods, to one involving ivory and then slaves, has been viewed as a 'major watershed' in Yao history. Thus during the 18th century the Yao chanelled most of their trade through Mozambique Island, which became a major centre of ivory trade. Alpers indeed concedes that the Yao ivory trade was fundamental to the prosperity of the Portuguese empire in East Africa, for the Portuguese had lost control of the East African coast north of the Rovuma River to the Arabs. For most of the 18th century the Yao dominated the ivory trade through to Mozambique (Alpers 1975: 97).

Shifting patterns of trade in ivory, and the development of the slave trade in the 19th century, tended, however, to undermine the importance of Mozambique Island as an ivory market.

Oral traditions emphasize the importance of muzzle-loading guns (*mfuti za gogodera*) that were acquired through the ivory trade, the Yao later learning to make their own, and the importance of beeswax, along with slaves and ivory, in the trade with the coast (*mbwani*). The Ngoni are said to have provided the Yao with slaves and ivory (Phiri et al. 1977: 89-122).

By about 1850 the Yao had firmly established themselves as a trading community, the wealth of whose chiefs was based on their involvement in the ivory and slave trade. But as Kings Phiri remarks, the most notable characteristic of the Yao trade was that it was controlled by a 'few men of means' - either local chiefs or men who had attached themselves to Swahili traders. Several of these chiefs acquired large quantities of wealth, which could be redistributed, as well as firearms. They used these new sources of wealth to expand their village communities into trading entrepots or small towns, attaching people from local communities, as well as acquiring slaves (Phiri 1975: 146). Also around the middle of the 19th century a number of Yao groups began to move into southern Malawi from northern Mozambique. The reasons for this exodus from Mozambique is far from clear, but famine conditions and conflict with the Makua and Lomwe people may have been important factors. Given their linguistic and cultural affinities to these people, some scholars have suggested that the Yao may originally have been Lomwe (Rangeley 1963: 13, Rashid 1978).

The Yao who entered Malawi seem to have come from the region immediately east of Lake Malawi, from the headwaters of the Rovuma and Lujenda rivers. They came to Malawi in three groups, each taking the name of a hill with which they were associated: Masaninga, Machinga, and Mangoche, the three groups to which Langworthy alludes. There were other groups of Yao, but only these three groups were represented in Malawi. These groups have been described as 'sub-tribes' but the Yao word used by Abdallah is either Lukosyo or Liwele, both refer to clan, or matrilineal kin group, Liwele also meaning 'breast'. But these clans or sub-tribes had less political significance than the various chiefdoms which began to form in Southern Malawi after 1850, coalescing around certain important entrepreneurial chiefs. The rise of such chiefs Alpers sees as very much a 19th century phenomena, and he sees the development of these chiefdoms as intrinsically linked to the ivory/slave trade. The power and status of these chiefs, though based on the wealth derived from this trade, nevertheless was closely linked to the number of followers that a chief was able to attract and control. Slave women acquired by raiding or through trade augmented the power of the chief, and became a common feature of Yao life in the 19th century (Rangeley 1963, Alpers 1969).

In his account of the Yao, W.H.J. Rangeley emphasized that until the development of the ivory trade by the Yao, the people of Southern Malawi had used elephant ivory locally for doorposts and seats, and as ornaments and that the opening up of Yao markets on the lakeshore had completely transformed their value. He notes the importance, too, of cowrie shells (*mpande*) and flintlock 'Tower' guns brought back from the coast, as well as of brass wire. With the price of ivory higher than that of a slave - a large elephant tusk could fetch between 30 and 60 yards of cloth as against 3 to 4 yards for a slave - ivory was the dominant commodity, and slaves were often procured to carry the ivory to the coast. Ivory became both the source and the symbol of the wealth of the Yao chiefs (Rangeley 1963: 14-24). These Yao chiefdoms became territorial domains, for the chief was described as the owner or guardian of the territory (*msyene chilambo*), headmen being simply guardians of the village community (*musi*). But Alpers stresses that although the Yao chiefs achieved their power through a combination of trading and raiding - a key factor in their political domination being the possession of guns - the Yao territorial chiefdoms had limited powers. For there was no standing army, or any formal administration, and though chiefs may also have had considerable ritual powers - with respect to rain-making - this too was limited in scope (1969: 415). The territorial chief also had important judicial functions and, according to McDonald, tribute in the form of elephant tusks, or the hindleg of any game animal killed, was given as a form of tribute through the headman, who would receive in return a present, such as a little gunpowder (1882: 152-58).

During the latter part of the 19th century, when the slave trade was at its height, Yao chiefs came to establish political dominance over much of the Southern Lakeshore, and the Shire Highlands. The more important of these chiefs were: Mponda (on the Shire, north of Mangochi), Makanjila (on the South-Eastern Lakeshore), Jalasi (on Mangochi Mountain), Kawinga (near the Chikala hills), Malemia and Mlumbe (near Zomba), Matapwiri (near the Fort Lister Gap, Phalombe) Kapeni (near Mount Soche), Liwonde (on the Upper Shire) and Pemba (on the lakeshore near the Linthipe River) (MacDonald 1982: 32-33, Phiri 1984: 58-61).

All these chiefdoms were strategically located for the control of the ivory/slave trade which, as Rangeley outlined, moved along several routes from East to West (1963: 20-21). Their rise to political dominance largely undermined the residual power of the local Chewa, Nyanja and Mang'anja chiefs. Langworthy has suggested that the Yao were directly responsible for the 'ending of the Kalonga dynasty' (1975: 14), but it seems by the middle of the 19th century that this chiefdom had long ceased to be a dominant political force.

Although largely illiterate, these Yao chiefs tended to adopt Islamic religion and culture. According to many 19th century missionaries, Islam was no more than a 'veneer' over traditional Yao culture, but, as Rangeley wrote, this veneer was not unimportant, for Islam was taken seriously by the Yao 'ruling class' - the chiefly dynasties. Yet the general spread of Islam amongst the Yao did not occur until after 1890, and has been interpreted as largely a response to the imposition of colonial rule (Rangeley 1963: 25-

26, Alpers 1969: 420, for important studies of Yao Muslims see Thorold 1995, Msiska 1995).

The power of the Yao chiefdoms, like that of the early Maravi states, was intrinsically bound-up with the hunting of elephant and the ivory trade - augumented towards the end of the 19th century by an expansion of the slave trade. The 'capital' villages of the chiefs (Msinda, Mbala), which developed into fortified towns with large populations, invariably held large stocks of ivory - which was readily convertible into slaves, gunpowder or guns. Mponda's village on the Shire, north of Mangochi had, for example, in the 1890s a population of some 5,000 people, and was protected by medicines, and each year ritually cleansed. The Catholic White Fathers at Mponda around 1890 noted the many conflicts over the ivory trade, and the 'numerous' ivory caravans that made their way to Quelimane a journey of 17 days. Mponda's chiefdom is said to have contained 110 villages (Linden 1974: 20-24, 1989).

The power of the Yao chiefdoms came to an abrupt end in the 1890s with the advent of the colonial administration under Harry Johnston. In a series of punitive raids using around 200 Sikh soldiers in 1895, Johnston completely routed the Yao chiefs - Makanjila, Mponda, Kawinga, Matapwiri and Liwonde '[s]weeping away all opposition to their progress, freeing slaves, intercepting and disarming fugitives, burning the villages of resisters and carrying off their stores of ivory and cloth, firearms and powder'. Johnston's lightning campaign of 28 days forced the Yao chiefs either to submit to the colonial authority or to flee the territory, now proclaimed a 'protectorate'. Although depicted as a crusade against the slave trade, Johnston's military operations were aimed primarily at destroying the Yao control of the ivory trade, and this it did completely (Oliver 1957: 259-265).

The Makololo Chiefdoms

When Livingstone left Malawi in early 1864, at the end of his Zambezi expedition, he left behind some of his Kololo porters, 16 in number. They had originated from Barotseland, and armed with muzzle-loading guns they quickly established themselves as petty chiefs over the local Mang'anja people in the Lower Shire Valley. The Makololo were ethnically a mixed group of men from Sekeletu's kingdom, and only two were true Kololo: Moloka and Ramakukan (the latter otherwise known as Kasisi, prophet or 'the refuge'). The terrible famine of 1862-63 (*chaola*) had greatly weakened the Mang'anja people of the Shire Valley, and the Makololo,

Rangeley writes, quickly achieved an 'almost bloodless occupation' of the country. They quickly achieved political dominance over the local Mang'anja chiefs, Mankhokwe, Lundu, and Kaphwiti, some traditions suggesting that Kaphwiti was shot by Kasisi as he was crossing the Shire River by canoe. Moloka and Kasisi proceeded to rule the Shire Valley south of the Nkurumadzi River as 'joint chiefs', the other Makololo settling at intervals along the Shire. They married local Mang'anja women. Their political dominance has been put down to a combination of circumstances: the decimation of the population as a result of the Yao invasions of the Shire Highlands; the famine; the weakness of the Mang'anja chiefdoms; and the possession of muzzle-loading guns. Once they had established their power they were able to sustain it by their control of the ivory trade, and through this trade to build their own wealth and power. They were also able to control salt production, and cultivation of oil seeds, like sesame (*chitowe*).

After the death of Moloka, who was shot by the Mang'anja chief Kabvina, who lived at Milolongo on the Mwanza River, Kasisi assumed complete control of the country. Chiputula, who was based at Chiromo, Mlauri, Mulilima and Maseya acted as sub-chiefs, although as Makololo they had a good deal of political autonomy. Mlauri had a great reputation as a hunter, as did Moloka, who acted as a guide to Henry Faulkner on the 1867 Livingstone search expedition. Chiputula was shot in 1884 by a former Scottish missionary, George Fenwick, in a famous incident. Having taken a consignment of ivory and sesame oil to Blantyre on Chiputula's behalf, Fenwick was accused by Chiputula of having cheated him. In the squabble that ensued, Chiputula was shot, and Fenwick was later speared by the chief's men. This episode created a crisis in the relationship between the Makololo and the newly formed African Lakes Company, whose own survival as a company depended on the ivory trade. Established in 1878, and managed by the brothers John and Fred Moir, the company had been formed to run a profitable export business from the Shire Highlands, particularly in such crops as sugar, tobacco and cotton. The company had been founded largely in response to the call of David Livingstone, namely to end the slave trade by combining Christianity with legitimate commerce (F. Moir 1923: 1). But as Hugh MacMillan has discussed, the company found it necessary, in order to remain solvent, to become involved in the ivory trade, for ivory was a highly profitable export. The Makololo resented what they considered to be the 'poaching' of ivory from their territories. Relations between the Makololo and the company were already strained when the Fenwick incident occurred, but, fortunately for the company and the Blantyre missionaries, Kasisi used his influence to re-establish a degree of peace in the Shire Valley, as well as to consolidate his own position as the paramount chief. Kasisi died in 1886, and six years later treaties were signed by the remaining Makololo chiefs, including Maseya and Mulilima, ceding their sovereign rights to the British Colonial administration. In 1894 a 'very fat cheery little man', John Bowhill, was appointed collector of revenue at Chikwawa. This marked the end of the independent power of the Makololo chiefdoms (Baker 1970: 99, for important discussions of the Makololo chiefdoms from which the above has been extracted see Rangeley 1959, MacMillan 1975, and Mandala 1990: 85-87, 90-91).

I have outlined above some of the various chiefdoms that emerged in Malawi during the 19th century. All of the chiefdoms indicate that a close relationship pertains between the power of the chiefly dynasties and control over the ivory trade, for it was ivory that was the essential source of both wealth and firearms. Thus the political history of Malawi during the 19th century is intrinsically connected with elephant hunting, and with the trade in ivory.

The Ngoni Chiefdoms

The history of the 19th century would not be complete without mentioning the Ngoni invasions. The Ngoni lie beyond the scope of my own studies, which are focussed on the matrilineal peoples of Malawi, all of whom are settled cultivators with important hunting traditions. The Ngoni, in contrast, are patrilineal people whose social and economic life was largely focussed around cattle-keeping. Although they did indeed hunt - especially for small mammals - Ngoni communal hunts tended to focus around predators, not on game animals.

The Ngoni have their origins in the rise of the Zulu empire in the Natal region of South Africa at the beginning of the 19th century. Shaka came to power in 1816, establishing a powerful centralized kingdom. In the conflicts and disturbances that followed, often described as the *mfecane*, several groups of Nguni-speaking people migrated north into Central and Eastern Africa. Two of these groups are particularly important in the history of Malawi, that of Zwangendaba, who is reputed to have crossed the Zambezi in 1835, and that of the Maseko Ngoni. These two groups entered Malawi between 1850 and 1860. The descendants of Zwangendaba, under M'mbelwa (Mombera), eventually settled in the Mzimba district, while an offshoot, under the leadership of Chiwere, established itself in the Dowa district. The Maseko Ngoni under Gomani eventually settled around Domwe and Dedza Mountains. Being pastoralists, although agriculture was also important, all these Ngoni groups settled in highland areas, where there was ample grazing and which were relatively free of tsetse fly. All these three groups, given their efficient military organization and the use of the short-handled spear, soon established political dominance over the surrounding peoples, in particular the Chipeta, Nsenga, Tonga, Chewa and Tumbuka. They thus created highly centralized chiefdoms, under a paramount who was also commander-in-chief. Only those chiefdoms, like Mwase at Kasungu, who had access to muzzle-loading guns, were able to maintain any political independence. These Ngoni chiefdoms were 'hybrid in composition,' as Kings Phiri (1988: 20) describes them, for a symbiotic relationship was formed with local village headmen, and the Ngoni freely inter-married with local people. The Ngoni appear to have adopted the Chewa language, social organization, and rituals to a great extent - especially after the turn of the century when the Ngoni kingdoms lost much of their power with the establishment of colonial rule - although the 1893 rinderpest epidemic had already undermined their social and economic foundations (Pachai 1972). Unlike the chiefdoms described above, the three main Ngoni chiefdoms - Mpezeni had created another kingdom near Chipata in Zambia - based their power, not on trade, but on the control of people and cattle. There is, however, plenty of evidence which suggests that although the Ngoni kingdoms were not directly involved in the ivory/slave trade, they did in fact provide ivory and slaves to Swahili, Bisa and Yao traders.

From the viewpoint of local people, the Ngoni immigrants are usually described in negative terms as *maviti* (terrible ones, *mfiti*: witch), or as *zirombo* (wild animals) and as causing 'devastation' throughout the highlands of Central and Northern Malawi. Some of the Maseko Ngoni, under Chikusi, who was based at Mlangeni, made raids into the Shire Highlands in 1882, plundering the Yao and Mang'anja, and causing great consternation among the Scottish missionaries (Pachai 1972: 190). Raiding seems to have been an important element in the dynamics of the Ngoni chiefdoms. Others, however, have suggested that the Ngoni by introducing a centralized system of government to the central 'Angoni' highlands and to the Mzimba district, brought 'law and order' to these areas. Desmond Phiri in his short history of the Ngoni of Malawi stresses the more positive aspects of Ngoni culture and of Ngoni rule (D.D. Phiri 1982, for further studies of the Ngoni see Elmslie 1901, Chibambo 1942, Read 1956, Rangeley 1966 and Ebner 1987).

THE COLONIAL IMPACT:
RINDERPEST AND TSETSE FLY

This study is not a history of Malawi, and I thus have no wish to go into the politics and culture of the colonial period. I have elsewhere described the social impact of the colonial game laws on local communities and the chequered history of wildlife conservation in Malawi - particularly as this effected local people. In this section, therefore, I want to examine the colonial period only in terms of two phenomena which directly effected local people's relationship with the environment, and particularly with mammalian life: the rinderpest epidemic of the 1890s and the problems associated with the tsetse fly. Both these issues have generated much debate among historians, although they are hardly mentioned in early Malawian historiography (e.g. Pachai 1972, 1973, MacDonald 1975).

In a now classic study of the social ecology of East Africa, specifically focusing on Tanzania, Helge Kjekshus (1977) sought to restore the people as agents in African history, shifting the focus of history away from state politics. His essential thesis is that prior to the colonial impact at the end of the 19th century African people had established and maintained a degree of ecological control over the natural environment - in spite of the inter-tribal conflict and the slave-raiding over a long period of time. He attempted to counter the widespread depiction of the pre-colonial period as one where people were at the mercy of the vagaries of nature, and that their political economy was one characterized by disorder, violence and underdevelopment. Three assumptions or factors were suggested by earlier colonial historians for this lack of control over nature: the state of constant warfare that was thought to be prevalent in the pre-colonial period; the widespread presence of tsetse fly; and the fact that the main form of agriculture - shifting cultivation - prevented any degree of environmental control. He thus sought to challenge the view of some early historians who saw the history of East Africa as nothing but 'blank, uninteresting, brutal barbarism' (Kjekshus 1977: 181).

Kjekshus argued that the presence of long-standing cattle traditions implied that local people had indeed achieved a degree of control over the environment, and were fully conversant with the problems of tsetse fly, especially in the transporting of cattle; that people had a developed trading economy and thriving small-scale industrial enterprises, particularly focussed around the production of salt, iron and cloth; and - citing Richard

Burton - he suggests that around the middle of the 19th century, before the full impact of colonialism, people in Tanzania lived in a state of 'wholesome prosperity'. According to Burton, their material conditions suggested 'comfort and plenty', and contrasted favourably with the conditions of peasants in India and Europe (1977: 4).

Acknowledging the vitality and the regenerative powers of nature in tropical Africa - its flora, fauna and microbial life - Kjekshus nevertheless felt that in the pre-colonial period humans had achieved a degree of control – 'ecological domination' are the words he uses - over nature. A certain balance had been established between human and mammalian life, and the dangers stemming from tsetse fly - both to cattle and humans - had been neutralized, or kept at bay.

The eruption of the tsetse-borne sleeping sickness epidemics in East Africa at the beginning of the 20th century, Kjekshus suggests, resulted from the colonial impact and the subsequent loss by African people of control over the environment (1977: 181, see M. Lyons 1992 for a similiar analysis of sleeping sickness in northern Zaire, for Lyons suggests that the outbreaks of this disease were intrinsically related to the social upheavals and ecological disruptions concommitant with the advent of colonial rule).

A similar thesis to that of Kjekshus was also presented by Leroy Vail with respect to Eastern Zambia. Like Kjekshus, Vail suggests that prior to the late 19th century people of this region were able to sustain a viable ecological relationship with their environment, a degree of control over nature, such that a 'finely balanced relationship' between humans and their environment pertained. But after 1895 the dual impact of expanding capitalism and colonial administration shattered this relationship, leading to a 'major ecological catastrophe'. Under the impact of colonialism, people lost control over the environment, and impoverishment and the spread of disease, particularly sleeping sickness, was the result. Again like Kjekshus, Vail suggests that the people of Eastern Zambia - the Chewa and Nsenga - prior to colonialism lived peacefully and were able to easily satisfy their basic needs - Vail citing the observations of Antonio Gamitto. The land was relatively fertile, and able to support a fairly high human population, and there was a flourishing trade in ivory and slaves with Mwase Kasungu.

It is important not to romanticize the economic conditions of the pre-colonial period, for subsistence agriculture is highly dependent on rainfall, and life is experienced as a constant struggle to survive, particularly against the depredations of wildlife. However, by the beginning of the 20th century a number of factors upset the ecological balance and of these Vail discusses the following: the invasion of the Ngoni 'warriors' which led to a settlement pattern of closely settled stockaded villages with large tracks of empty land inbetween; the restrictions on the sale of gunpowder to Africans; and the proclamation of game laws which prohibited hunting by local people. Together these led to the development of large tracts of 'bush' (savanna woodland), in which an ever-expanding population of game animals flourished, and these, in turn, set the stage 'for one of the major ecological reverses' in the history of Eastern Zambia - the spread of tsetse fly. This affected both cattle and humans in the form of sleeping sickness (1977: 138).

In a later paper, discussing the impact of capitalism on East Central Africa, Vail suggests that the daily realities of colonial rule, labour migration and the consolidation of village communities, coupled with the natural disasters of the 1890s like the rinderpest epidemic, precipitated an 'ecological collapse'. This entailed the reversion of cultivated land to woodland, a substantial increase in the numbers of wildlife, and thus to the spread of tsetse fly, with its negative impact, and to an increase in crop depredations by wild mammals. As with Kjekshus, Vail suggests that the villagers of Eastern Zambia became 'out of harmony with the countryside' and thus experienced increased impoverishment, epidemics of disease, and a general decline in living standards (1977: 154-55, 1983: 228-29).

Malawi, of course, is situated between Tanzania and Eastern Zambia, and John McCracken (1987) in an important paper has attempted to assess the validity of the Vail/Kjekshus thesis as it applies to Malawi. I will follow some of his guidelines here.

During the latter part of the 19th century, before the advent of colonial rule, village communities in Malawi, and their ecological environment, were subject to the impact of two complex social forces, the Ngoni invasions and the development of the ivory/slave trade. We have discussed both of these earlier; both made their impact at roughly the same time - the decades after 1850. And the impact of both was similar, for throughout Malawi they forced communities to concentrate their settlement in fortified villages as on the Kasungu Plain or to live in rather remote or inaccessible localities - on the rift valley escarpment along the lakeshore, high on the mountains of Zomba or Mulanje, or hidden on Chisi Island in Lake Chilwa, or on islands in the River Shire. Whether escaping from the slave trade or from the Ngoni raiders, settlements took the form either of fortified villages or refugee camps (McCracken 1987: 67, Mandala 1990: 76).

A consequence of this change in settlement pattern was that large sections of the Kasungu Plain, the Shire Highlands, particularly the Thuchila/Phalombe Plain, and the Lower Shire Valley became depopulated. This allowed the regeneration of the savanna woodland and within a short period of time game animals began to flourish in these areas. Following the analysis of Kjekshus, and emphasizing the dramatic impact of the slave trade and the great famine of 1862-63 (*chaola*), Elias Mandala suggests that the Mang'anja of the Lower Shire Valley were unable to control nature through the labour process and, with this loss of control, came the bush and the wild animals (op. cit. 78). It was in such circumstances that the tsetse fly 'belts', which had previously been limited in range, began to spread in Malawi - with the subsequent loss of both cattle and human life. In the first three decades of the present century tsetse fly thus constituted a serious problem, and a focus of ongoing concern for the colonial government.

All tsetse flies belong to the genus *Glossina*, and they are found only in Africa south of the Sahara. They are active only in daylight hours, and two species are important: *Glossina palpalis* which is a riverine species found mainly in West Africa, Zaire and Uganda, and *Glossina morsitans* which is a savanna species, once common in Central Africa, and the commonest of the genus in Malawi. This fly still flourishes in Kasungu and Nkhotakota game sanctuaries. *Glossina morsitans* (*kanzemba*), as is the case with other members of the genus, feeds on blood, sometimes of humans, but mainly of bushbuck, warthog and buffalo. According to Selous 'tsetse' is a word derived from the Tswana (Bechuwana) language (1908: 170). The tsetse fly is the vector both of the cattle disease *nagana* - which is a Zulu word meaning to be depressed or low in spirits - and of human sleeping sickness, both of which are caused by the parasitic *Protozoa trypanosoma*. The trypanosome responsible for sleeping sickness in Zambia and Malawi was discovered in 1912 by Warrington Yorke and Allan Kingham, and was shown to be trypanosome rhodesiense which is transmitted by the common tsetse fly *G. morsitans* (Pollock 1969, Lambrecht 1970).

It is possible that both nagana - caused by the trypanosome *T. Brucei* - and sleeping sickness have existed in Africa since the earliest times. The trypanosome are normal parasites on several species of ungulates and do not cause illness either to the fly or to their main hosts, an indication of 'ancient, well adjusted parasitism'. It has been suggested that because these parasites produced such debilitating illness in humans, this has been conducive to the survival of the African ungulates (M. Lyons 1992: 51). But throughout much of East Central Africa, the opening up of land for settlement, and the cleaning of the woodland through bushfires, allowed some degree of control by humans over the tsetse fly - a balance which, both Kjekshus and Vail suggest, was disrupted only at the end of the 19th century. It was then that epidemics of sleeping sickness began to sweep through Africa, causing a serious loss of human life (Lambrecht 1970: 93).

Compared with neighbouring countries Tanzania and Zambia, Malawi in pre-colonial times had a fairly high population density - especially around the lakeshore and in the Lower Shire Valley, and it lacked communities with a pastoral economy, apart from the Ngonde in the extreme North, and the Ngoni immigrants. The Ngoni, as noted, settled mainly in the Mzimba, Dowa and Dedza highlands. But, as McCracken has discussed, the colonial administration in Malawi followed the patterns of that described by Vail and Kjekshus, in attempting to consolidate village settlement in order to have effective control over the local population, in limiting the use of firearms by Africans, and in enacting game laws that were aimed to curtail local subsistence hunting, particularly the communal hunts. These colonial policies only had a limited success. But there can be no doubt that game animals increased substantially during the early colonial period, and crop depredations became an increasing cause for concern among local communities in certain areas. McCracken suggests that in the Kasungu district and on the South-Eastern Lakeshore, the colonial occupation was marked 'by an increase in the number of wild animals' (1987: 71).

But equally important in disturbing the ecological balance between humans and wildlife at the end of the 19th century was the rinderpest epidemic. Kjekshus suggests that it was the rinderpest epidemic that initiated the 'breakdown' of the long-established ecological balance between humans and nature (wildlife), and placed 'nature again at the advantage' (1977: 126).

Rinderpest is reputed to have first made its appearance in Somaliland in 1889. By 1890 it had reached Uganda, and then spread like wild fire throughout Eastern Africa. Its impact was 'catastrophic' on many pastoral people, like the Wagogo and Maasai, in East Africa, for it had a destructive impact on their herds of cattle. In some regions it almost wiped out the cattle population, causing widespread famine, and the attendant diseases that were an effect of the famine (Kjekshus 1977: 126-131). In 1892 rinderpest reached Zambia; by 1896 it had spread to Botswana and Southern Africa, and besides its economic impact on local pastoral people, it had far-reaching social and political effects, paralysing the transport system (which utilized oxen) and initiating political revolts (Van Onselen 1972). The rindepest epidemic reached Malawi in the dry season of 1893, and according to the Rev. Stewart of the Ekwendemi Mission almost all the cattle in Mombera's (M'Mbelwa) kingdom had perished before the rains broke. The epidemic seems to have completely undermined the economic power of the Ngoni - although the cattle soon recovered their numbers. Equally important the rinderpest also had a devastating effect on wild game - for although elephant, rhinoceros and hippo were immune from this 'malignant fever', buffalo, kudu and eland were especially susceptible to the virus disease and large numbers succumbed. The Henga Valley, and the Rukuru River basin - near Lake Kazuni - were prior to the rinderpest epidemic, teeming with wild game and with tsetse fly. After the epidemic buffalo and eland had almost disappeared - and also, the Rev. Steward records, so had the tsetse fly. By the 1920s, he continued, the game had increased in numbers in its old haunts, together with the tsetse fly (MNA/S1/1721A/123).

The exact distribution of tsetse fly in pre-colonial Malawi is difficult to ascertain, but it is probable that it was restricted to uninhabited woodland on the lakeshore and the Upper Shire, and on the

NOTICE.

In pursuance of the clauses of the "Regulations for the Prevention of Rinderpest (or other Diseases attacking Domestic Animals) within the British Central Africa Protectorate," I hereby publicly notify:—

1. That the importation of Cattle or any other Domestic Animals into the British Central Africa Protectorate from

(a). Portuguese Territory lying to the east, south, and west of the British Central Africa Protectorate,'

(b). The Territory administered by the British South Africa Company lying west of the British Central Africa Protectorate,

is for the present strictly prohibited.

2. It is also for the present forbidden to move any cattle or other domestic animals across the River Shire.

3. Any person contravening the terms of this notice will be at once proceeded against and punished in accordance with the provisions of the above cited Regulations and of the "Africa Order in Council, 1889."

(Signed) ALFRED SHARPE.

H. M. Acting Commissioner & Cont-Genl.
Zomba, December 30th, 1896.

Thuchila/Phalombe Plain. Harry Johnston suggested it was not found over 3000 ft (900 m), nor was it found in low-lying areas, like the Lower Shire Valley, where there was extensive human settlement, although it abounded near the Elephant Marsh. He noted that the wild game of Africa - the buffalo, zebra and the antelopes - were quite unaffected by the bite of the tsetse fly, but their nearest congeners among domestic animals - cattle, goat and horse - were killed by the fly. As an observant naturalist, Johnston fully understood the close association between tsetse fly and wild game, and noted that the tsetse 'tends to disappear before the presence of man'.

A certain cure then for tsetse fly, he suggested, would be human settlement and putting the low-lying parts of the protectorate under cultivation (1897: 377-80).

In the early years of the present century the spread of tsetse fly threatened Malawi in ways comparable to that of Tanzania and Eastern Zambia, and heralded what McCracken, following Kjekshus, has described as an 'ecological catastrophe' (1982: 105). Although in the late 19th century the missionary Dr Elmslie and a hunter-naturalist Richard Crawshay had reported that both larger game animals and tsetse fly to be common in the Henga Valley, the area from the South Rukuru River in the Mzimba district south to Dedza appeared to have been completely free of tsetse fly. According to Dr George Prentice, a missionary at Kasungu, no tsetse fly existed in the Kasungu district in 1900 when he established the Livingstonia Mission there (McCracken 1987: 66). But the tsetse fly belt soon spread eastwards from the Luangwa Valley, and in 1908 a case of sleeping sickness appeared at Dowa, and substantial numbers of cattle became infected with the trypanosomiasis disease. In 1910 Dr Prentice, who did pioneering medical work at Kasungu, diagnosed the first case of sleeping sickness at Kasungu, and between 1909-1911 around 42 cases of the disease were recorded, particularly in the Dowa district. In 1909 Dr Hallam Hardy, the medical officer in charge of West Nyasa district, succumbed to the disease. By 1913 there had been 163 confirmed cases of sleeping sickness (King 1992: 114-119). In addition, there had been great loss of cattle through the disease trypanosomiasis (Nagana), particularly in Northern Ngoniland - the Mombera (Mzimba) district.

The causes of the spread of tsetse fly and the outbreak of sleeping sickness are undoubtedly complex. McCracken suggests that the causes include 'the changing settlement patterns of the late 19th century, the impact of the rinderpest epidemic of 1893, the effect of government game policies and the drain of labour from the north' (1982: 105-106), and, following the perspectives of Iliffe and other scholars, he suggests that the effects of these changes were devastating on local people for they essentially led to an increase in wildlife and tsetse fly: 'Nature was reconquering the land'. This included increasing crop depredations, problems with predators, especially with lions, and diseases both of cattle and humans (op. cit. 106).

The expansion of the tsetse fly belt continued, and in 1922 there was a serious outbreak of sleeping sickness on the Kasungu Plain. As we have discussed below, this led to the evacuation of many villages from the Lingadzi Valley, and the subsequent establishment of the Kasungu Game

Reserve. But this, and the proclamation of a free shooting area, did little to halt the spread of the tsetse fly belt, which moved progressively southwards. It eventually reached the outskirts of Mchinji, and stretched between Kasungu and Nkhotokota, thus cutting off the northern cattle from markets in the South. Throughout many parts of the protectorate there was a serious loss of livestock, particularly cattle, and large areas of the territory reverted to 'bush' (woodland) because of the prevalence of the tsetse fly (McCracken 1982: 106-7, 1987: 66-67).

Like Harry Johnston, the missionary Dr George Prentice saw a clear link between tsetse fly (and sleeping sickness) and the prevalence of game animals. In a series of communications with the government he had continually urged that the only satisfactory measure to repel the tsetse fly, would be the decimation of the larger game animals. Since game animals are carriers of the trypanosomes that cause sleeping sickness then wildlife, Prentice contended, should be eradicated. The increase of the tsetse fly, he wrote, 'is due entirely to the European policy of game protection'.

Although he was himself, like many other missionaries, a keen hunter, Prentice was very critical of wildlife preservation and tersely noted, 'One might say that a huge culture medium is being prepared under the protection of European powers or European sportsmen for the spread of trypanosomiasis...the protection of game, and the consequent spreading of tsetse with sleeping sickness threatening this country, is about as sane a policy as the protection of rats when bubonic plague is threatening a home community' (King 1992: 118).

He therefore repeatedly demanded the introduction of free shooting zones, where African hunters could hunt without hindrance, and thus eliminate the wild game - and the tsetse.

In the early decades of the century a great debate sprang up among European hunters as to whether there was indeed any link between wild game and the tsetse fly. This was aired in the famous sporting magazine *The Field* in 1907, and the two figures in the controversy were both famous hunter-naturalists, who had travelled extensively in Central Africa as elephant hunters. Alfred Sharpe, who had spent 20 years in the region, and was later to become governor of Nyasaland, firmly believed that the existence of tsetse fly was not dependent on wild game, and that the presence of tsetse was related to altitude and to the type of local vegetation. Frederick Selous, on the other hand, stressed the close relationship between tsetse and the buffalo, for where buffalo had been exterminated, it was his experience that tsetse too disappeared. This was particularly evident at the time of the rinderpest epidemic, for when buffalo disappeared from any locality the 'fly' soon followed suit; when the buffalo returned to its former abundance so the tsetse fly again became prevalent (Selous 1908: 149-158). Another big-game hunter, Reginald Maugham, who travelled extensively in Northern Zambezia in the early part of the century, sided with Sharpe, and felt that the tsetse fly also found nourishment from sucking plants. He observed that tsetse fly was found in areas of Malawi where 'game is decidedly scarce'. On the other hand, the research scientist Warrington Yorke, who had conducted researches in Zambia in 1912 and shown that the tsetse fly *Glossina morsitans* was indeed the vector of the sleeping sickness pathogen, agreed with Johnston, Prentice and Selous that there was a close connection between game animals and tsetse fly. Thus Yorke advocated driving back game from the neighbourhood of human habitations (Maugham 1914: 347-355).

At the end of the First World War a new initiative against the tsetse fly was launched, and the Nyasaland government appointed a medical entomologist Dr William A. Lamborn to study the problem, and to offer practical suggestions for dealing with both the cattle disease trypanosomiasis and the human sleeping sickness. Lamborn apparently was short-sighted and a poor shot, but he travelled extensively throughout Malawi on *ulendos* (*ulendo*, journey or hunting expedition) and based himself at Fort Johnston (Mangochi) far 'from the urban delights of the capital Zomba' (McCracken 1982: 108). Lamborn was opposed to the policy suggested by Prentice for dealing with tsetse fly, namely the complete eradication of game animals. This he felt was entirely impracticable, and the shooting would result in the dispersal of the game animals into other areas, taking the fly with it. On the recommendation of Dr Prentice, the government had indeed, in 1915, suspended the Game Ordinance of 1911, and allowed the free shooting of game to the south and east of Kasungu Game Reserve. But on his return to the country in 1919, after an absence of two and a half years, Lamborn found that the tsetse fly belt had actually advanced southwards. He thus concluded that, 'If free shooting did not actually hasten the spread of fly it had certainly been ineffectual in preventing it'. The free-shooting proclamation was therefore revoked in December 1919.

Lamborn was adamant, and in this he was supported by colonial administrators like W. Kirby-Green and A.G.O. Hodgson, that the 'game extermination' policy was counter-productive in the control of tsetse, for it was felt that the 'disturbance of game' simply helps to 'spread the fly'. Thus, although the free shooting policy in the Kasungu district had led to over 1200 game animals being shot, this had not led to a reduction in the tsetse fly belt, but rather to its expansion southwards (MNA S1/700/20, McCracken 1982: 108).

Having abandoned the eradication of game animals as a policy, Lamborn, following the suggestions made by Charles F.M. Swynnerton in Tanganyika, decided that the best strategy in dealing with the problem of tsetse fly involved combining several methods. These included: firing the woodlands inhabited by tsetse, the judicious settlement of local people so as to form a barrier against the spread of the fly; the encouragement of both local and commercial agriculture, with the growing of such crops as tobacco and cotton; the breeding and release of parasites that were destructive of the tsetse fly; and the clearing of bush to create a 'defensive line' to stop the spread of the fly southwards.

When Lamborn made his initial surveys in the early 1920s he found that the tsetse fly belt stretched over much of the Kasungu and Dowa districts, that there had been a substantial loss of cattle, and that the only area free of tsetse fly in the Central Region was between Ntchisi Mountain and the Dowa boma. Although he experimented with various methods of controlling the spread of the fly, none were much of a success, and Lamborn himself was sceptical of firing the bush as a means of control - for the tsetse were strong fliers, and the warthog, which was a favoured host of the fly, actually favoured the burning of the undergrowth. Between 1925 and 1927 Lamborn supervised the construction 'buffer line' of cleared bush between the Bua and Nkamyo Hill near Kabuadula. But even this was not a great success.

Lamborn seems to have come to the conclusion, along with the chief veterinary officer J.A. Griffiths and the District Resident at Dowa A.G.O. Hodgson, that the only solution to the 'tsetse fly menace' (as he called it) was not the eradication of game - a policy that did more harm than good by causing the game to scatter - but human settlement. Opening up the land to human settlement, it was contended, was the only satisfactory method of clearing the area of tsetse fly. In 1927 he concluded that tsetse fly then covered at least two-thirds of the country, and the main infected areas comprised two zones - one covered the Shire Valley from Chikwawa to the Lake, and thence along the lakeshore to the Dwangwa River in the Nkotakota district; the other covered most of the Kasungu and Lilongwe districts embracing the Bua, the Rusa and the Namitete rivers (MNA S1/700/20).

Malawi was thus spared the wholesale destruction of game animals such as occurred in Tanzania, Zambia and Natal (McKelvey 1973: 148-154). McCracken points out that the major hosts of tsetse were the bushpig and warthog, and that as late as 1954 one of the heaviest concentrations of tsetse fly in the country was near Mangochi, where, apart from warthogs, all game animals had been eliminated (Mitchell and Steele 1956, McCracken 1987: 72).

Just as the advent of colonialism and the penetration of capitalism at the end of the 19th century stimulated the expansion of tsetse, so, some 30 years later, McCracken writes, the expansion of commercial agriculture, in the form of tobacco estates, signalled the eradication of tsetse fly over large areas of the Central Region. Initiated by A.F. Barron in 1922, tobacco cultivation expanded greatly and rapidly, to the extent that by 1928, over 25,000 growers had been registered. European settlers purchased leasehold estates in the vicinity of the Mudi, Bua and Ludzi rivers - areas which had earlier been teeming with game - as MacPherson (1973) records, and infested with tsetse fly. Hundreds of African cultivators took up the tenancies, and extensive areas of savanna woodland were cut back to make way for tobacco cultivations. This immediately curtailed the spread of the tsetse fly. In a similar fashion, increasing human population and settlement in the Lower Shire Valley and on the Thuchila/Phalombe Plain resulted not only in the eradication of most of the larger mammals but also of the tsetse fly in these regions.

McCracken thus concludes that the colonial administration was much less effective and powerful than it is often assumed to be, and that the impact of capitalism on African communities, those of Malawi in particular, was both complex and contradictory in character (1987: 72).

By 1954 tsetse fly had been eradicated over much of Malawi, the remaining belts roughly corresponding to areas where game animals were still to be found - the Vwaza, Malsh, Nkhotakota and Kasungu game sanctuaries, the Phirilongwe region and parts of the Upper Shire, and the western scarps of the Lower Shire Valley (Mitchell and Steele 1956). It was thus estimated that at the end of the colonial period some 12% of the total land area was still covered by tsetse fly belts. However, with tsetse having been eradicated over much of the Central Region and the Lower Shire Valley, the number of livestock increased substantially in both these areas (Pike and Rimmington 1965: 193-96).

CHAPTER TWO

THE LAND AND
ITS MAMMALIAN LIFE

INTRODUCTION

The writer James Riddell was a formidable traveller and alpine climber. In the mid-1950s he travelled through Malawi, then Nyasaland, and was greatly impressed by both the country and its people. He entitled his book *African Wonderland*, and described the country as a 'Happy Land' (1956: 32). This theme has been taken up by the tourist trade for whom Malawi has become 'the warm heart of Africa'. Tourism in Malawi is a relatively recent phenomenon, but in holiday brochures the country is now being described as an 'unspoilt Eden' and as perhaps 'Africa's most beautiful country', its great lake being set 'against a profusion of exotic foliage and rolling hills'. Malawi has indeed a unique combination of lakes, rivers and mountains that is unmatched in scenic value anywhere else in Africa. Yet the way the country is often described one might be excused for thinking that Malawi is devoid of human life, although, in fact, it has one of the highest population densities in Africa (87 persons per sq km). Its total population is around 10 million people, about the same as that of Zambia, whose land area is over six times that of Malawi. By African standards, Malawi is thus a small country, and it has comparatively little urban development, only 11% of the population living in urban areas - mainly in Lilongwe, Blantyre-Limbe, Mzuzu and Zomba. Yet in spite of its high population - which has more than doubled since I first arrived in Malawi in 1958 - much of the country is estimated to be still under 'natural vegetation' (33%) while some 20% of the land comprise either game sanctuaries or forest reserves (Bell 1987: 83). Its land area (92,067 sq km) is slightly larger than that of Scotland to which, scenically, it has often been compared, but it is much narrower being about 830 km long, and varying between 80 and 208 km in width. The major biotic communities are indicated in the following table.

TABLE THREE
The Major Biotic Communities of Malawi, Their Sizes, and Percentage Occupancy of the Country

No.	Name of community	Size (km²)	Occupancy %
1	Montane evergreen forest	324	0.27
2	Montane grassland	4,546	3.98
3	Semi-evergreen forest	963	0.81
4	Woodland of plateaus, hills and scarps (*Brachystegia/ Julbernadia/ Isoberlinia*)	60,959	51.44
5	Open canompy woodland of fertile areas (*Piliostigma/ Acacia/ Combretum*)	5,629	4.75
6	Mixed thicket/woodland of drier uplands	1,772	1.50
7	Mopane woodland	2,107	1.78
8	Woodlands of fertile areas (*Adansonia/ Cordyla/ Acacia albida*)	2,729	2.30
9	Thicket/savanna of poorer areas (*Combretum/ Acacia*)	1,899	1.60
10	Woodland/savanna (mixed species)	5,060	4.27
11	Sand dune vegetation	378	0.32
12	Woodlands of wet fringes (*Terminalia sericea*)	1,899	1.60
13	Grasslands	5,252	4.43
14	Lakes	24,926	21.04
15	Islands	38	0.03
Total		118,484	99.98

Source: Shaxson 1977

Malawi forms the Southern Section of the great African Rift Valley, which incorporates Lake Malawi and the Shire River Valley. Its western boundary consists of the watershed between the Luangwa and Zambezi Rivers, and Lake Malawi, and its most southern township Nsanje lies only about 65 km from Sena on the Zambezi. Both ecologically and culturally Malawi forms part of the Northern Zambezia region.

The climate of Malawi, which is typically that of Southern Africa, is popularly divided into two seasons, comprising the wet and dry parts of the year. The wet season begins in November or December, earlier in the South, and the rains last until March or April. Then comes the long dry season, generally cool from May to August, but becoming increasingly hot until the break of the rains. September and October are the hottest months, and in the Lower Shire Valley temperatures may reach over 100°F (24°C). Both temperature and rainfall vary according to altitude and region, but the mean average rainfall for the country as a whole is around 45 inches (114 cm). In the dry season, in June or July, periods of cold weather may occur, with light rains and mist coming from the South East. These are locally known as *chiperoni*, a name derived from the mountain in Mozambique (Pike and Rimmington 1965).

Malawi is a land of contrasts, and its landscapes or physiography is usually described in terms of three main regions: The Shire Valley and the Lake Malawi littoral, which ranges in elevation from 36 to 600 m; the hill areas or the Shire Highlands, the Namweras, and the Lilongwe and Mzimba Plains which together form part of the Central African Plateau (900-1200 m); and the highland areas, consisting of the high mountains and plateaux of Mulanje, Zomba, Dedza, Viphya, Nyika and the Misuku.

I shall, however, discuss the physiography of Malawi in relation to five bioregions, focusing on the history of the 'game' sanctuaries in these regions, and the mammalian fauna to be found there.

THE LOWER SHIRE VALLEY

In the past, Nsanje was the first port of call for visitors to Malawi who reached the small township by rail from Beira. Nsanje is only some 60 m above sea level, for the region is actually a narrow extension of the Mozambique coastal plain into Malawi. The region is thus hot and dry, and the annual rainfall often less than 30 inches (75 cm). The scenery is varied, much of the valley consisting of a fertile alluvial plain which is nowadays extensively cultivated with cotton, sugar and other crops. An important feature of the landscape of the valley floor is the Elephant Marsh. This is a huge area of marsh and swamp, a mosaic of islands and lagoons, contiguous to the River Shire, stretching for some 40 km above Chiromo. At its widest it is 15 km across. When Livingstone came up the Shire in 1859 the Marsh was frequented by vast herds of elephants. Livingstone counted 800 elephants in sight at once. He noted too that the Marsh and river had a high population of hippopotamus and supported a prodigious number of waterfowl (1887: 68-69). When the protectorate was established in 1896 the Elephant Marsh was immediately declared a game reserve - along with Lake Chilwa - and hunting within these reserves was forbidden without possession of a game licence costing £3 (Johnston 1897: 328-9). The area was thus essentially made into a private hunting preserve for Europeans.

BRITISH CENTRAL AFRICA.

Regulations for the preservation of wild game in certain parts of the Protectorate of British Central Africa.

WHEREAS, under the provisions of the Africa Orders in Council, 1889 and 1893, H. M. Commissioner and Consul-General for the British Central Africa Protectorate (hereinafter referred to as the Protectorate) has power from time to time to make Regulations for peace, order, and good government:—

It is hereby notified that the Acting Commissioner and Consul-General has, in pursuance of the powers aforesaid, made the following

REGULATIONS.

1. From and after the 15th day of September, 1896, the piece of country included within the limits laid down in Schedule I of these Regulations shall be considered and treated as a "Preserve."

2. It shall be illegal for any person or persons to shoot, trap, net, or in any way molest, any description of wild game within such limits without a written permission from H. M. Commissioner and Consul-General.

3. Such written permit shall be in the form given in Schedule 2 of these Regulations.

4. Any person holding such a permit and making use of it shall be required to produce it for inspection to any officer of the Administration of the Protectorate, whether European or native, who may request it to be shown to him.

5. It shall be in the discretion of the Commissioner to issue as many or as few of such permits, and to such persons as he may deem advisable.

6. It shall be in the power of the Commissioner at any time to withdraw and cancel any permit issued by him.

7. Any breach of any one of the above Regulations, or of any part of their conditions, or failure to comply with them, or with any part of their conditions, is an offence against "The African Order in Council 1889" as amended by "The Africa Order in Council 1893," and will be punishable accordingly.

(Signed) A. SHARPE,

H. M. Acting Commissioner & Consl-Genl.
Zomba, 9th September, 1896.

But the hunting for ivory and the increase in the human population in the valley at the turn of the century soon decimated the elephants. The Elephant Marsh was only a game reserve for some 14 years, but its name is still a nostalgic reminder of a former era (Carter 1987: 118). The marsh is still a bird-watchers' paradise, with abundant wildfowl and water birds such as the pied kingfisher, squacco heron and jacana.

The valley floor is characterized by such common trees as the baobab *mlambe* (*Adansonia digitata*), *mtondo* (*Cordyla africana*), the fever tree *mchezime* (*Acacia xanthophloea*), *mnjale* (*Sterculia appendiculata*) and the ubiquitous sausage tree, *mbvunguti* (*Kigelia aethiopica*). But given the high population density in the valley, (between 77 and 154 persons per sq km), both woodland and mammalian life is now scarce in the more fertile areas of the valley - although small mammals such as the vervet monkey, bush squirrel, civet, bushbaby, side-striped jackal and cane rat are still common. But it is evident from the Lower Shire District Book (1907) that reedbuck, waterbuck, zebra, buffalo and impala were all found in abundance around Chiromo at the turn of the century. While large mammal species have generally disappeared from the valley itself - though not in the forest reserves and sanctuaries - what is significant is the large increase in domestic livestock within the region. While pigs and goats were kept in the past, cattle were uncommon, mainly due to the presence of tsetse fly. Since the Second

World War, however, the cattle population has increased in spectular fashion, and there are now perhaps over 60 thousand cattle in the valley.

The larger mammals in the Lower Shire are confined mainly to the *Brachystegia* woodland that still clothes parts of the Thyolo escarpment, the Matandwe Forest Reserve covering the hills west of Tengani (which includes the Malawi Hill with its evergreen forest), and three important game sanctuaries - Majete and Mwabvi Game Reserves (these have been renamed as Wildlife Reserves) and Lengwe National Park. I shall discuss each of these sanctuaries in turn.

Mwabvi Game Reserve

Mwabvi is one of the most remote and little known game sanctuaries in Malawi - and even these days it is only occasionally visited by tourists. In the early 1960s I regularly visited the reserve at weekends from Zoa, and its establishment as a game reserve was undoubtedly due to similar weekend visits. For in the years after the First World War, Rodney Wood, who worked on a cotton estate near Chiromo regularly visited the area on hunting expeditions. He was particularly attached to the woodland thickets at Namalamba, near the River Thangadzi, some 20 km from Chiromo. His experiences in hunting the nyala antelope I describe elsewhere in the study. In the 1920s a new road was built down the Chiromo escarpment, and although the nyala was a protected species, Wood was concerned that some 'fool with a gun' might mistake a nyala for a bushbuck. He therefore advised the Governor, Charles Bowring, to declare the 'Nyala haunt' a game reserve (MNA S1/1721A/23). This was duly done, with the creation of Thangadzi Game Reserve in 1928. It consisted only of 23 sq km. In 1953 the area was extended further, to encompass 131 sq km, and renamed Mwabvi Game Reserve, Mwabvi being one of the main tributaries of the River Thangadzi. (Mwabvi is the name of the tree whose bark was used in the past for poison ordeals, *Erythrophleum suaveolens*.)

The main motive behind this extension was to create a reserve that was sufficiently large to support a small population of black rhinoceros. In 1975 the game reserve was further extended to cover an area of 340 sq km, to include a strip of land between the existing reserve and the Mozambique border. This was done on the grounds that the land was unsuitable for cultivation, and that it formed part of a water-catchment area that needed protection. This involved the removal of some 500 people who were cultivating in the area (WRU {Wildlife Research Unit} 50/7/0).

Mwabvi Game Reserve has a varied landscape, with open woodland, grassy dambos, rocky hillsides, and dense evergreen thickets - the latter being especially frequented by the rhinoceros and nyala. Although elsewhere the black rhinoceros is catholic in its choice of habitat, in the Mwabvi reserve it is restricted to the dry forest thickets. The common trees in these thickets are *mtwana* (*Brachystegia bussei*), *mlombwa* (*Pterocarpus angolensis*), *mlimbauta* (*Zanha africana*) and the silk cotton tree (*Ceiba pentandra*) (Ridding 1975), the latter indicating early human settlement. It is evident from notes in the Lower Shire District Book (1907) that larger mammals were common in the vicinity of what is now Mwabvi Game Reserve. Impala, klipspringer, waterbuck, eland, sable, hartebeest, kudu, Sharpe's grysbok and buffalo were all noted as 'fairly plentiful', but even then a note dated 14 April 1919 suggests that 'all game is fast disappearing from the district'. However, Reports of the Department of Game and Tsetse Control 1959-62 indicate that game animals were then plentiful - although the records are not entirely reliable. These note the following mammals as frequently seen in the Mwabvi reserve: black rhinoceros, zebra, buffalo, waterbuck, sable, grey duiker, kudu, klipspringer, impala, bushpig, reedbuck, warthog, bushbuck, nyala, Livingstone's suni, and Sharpe's grysbok.

What is of interest is that there were no records of elephant, lion, roan, eland, hartebeest, and oribi. Only wild dog was seen on one occasion. My own records in the period 1959-60 noted that the following mammals were widespread: bush squirrel, vervet and blue monkey, antbear, yellow-spotted hyrax, porcupine, slender mangoose, hyena and the side-striped jackal. Anderson, the game guard, estimated that there were 3 lion, 67 buffalo and 17 rhinoceros in the reserve (Journal 1959: 202). As far as the larger mammals were concerned, an Ecological Survey undertaken by members of Aberdeen University in 1975 tended to confirm these observations (Ridding 1975, Evans 1979, for a detailed list of the mammals of the Nsanje district see Long 1973).

In 1976 Ian Parker published a consultative report on Mwabvi Game Reserve, particularly focusing on the black rhinoceros. Although the report of the Aberdeen University survey had noted that there 'are probably between 15-30 animals in the reserve' (Ridding 1975: 16) and the African game guards were constantly reporting around 17 rhinoceros in the reserve, Parker was highly skeptical of these figures. Scrutinizing the earlier records, and conducting an aerial survey of the Mwabvi reserve, he estimated that there were probably between 4 and 7 rhinos resident in the reserve, and that over the past 50 years the population of black rhinoceros had always consisted of a small group of about 10 individuals (1976: 17). Thus, although there were undoubted movements of animals between the reserve and the Zambezi Valley, this number, he concluded, could not be considered a 'viable' population. During the aerial survey to locate the rhino, other larger mammals were recorded. Those clearly in evidence included: nyala, kudu (probably the commonest of the larger antelopes), sable, impala, bushbuck and warthog. No buffalo, hartebeest, zebra or elephant were seen.

What Parker's survey also indicated was the following: that there was widespread and intensive hunting and trapping of mammals along the boundaries of the reserve, as well as within the reserve to some degree; that people entered the reserve to collect firewood, to fish in the Thangadzi pools, and as a right of way when travelling to Mozambique; that local police were reluctant to prosecute local people for trespass; that there was much hostility between the game guards and people living in the vicinity of the reserve; and that there was still widespread cultivation within Mwabvi reserve itself. There was a 'wide chasm', he concluded, between local interests and the official attitudes of the Department of National Parks and Wildlife (DNPW) (1976: 34). He recommended that restrictions on local people entering the reserve to collect firewood and to fish should be relaxed, and that the reserve should be run for the benefit of local people, as long as this did 'not compromise the welfare of the black rhino' (41). He also suggested that immediate research should be undertaken to explore the interactions between the people and wildlife in the vicinity of Mwabvi. Parker did not see any conflict of interest between the existence of a game sanctuary, and the subsistence needs of local agriculturalists - such as their need for land, for meat, and the need of protection of local crops from depredation by the larger game animals.

In his reflections on the report, the secretary of the Nyasaland Fauna Preservation Society (NFPS), G.D. Hayes (1976) emphasized that the establishment of the reserve had been for the protection of its wildlife. It should not then be expected to function as a provider of local fuel-wood. While Parker had posed the question of *why* local people around Mwabvi hunt, for Hayes this was self-evident; it was in order to obtain meat. He also stressed that 'poaching', the hunting of game animals in protected areas, was incompatible with the aims of the reserve. While Parker criticized the game guards for their inefficiency Hayes emphasized their difficulties: their lack of adequate support, and the harassment and intimidation they faced from local people, especially from poachers who were a law unto themselves. Local people had refused to sell the game guards food, and the guards had even had their houses burned down. Many of the game guards were in fact, Tumbuka from the Northern Region.

Given this state of affairs, the DNPW commissioned a university sociologist to make a study of the attitudes of the people living in the vicinity of Mwabvi Game Reserve towards its wildlife. Although he seems never to have actually visited the reserve, John Kandawire wrote two papers on the Mwabvi reserve, a preliminary report and an article on the political economy of game reserves (1980, 1982). Almost 300 local people were interviewed in the Mbenje area. It emerged that almost half the respondents were in fact immigrants from Mozambique.

The survey confirmed what had long been suspected, namely, that there was a serious conflict between the conservation measures instituted by the national government, and the need by the local communities to utilize the natural resources of the area. Kandawire emphasized that this conflict had arisen not simply because of the creation of Mwabvi Game Reserve, but also because of several other factors: the occasional droughts in the Shire Valley; periodic floods; the substantial increase in the human population, and thus extreme pressure on both land and on woodland for fuel; the competition for land between food and cash crops, particularly cotton; and the great expansion in cattle production - although traditionally the Mang'anja were not pastoralists (1982: 56-58).

Kandawire noted that the concept of 'preserve' or conservation was not unknown to local people, and he distinguished between two main conceptions of 'reserve'. The first is denoted, he suggests, by the term *dambwe* which is the site where members of the *nyau* meet in graveyards. As we have explored elsewhere (1995), throughout Malawi, graveyards (*manda*) and shrines associated with the ancestral spirits (*mizimu*), are protected areas. The trees in these areas are not cut, and they are kept free of fire, and any killing of wild mammals is believed to disturb the 'peace of the spirits' (Kandawire 1982: 54). The second conception is *lizaya*, which denotes a government game sanctuary. People are not necessarily opposed to this type of reserve, and as one of the field researchers wrote, most people in the vicinity of Mwabvi reserve, tended to respect the integrity of the area, although a few people did poach - mainly for warthog, kudu and hyrax. What, however, was particularly resented by local people, especially the people of Kanyimbi village, was the expansion of the reserve in the 1970s, and their removal from the area. The area contained good, fertile land (*dimba*), where they grew bananas and mangos. The move was initially prompted by Frelimo (one of the parties in the civil war in Mozambique) activities in this area, and though compensated, they clearly felt that they would be allowed to move back there in the future.

Enquiries regarding the impact of the game reserve on local people focussed on two issues: crop depradation involving mainly monkeys, baboons, porcupine and bushpig which were perceived as a real nuisance by almost all of the respondents; and the lack of firewood and building materials in the area, which necessitated entering the sanctuary for supplies. Interestingly, the majority of the respondents considered fire to be a positive thing, facilitating the clearing of cultivated land, and the hunting of mammals. Hunting per se did not feature at all in Kandawire's report, although G.D. Hayes and many others who knew the area well reckoned that it was the intensive hunting within the reserve by local hunters, which was responsible for the low population density of the larger mammals. Hayes noted that only 20 years ago, there was a large population of impala in the tsanya woodlands (*Colosphospermum mophane*), and that both buffalo and zebra were commonly seen on the Thangadzi Stream. Parker queried the connection between illegal hunting and the low mammal densities, but offered no suggestions himself as to why densities should be so low (1976: 24).

Kandawire concluded his report on Mwabvi by noting that the reserve is 'not liked' by people living within its vicinity, and suggested that the DNPW should adopt a more educational approach towards wildlife conservation, and should consider either devolving some of its responsibilities to local authorities, or 'de-gazette' the reserve.

From the discussions which emerged from Ian Parker's report and the sociological survey, three important themes were highlighted. One was the need to change the colonial 'image' of the department, as game sanctuaries were perceived to be closed 'except for Europeans to enjoy'. The second theme suggested the crucial need to begin 'educating the ordinary people of the villages' as to the value of protecting wildlife - as Mark Tembo (1980) put it. And finally, the third theme stressed the crucial importance of Mwabvi as one of the last strongholds of the black rhinoceros - even though it was only a remnant population. The rhinoceros is one of Africa's most endangered species, and during the last two decades its numbers have fallen drastically. This is due mainly to increased poaching activities and the high demand in Asiatic countries for rhino horn, which is thought to have potent medicinal properties. In such circumstances the small population in Mwabvi Game Reserve of these 'prehistoric monsters', as Bruce Liggit (1979: 79) described the rhinoceros, takes on a new significance (WRU. 50/7/0).

When I stayed in Mwabvi Game Reserve in November 1990 conflict between the game guards and the local villagers was still in evidence.

During the four days I was there I noted plenty of signs of nyala, rhinoceros, antbear, buffalo and porcupine, but actual sightings of game animals were rather infrequent. These included: baboon, suni, klipspringer, bushbuck, grey duiker, bushpig, warthog and kudu, the last still fairly common. The status and viability of Mwabvi Game Reserve has long been questioned, but one cannot but agree with Jachmann's conclusions that this is an important conservation area which ought to be preserved. The reasons are these: firstly, it is one of the last domains of the black rhinoceros; secondly, it still contains many of the larger antelope, sable, kudu, and nyala; thirdly, it forms part of the extensive range of several packs of the now rather rare wild dog; and fourthly and finally, most of the reserve is unsuitable for cultivation and it is an important water-catchment area (Jachmann 1984; 88). Sadly, recent reports suggest (1995) that the black rhino is no longer in evidence in Mwabvi. The estimated number of larger mammals in Mwabvi reserve in 1989 was as follows:

Buffalo	10
Impala	100
Klipspringer	25
Kudu	200
Nyala	100
Sable	100
Warthog	200

(Simons 1989).

(For general accounts of Mwabvi Game Reserve see Carter 1987: 151-55, Hough 1989: 155-163.)

Lengwe National Park

Lengwe, situated only 72 km south of Blantyre - and most of that distance is covered on a good tarred road - is now a familiar tourist resort. Its attraction is the famous nyala antelope, one of the most beautiful of the African antelopes. They now number (1990) around 3,000 individuals. As with Mwabvi, the reserve initially owed its existence to Rodney Wood, and in 1928 some 520 sq km was set aside as a reserve, specifically to conserve the nyala. The unique experience in which Wood killed three nyala bulls with two shots seems to have occurred near Namalamba Hill rather than

in Lengwe - as Carter (1987: 143) pre-
sumes. Even so, remorse at having shot
3 nyala, led Wood to become a 'penitent
butcher' and he was instrumental in the
formation of both Lengwe and Mwabvi
reserves. It is of interest that when the
game ranger C.J.P. Ionides from
Tanzania came to Nyasaland in 1944 to
hunt a bull nyala under special licence,
he was advised that he would have a
greater chance of success at
Namalamba Hill, near Chiromo, rather
than in the Lengwe reserve (MNA/NSB
3/6/1). (The location, it is worth noting,
was originally called Nyamalambo
{nyama: animal, lambwe: buffalo bull}.)

Kudu

This was due to the fact that in 1934 a greater part of the reserve was
deproclaimed, and during the war years there was a big influx of people into
the area, mainly from Mozambique, who settled in the Mwanza Valley. This
had a major impact on the wildlife of the Lengwe area, for it separated them
from the major source of water during the dry season. The original reserve
boundaries were the Mwanza River in the North, the Pwadzi River in the
South, and the Shire River itself as the eastern boundary. The area had been
a favourite hunting ground of the Chikunda, the Kololo chiefs and
Europeans throughout the early part of the century - and the game population of the region had been much reduced. The Chikwawa District Book
(1904-5, nsc 3/2/1) had noted the following mammals in the Mwanza and
Chikwawa localities: 7 elephant, 1 black rhinoceros, 40 zebra, 30 sable, 15
kudu, 30 eland, 30 warthog, 100 hartebeest, 25 impala, 20 reedbuck, 60
waterbuck, 60 bushbuck, 60 hyenas, and 15 lion. Buffalos were also noted,
but these numbers do not indicate a wealth of fauna. The human population of the Chikwawa district in 1931 was around 35 thousand people,
mostly Mang'anja, and there were only some 148 cattle (Murray 1932: 189).
At the end of the Second World War, due to the settlement of people in the
Mwanza Valley and the widespread hunting of game animals (there was a
flourishing trade of meat between Chikwawa and the Shire Highlands) the
game population, and particularly the number of nyala, was at a very low
ebb. In 1945 G.D. Hayes returned from active war service, to find this state
of affairs especially worrying. He had worked as an agricultural officer in
the Chikwawa district for five years (1935-1940), knew the Lengwe area

well, and in 1939 was appointed an honorary game warden. He toured the Lengwe area in 1945, and reported to the District Commissioner (DC) Blantyre (C.W. Benson) his concerns: a serious decline in the numbers of the larger mammals; the widespread hunting with muzzle-loading guns of game animals, particularly bushbuck, kudu and buffalo; the regular traffic in meat between Chikwawa and the markets of Blantyre and Limbe; and the fact that the meat obtained from animals shot to protect local gardens went to these markets, rather than to the local people whose crops had been damaged - especially by hippopotamus and elephant. By then, Lengwe reserve had been reduced to 104 sq km. Hayes pleaded for the Lengwe area to be properly protected, and stressed the considerable benefits that might be attained by the creation of a 'minor Kruger National Park' (MNA/NSB/3/6/1). G.D. Hayes was instrumental in the forming of the Nyasaland Fauna Preservation Society (NFPS) in 1947, whose energies in the early years were largely devoted to establishing Lengwe as a viable game sanctuary. When I joined the Society in 1958, 'G.D.' - as he was affectionately known - was, to an important degree, the NFPS. The main credit for the establishment of the Lengwe National Park belongs essentially neither to Rodney Wood nor to President H. Kamuzu Banda (as both Hayes and Carter implied), but rather to 'G.D.' himself. For over 50 years he worked tirelessly and enthusiastically for the cause of nature conservation, particularly for the preservation of the larger mammals. I shall discuss the history of conservation in Malawi later in the study; but suffice to record here the important contribution that G.D. Hayes made to the establishment of the Lengwe game sanctuary. Hayes wrote a number of important short essays on the nyala and Lengwe Game Reserve (1948, 1967), as well as the first guidebook to Malawi's national parks and game reserves (1978).

Around 1960 Lengwe as a game reserve was in the 'doldrums', and in 1963 a proposal was considered to abolish it as a reserve. It was largely through the efforts of G.D. Hayes and the NFPS, that the government was induced in 1964 to take active steps to develop Lengwe, with a view to it becoming a tourist attraction. A number of boreholes were sunk, and pumps installed to provide dry season water, and a network of roads and a restcamp for visitors was constructed. These initiatives proved to be a great success, and in 1970 Lengwe was given national park status. It became the responsibility, three years later, of the newly formed DNPW, and in 1975 an extension of 780 sq km was added to the park. This area, to the west of 'Old Lengwe' and stretching to the Mozambique border, was considered to be unsuitable for agriculture, and in need of protection as a water-catchment area. This gave Lengwe as a protected area, a total area of 887 sq km (Bell 1981: 5, Sherry & Ridgeway 1984: 4-5).

Lengwe lies on the edge of the flood plain of the Shire River, on the floor of the rift valley. It is low-lying, between 100 and 150 m, and very flat. The climate is semi-arid, with an annual rainfall of around 83 cm (33 inches). Areas of the park are subject to seasonal flooding, and there are numerous pans scattered throughout the area, utilized mainly by buffalo and warthog. The vegetation of the park is varied, consisting of dry deciduous forest/thicket, various types of woodland and grassland savanna. The thickets are particularly common in 'Old Lengwe', and are characterized by such trees as mpanje, *Pyerocarpus lucens, Newtoni hildebrandtii*, and *chitunya, Acacia welwitschii*. Such mammals as the bushpig, suni, blue monkey, bushbuck and suni squirrel are common in the thickets, as well as the nyala. The woodlands are of three major types: the tsanya woodland, consisting of a closed forest of *Colosphosperum mopane* - which are particularly associated with sable and impala; the *Combretum/Terminalia* woodlands; and the *Brachystegia* woodlands that are common on the sandstone hills in the western areas of the park. Mammals associated with the woodlands include kudu, sable, zebra, hyena, grey duiker, and hartebeest. In the grassland savanna, found in low-lying areas that are frequently water-logged, such mammals as reedbuck, buffalo and warthog - all grazers - are found (Hough 1989: 111-114).

Lengwe National Park has, compared with other conservation areas, many distinctive features. It is easily accessible, being only an hour's drive from Blantyre and it contains a high density of wild mammals, making it a tourist attraction in terms of good game viewing. But what makes it unique is that it contains the largest area of dry decidious thicket to be found in Malawi, and it harbours most of the country's population of nyala antelope. Lengwe, in fact, is the local term for 'thicket'. With regard to the larger herbivores the following numbers have been estimated in 'old Lengwe' (1980).

Buffalo	200
Bushpig	100
Bushbuck	200
Grey duiker	100
Impala	50
Kudu	50
Nyala	3000
Reedbuck	50
Sharpe's grysbok	100
Suni	50
Warthog	100

Source: Bell 1981

Table Four also gives some idea of the numbers of the commoner species.

TABLE FOUR
Lengwe National Park (Game Reserve)
Average Numbers of Game Seen per 10 Patrol Days (1959-62)

	1959	1960	1961	1962
Buffalo	0.95	0.02	2.50	4.35
Bushbuck	1.10	1.42	1.27	1.50
Bushpig	1.00	3.15	2.75	2.45
Grey duiker	1.44	1.62	1.12	1.23
Hartebeest	0.84	1.17	1.72	2.95
Impala	0.86	1.82	2.10	2.05
Kudu	2.76	3.80	4.12	5.40
Leopard	-	seen	seen	seen
Nyala	4.51	1.30	1.17	1.00
Reedbuck	0.38	1.12	1.17	1.17
Sable	-	-	0.17	-
Sharpe's grysbok	-	seen	0.10	seen
Suni	0.10	-	0.35	seen
Warthog	1.84	seen	1.05	1.03
Waterbuck	-	-	0.95	seen
Zebra	0.40	0.07	0.05	-

Source: Annual Reports of the Department of Game, Fish and
Tsetse Control 1959-62

The most recent estimate of wildlife numbers is as follows:

Buffalo	300
Bushbuck	200
Bushpig	100
Grey duiker	100
Impala	600
Kudu	200
Nyala	1800
Sharpe's grysbok	100
Suni	400
Warthog	800

Source: Simon 1989

No elephant or reedbuck were recorded.

Elias Mandala (1990: 221) remarked that with the conservation measures, elephant, lion, kudu, eland, waterbuck and other animals had repopulated the Lengwe area. Yet there are few recent records of eland, elephant (the last killed by poachers in 1964), lion, rhinoceros, roan, hartebeest, waterbuck, wild dog or zebra. Hartebeest and zebra, both grazers, may however still occur in small numbers in the wooded western escarpments.

In conservation terms, Lengwe has been a great success story. So much so that by 1980 it was estimated that the population of nyala - whose numbers the NFPS had attempted to monitor since 1967 in their annual Lengwe 'game counts' (Hutson 1977, Dudley & Osborne 1980) - was around 3,800. This had entailed an annual increase of some 23% since 1968, when the nyala population was estimated at 279. Then disaster struck. In the drought year of 1980 a number of nyala were found dead, apparently of starvation. The reek of rotting flesh was noted by many visitors to the park, and it was estimated that between 50 and 100 nyala had died. Eruptions and the subsequent 'die off' of ungulates are a common phenomenon, particularly in areas where environmental constraints (water shortage, hunting) have been removed. But in Lengwe there was also evidence of environmental degradation - particularly of the dry deciduous thickets. The DNPW therefore faced a serious problem as to what course of action to take. Richard Bell (1981) produced a lucid report outlining the issue, and the pros and cons of the various management strategies. Basically there were two options. The first was to take no action at all, to let 'nature' take its course. But the concept of nature, and its use as a guiding principle, is highly problematic in terms of wildlife management, as Bell emphasized. For the situation at Lengwe was by no means natural - for its creation as a reserve involved artificial boundaries, the construction of boreholes, and the protection of the mammals, to some extent, from hunting pressures. Although writers like Bill McKibben (1990) speak of the recent 'end of nature' (see my critical review 1993), it is doubtful if there is any part of world where nature is 'pristine', that is, untouched by human activity. Hall-Martin indicated that in the Lengwe area there was evidence of much slash-and-burn cultivations in the past (1977: 4-5), such that the area could not be considered entirely 'natural'.

The option of taking no action - 'doing nothing', it was quipped, was what the DNPW did best - had certain advantages. It reaffirmed the ethos of the park as a place where hunting was proscribed, and no violence was done to its wildlife, which were not even considered as an economic resource. It was also felt that doing nothing was desirable on ecological grounds, for eventually a balance would emerge between the park's vegetation and its fauna.

The second option was to reduce the number of nyala by 'culling'. This was felt not to be incompatible with one of the aims of the park which was to preserve in perpetuity a representative sample of its fauna and flora. This had the advantage of both maintaining the ecological status of the park and of providing local communities with meat. The second option would create a favourable attitude towards the park by such communities, and undercut the sale of illegal meat by poachers. Cropping (culling) was thus deemed to be beneficial, while simply allowing a population crash was deemed both inhumane and wasteful. Bell himself did not feel strongly either way, but emphasized that if cropping was the option taken, then the only feasible method was by shooting. This was efficient, could be controlled, and it provided meat for sale (Bell 1981: 19-28).

In 1981 culling was begun by the DNPW and that year 400 nyala were shot. In the following years further nyala were culled, with a view to reducing the nyala population to around 2,000. This was felt to be the level which the Lengwe habitat could support without adverse effect. Carter concluded that 'meat from the cull was sold locally at low prices, a tangible benefit of the park for the local people living nearby' (1987: 145). But the impression one has talking to game guards and local people is that much of the best meat went to the *akulu* (meaning important people and hotels in the urban areas) and to *Sanjika* (President Banda's residence) and that local people tended to be sold 'offal'. However, Alfred Kombe, who was game warden at Lengwe from 1974 to 1980, stressed that every effort was made to ensure that all local people had a chance to buy meat. He also concluded that the first culling operation had been completed satisfactorily and that the general consensus had been that it was both necessary and successful (1983: 245-6). In a survey of local attitudes towards the culling of nyala (and also of the warthog), very few people disapproved of the reasons for establishing the park, and the majority of respondents (93.7%) felt that the availability of the culled meat did not effect their 'feeling negatively' about the park. On the whole, people living in the vicinity of Lengwe, only had a 'vague idea' of why conservation areas were established, and clearly felt that the area belonged to them, and that they were 'currently getting very little or nothing out of it' (Munthali & Banda 1985: 77-79).

What was clear, however, and hinted in their report, was that with a relatively high population of mammals in the 'Old Lengwe' area, and also a high population of humans living in nearby villages, poaching was rife in Lengwe. Wire snares and spring traps were to be found even close to the main camp, and they were common in thickets and close to waterholes.

Hunting in the park was widely practised, especially in the western extension, but there were limited deterrents against such poaching. One game guard told me (1993) that meat from a waterbuck might bring the hunter anything up to K300, and yet the fine for poaching - if caught - only amounted to K40.

In recent years, sensing that there was potential conflict between tourist activities and culling strategies, which were temporarily suspended in 1988, suggestions were made with regard to the establishment of a 'nyala ranch' in the western extension (Chiwona 1990). (For further information on the ecology of Lengwe National Park, and on small mammals see Hall-Martin 1977, Sherry & Ridgeway 1984: 8-16, Carter 1987: 144-48, Happold & Happold 1991).

Majete Game Reserve

Some 30% of the area of the Lower Shire Valley has been designated as a conservation area, either as game sanctuaries or forest reserves. Of this, Majete constitutes a fairly small reserve of some 690 sq km. It forms part of the Middle Shire Valley, an area of rugged hills and wild country to the west of the Shire River, north of Chikwawa. It ranges in altitude from 100 to 500 m. Majete Hill lies in the centre of the reserve. The Shire River, which forms the eastern boundary, descends from Mpatamanga Gorge in a series of rapids and falls, including the famous Kapichira Falls, which formed a notable barrier to Livingstone's early exploration of the Shire. Much of the reserve is covered with lowland *Brachystegia* woodland, and although there is evidence of cultivation in the past, the soils of Majete are shallow and stony, and generally unsuitable for cultivation. B.L. Mitchell described the region around Majete Hill as 'barren and uninhabitable' (1953: 102). Along the banks of the Nkurumadzi and Shire rivers there are riverine forests, dense thickets and some narrow strips of floodplain grassland. Here game animals tend to congregate during the dry season.

With increasing population during the early years of the present century, most of the larger game animals - such as eland, elephant, kudu and waterbuck - became eradicated over much of the Shire Valley. Thus Majete (Majeti) became a kind of refuge for these mammals, although hunting was always common in the area. Soon after its formation, the NFPS, through its secretary G.D. Hayes, made proposals to the colonial government that Majete should be declared a game sanctuary, principally to protect the remnant herds of elephants which once ranged throughout the valley. In 1951 the area around Majete Hill was declared a non-hunting area, and in July 1953 a game guard was appointed to patrol the reserve. A local *sing'anga* Biton Balandow sent monthly reports on the reserve to the DC in Chikwawa. In 1953 he reported seeing elephant, eland, kudu, waterbuck and warthog in 'fair numbers', as well as several herds of sable and hartebeest. He also reported reedbuck, bushbuck, klipspringer, grey duiker, Sharpe's grysbok, zebra, lion, leopard, and jackal (Hayes 1954). B.L. Mitchell (1953: 102) also noted roan from the area - but there is no evidence of the latter being recorded in Majete, and neither Hayes nor Balandow reported seeing roan. In 1955 Majete was declared a game reserve of 500 sq km, one of the motivations being to confine the elephants to this restricted area, for the elephants of the Upper Shire were prone to raid maize gardens of local people, particularly in the Mwanza Valley to the south. In 1969 the reserve was extended as far as Nkurumadzi and Shire rivers, to allow the animals access to dry season water. Throughout the period 1954-1960 the game department maintained a cordon of hunters around the 'elephant country of the Majete' to defend the cotton lands of the Mwanza Valley.

Table Five gives some indication of the relative numbers of the larger mammals, and although these figures are not entirely reliable, they do indicate a decline in the numbers of zebra, eland and hartebeest. This was acknowledged in the game department's reports for 1961-1962 which noted a decline in the game population of all the major species in Majete as well as in Mwabvi Game Reserve.

Majete Game Reserve only supports a relatively small population of the larger mammals, mainly because the area has long been a favourite hunting ground of local professional hunters. Its importance lies in the fact that it contains the only remaining herds of eland and waterbuck to be found in the Shire Valley, and, until recently, a herd of around 200 elephants. In a pioneering study, Brian Sherry (1989) estimated that there were, perhaps, around 300 elephants in the Middle Shire Valley, which dispersed widely in the wet season, but during the late dry season concentrated close to the major rivers. He noted that there existed a fairly healthy 'natural respect' between elephants and humans in the region, for they tended to give each other as wide a berth as possible. Only a few hardened hunters were prepared to make elephants their quarry, and he noted that between 1982 and 1986 of the five people killed by elephants, three were poachers, who were killed while illegally hunting in Majete Game Reserve. With regard to the elephant, he wrote, that while illegal hunting was not then (in 1989) a problem, 'there is a real danger it could become so'. His words have a certain pre-

TABLE FIVE
Majete Game Reserve
Average Numbers of Game Seen per 10 Patrol Days (1959-62)

	1959	1960	1961	1962
Buffalo	0.15		-	-
Bushbuck	3.04	1.20	1.60	1.42
Bushpig	1.19	4.05	2.75	2.95
Eland	13.51	4.67	2.85	2.20
Elephant	13.2	4.72	4.82	5.40
Grey duiker	1.03	0.82	1.60	1.57
Hartebeest	6.57	2.40	1.20	0.27
Impala	-	1.52	0.15	-
Klipspringer	0.29	0.90	0.55	1.95
Kudu	5.70	5.47	4.87	3.07
Leopard	-	0.10	0.05	0.05
Lion	0.11	1.40	0.75	0.12
Reedbuck	3.89	2.00	4.42	0.57
Sable	7.36	6.72	8.10	2.23
Sharpe's grysbok	-		0.15	0.10
Suni	-	0.22	0.10	-
Warthog	1.91	0.75	1.82	2.20
Waterbuck	-	-	0.07	-
Wild dog	0.44	-	0.17	-
Zebra	13.13	10.02	7.47	4.95

Source: Annual Reports of the Department of Game, Fish and
Tsetse Control 1959-62

science, for within five years, given inadequate protection by the DNPW, poachers with high-powered rifles entered Majete and virtually decimated the elephant population. Letters to local newspapers by Malawians bewailed the incompetence and inertia of the government, and the loss of this precious heritage (Wildlife Society of Malawi {WSM} Newsletter June 1995). Sherry was of the opinion that hunting in the reserve was common and virtually uncontrolled, to the extent of being no different from that in unprotected woodland. The wild animals were left to fend for themselves with minimal protection. As with the Mwabvi reserve, this accounts for the low-density levels of the larger mammal species (1989: 123). In his 'Ulendo Notes' (July 1984), Richard Bell noted plenty of evidence of illegal activity within the reserve, and came across four poachers' camps, with drying racks, two of which were only a short distance from the Phwadzi game scout camp (WRU 50/5/0). He concluded that the game scouts were completely ineffective in controlling illegal hunting in the reserve.

With regard to the current status of the larger mammals in Majete, from my own observations and from discussions I had with game scout Nicholas Nkonjiwa, baboon, klipspringer, hippopotamus, Sharpe's grysbok, reedbuck, eland, sable, waterbuck, bushpig, warthog, bushbuck, hyena, porcupine, grey duiker, kudu and leopard are still to be found in the reserve, although some of these species are far from common. Hartebeest and zebra seem restricted to the woodlands in the west and are rarely seen. Buffalo, and now the elephant, are almost non-existent in the reserve. In 1989 the following numbers of the larger mammals were estimated:

Buffalo	16
Bushbuck	28
Elephant	125
Grey duiker	117
Hippopotamus	17
Kudu	228
Sable	500
Warthog	20
Waterbuck	248

Source: Simons 1989: 64

(For general information on the Majete see Carter 1987: 134-139, Hough 1989: 145-153)

THE SHIRE HIGHLANDS AND THE LAKE CHILWA BASIN

The Shire Highlands - the Mang'anja Hills of the early botanists - are roughly 7200 sq km in extent and lie at an altitude of between 600 and 1200 m. The area is flanked on the west and south by the scarps of the Shire and Ruo rivers, while the eastern limits are marked by the Phalombe-Chilwa depression. The plateau is surmounted by the high mountains of Zomba, Mulanje, Chiradzulu and Thyolo, all over 1,500 m, as well as by numerous other smaller hills, such that the highlands have been described as a 'lunar landscape' by Debenham (1955: 26). The Shire Highlands were at the heart of early colonial development in Malawi, the Church of Scotland Mission being established at Blantyre in 1876, and much of the land was alienated around the turn of the century to European planters who established cotton, coffee, tobacco, and later tea plantations in the highlands. Although the area was by no means a 'comparatively empty land,' as Debenham suggests (24), nevertheless at the end of the 19th century much of the highlands was covered by *Brachystegia* woodland and human population was comparatively low. The dominant trees of this woodland are *Brachystegia* spp., especially *mombo* (*B. longifolia*) and *chumbe* (*B. spiciformis*), *mlombwa* (*Pterocarpus angolewsis*), *msuku* (*uapaca kirkiana*), and *muula* (*Parinari curatellifolia*), while in riparian tracts one finds such trees as *mpindimbi* (*Vitex doniana*) and *mbawa* (*Khaya nyasica*). Evergreen forest is found in the galleys and ravines of the larger mountains, and above 1,500 m clothes the summits of all the hills and mountains. On Mulanje, one finds a unique cedar forest with closed stands of *nkungudza* (*Widdringtonia cupressoides*), whose ecology has been fully discussed by Chapman (1995). (For a full discussion of the vegetation of the Shire Highlands see Morris 1970: 7-14.)

Evidence from the writings of the early missionaries and travellers suggest that at the end of the 19th century the Shire Highlands was a 'well-wooded' country with an abundance of the larger mammal species. John Buchanan called the country 'delightful', and although he was more of a botanist and agriculturist than a hunter, he records, on a journey from Blantyre to Mulanje across the Thuchila Plains, encountering elephant, rhinoceros and kudu (1985: 156-160). To what degree this abundance of larger mammals was a concomitant of the dispersal of the human population through the ravages of the slave trade and Ngoni raids - and their concentrations in more remote and inaccessible regions such as the Domasi Valley, Nchisi Island and the higher slopes of Chiradzulu and Mulanje - it is difficult to say. But nonetheless over many areas of the Shire Highlands larger mammals were common at the end of the 19th century. Many place names reflect the presence of mammals: Chowe (oribi) village, Ngoma (kudu) Hill, Masambanjati (where buffalo wash), Nchefu (eland) Estate, Mafisi (hyena) Estate, Bvumbwe (wild cat) and Namikango (lion) are examples.

Henry O'Neill, who was the British consul in Mozambique, made a journey to Lake Chilwa in 1883-84. He described the area as the 'best game country' in East Africa, and noted zebra, buffalo, hippopotamus, eland, elephant, bushpig and rhinoceros as well as, more questionably, giraffe

(W.Y. Campbell n.d. 126-127). Henry Drummond, who visited the Blantyre Mission around the same period, described Central Africa in rather lyrical fashion as 'the finest hunting country in the world. Here are the elephant, the buffalo, the lion, the leopard, the rhinoceros, the hippopotamus, the zebra, and endless species of small deer and antelope'. And he concludes this sentiment, with the remark that 'the whole country is covered with traps to catch these animals' (1889: 106). Although a Scottish divine, and very conscious of the moral superiority of the 'white man' (105), Drummond was a keen hunter. It is of interest that he writes that nowhere else in Africa did he see such splendid herds of larger game animals than near Lake Chilwa, zebra being especially abundant (1889: 30).

Such observations are confirmed by Hector Duff, who was a self-confessed 'reactionary' and also, at the turn of the century, was 'resident', i.e. colonial administrator, at Mulanje. Duff was an avid hunter, but also a keen and accurate observer of game animals. In the Mulanje District Notebook of 1904, Duff has a note on the 'game statistics' of the district, with maps indicating the 'good hunting grounds' of the European planters living at Mulanje. The main hunting areas indicated were *Mtima nyama* ('heart of

Mount Mulanje

Source: Archives of the Society of Malawi.

game animal'), north-west of Mt Mauze, Chimombo's village near where the Phalombe River enters Lake Chilwa, and Tamanda and Milambi in the Tuchila River basin near Mlombo Hill. In these areas Duff records hartebeest, reedbuck, elephant, blue wildebeest, kudu, as well as the smaller antelopes like the grey duiker and oribi. With respect to the Shire Highlands more generally, Duff noted that the hartebeest was the 'commonest antelope'; that sable was 'still abundant', the highlands being 'full of them'; that buffalo and elephant were frequent around the Chikala Hills; that the eland was 'fairly common'; and that four rhinoceroses had been killed in the Zomba district between 1898 and 1903. Reedbuck was 'everywhere plentiful', and bushbuck and klipspringer common in the hill areas. Of the carnivores, Duff noted that the wild dog, hyena, leopard and lion were all common (Duff 1903; 140-165).

The larger mammals known to have existed and, in many cases, known to have been common in the Shire Highlands at the end of the 19th century, can be listed as follows:

Black rhino*	Kudu*	Sable*
Buffalo*	Lichtenstein's hartebeest*	Serval
Bushbuck	Lion	Side-striped jackal
Bushpig	Oribi*	Spotted hyena
Cane rat	Otter	Vervet monkey
Civet	Pangolin	Warthog
Eland*	Sun squirrel	Waterbuck*
Elephant*	Bush squirrel	Wild cat
Genet	Porcupine	Wild dog*
Grey duiker	Hare	Yellow baboon
Hippopotamus	Redforest duiker	
Klipspringer	Reedbuck	

* No longer occurs in the Shire Highlands.

Neither impala nor nyala were common in the Shire Highlands, and there is a questionable record of the roan antelope from near Namadzi in 1902 (Duff 1903: 153). Within only a few decades many of the larger game animals of the Shire Highlands had been eradicated, and there was a serious decline in the mammalian fauna. This decline has been discussed in seminal essays by Hayes (1972) and Dudley (1979), and three factors seem to have been involved: the 'population explosion' that occurred within the Shire Highlands, for with the opening-up of estates, there was a large influx of Lomwe people into the highlands, particularly into the Thyolo, Mulanje and Chiradzulu districts; the increasing availability of firearms, specifically muzzle-loaders among African hunters, thus Duff MacDonald was to write that 'men go armed generally with guns', and that the country was 'full of flint muskets marked the Tower' (1882: 19); and finally, the fact that hunting was the favourite past-time of the majority of European settlers - whether administrators, planters or missionaries. G.D. Hayes was adamant that the decline of the larger mammals could not be blamed on local people and he stressed the fact that the country was 'teeming with wild animals' before the arrival of Europeans, and, drawing on the suggestions of Father Schoffeleers, stressed aspects of the local culture that were conducive to the conservation of mammals (1972: 22-24). Hayes was not alone in stressing the negative impact of European hunting on the game population. Hector Duff, while emphasizing the destructive aspects of African hunting, nevertheless suggested that game was often found in abundance near local villages, while once there was European settlement game animals soon disappeared (1932: 141). Murray noted, significantly, that in 1932: 'game is still fairly plentiful in Nyasaland, except in districts that have been thickly populated by Europeans' (1932: 327) and this applied specifically to the Shire Highlands. Judging from the District Notebooks (1910-1912) for Blantyre, Zomba and Mulanje, a high proportion of Europeans, including many missionaries, had taken out a Protectorate Game Licence 'B'.

Given the opening-up of land to European estates, and the substantial increase in human population, trees were becoming scarce in the Chiradzulu district, wrote its Resident in 1915, who advocated the need for village plantations of blue gums. This, together with the intensive hunting of the larger mammals by both European and African hunters, meant game animals quickly disappeared from the Shire Highlands. By 1930 practically all the larger game had been eradicated. For the Zomba district Murray noted: 'with the exception of baboons on the slopes of the mountain, bushbuck on the plateau, and an occasional leopard or lion, there is very little game of any kind in the district' (1932: 163). For the Chiradzulu district both the District Book (1910-13) and Murray's Handbook (1932) recorded that there was 'very little game' left, apart from some kudu near Magomero, and a few antelopes in the Chiradzulu Forest Reserve. For the Thyolo district, which formerly had 'a good reputation' for game, intensive European cultivation and the opening-up of estates, Murray wrote, had resulted in there being 'practically no game left' (183). With regard to the Blantyre district, which was, according to Duff, a 'good hunting centre' as late as 1895, there was no longer any game found there by the 1930s (Murray 1932: 173).

Thus by the 1930s the only area of the Shire Highlands where game was still to be found was in the Mulanje district, specifically on the Thuchila Plain near Sambani and Mlombo hills, where kudu, sable, hartebeest, oribi and reedbuck were still hunted. Bushbuck and klipspringer were common on Mulanje, Michesi and Mausi mountains, and lions and leopard were also still plentiful in the area. By then the blue wildebeest was extinct in Malawi - the Thuchila Plain being its main and last haunt. But within a few decades hunting pressure and increasing human population, and thus cultivation of the area, had led to the demise of these other five antelopes (Murray 1932: 161-183, MNA/NSB 3/13, NSD 1/3/1, NSE/1/22).

Although the elephant, rhinoceros, zebra and many of the larger antelopes have long since disappeared from the Shire Highlands, mammalian life still flourishes, though it is mainly confined to the woodlands and forests that still clothe the larger hills and mountains - Mulanje, Michesi, Zomba, Malosa, Thyolo, Chiradzulu, Michiru, Soche, Chikala and several of the smaller hills. Bushpig, grey duiker, bushbuck, klipspringer, red forest duiker, blue duiker, baboon, vervet and blue monkey, and porcupine are still to be found in protected areas, and, in suitable habitats, are common. Leopard and hyena are still in evidence, and the occasional itinerant lion has been observed - particularly on the plateaux of the higher mountains. I noted one at Likabula, Mulanje in 1964, and at Makwawa, near Zomba, in 1979. Of the smaller carnivores, zorilila, side-striped jackal, serval, civet, genet, otter, and various species of mongoose are still to be found although their numbers have certainly decreased over the last two or three decades. The smaller mammals, of the Mbewa category, and bats are still plentiful. It is of interest that Laurens van der Post on his expedition to Mount Mulanje in 1949, graphically described in his best-selling travellogue 'Venture to the Interior' (1952), never seems to have observed a single mammal while on the mountain. Nobody has ever discerned what his secret 'mission' to the mountain entailed, although in his romanticism he not only conceived of Africa as 'unconscious' and 'feminine but also thought that gazelles lived on the mountain. He did not observe any! (For useful checklists see Morris 1964, Happold & Happold 1989, Van Strien 1989: 75-76.)

THE UPPER SHIRE AND
THE SOUTHERN LAKESHORE

The Upper Shire is a wide flat valley extending from the southern shore of Lake Malawi south to Matope, some 22 km north of the Nkula Falls. The gradient of the Shire Valley is extremely flat, and between Mangochi and

Matope, some 130 km, the river falls only about 9 m. The Shire River leaves Lake Malawi just north of Mangochi, and after flowing south for a few kilometres, spreads into the wide but shallow Lake Malombe. South of the lake, on the eastern bank of the river, is the Liwonde National Park. The Upper Shire Valley is flanked to the east by the scarps of the Namwera Hills, lying at an elevation of between 900 and 1,050 m, the highest point of this plateau being Mangochi Mountain (1,700 m). Its summit is clothed with evergreen forest, and high on its slopes are the remains of Fort Mangochi, which had a strategic importance in the fight against the slave trade at the end of the 19th century (see Cole-King 1972). To the west of Mangochi Mountain is Phirilongwe Hill (1,529 m), while to the north is the Cape Maclear pennisula, with its rocky islands and steep wooded hills. This area, of some 875 sq km, now forms Lake Malawi National Park. This was gazetted in 1980 mainly to conserve the unique *mbuna* (cichlids) fish found there.

The vegetation of the Upper Shire Valley is extremely varied ranging from *Brachystegia/Combretum* woodland on the rocky hills, through woodland savanna, where the conspicuous trees are *mlambe* (*Adansonia digitata*), *mkunga* (*Acacia nigrescens*), *mfula* (*Scelerocarya caffra*), *nkongomwa* (*Afzelia quanzensis*), and *msetanyani* (*Sterculia* spp.), to palm savanna and flood plain grasslands near the River Shire. These areas, which are subject to wet season flooding, are associated with such trees as *mgwalangwa* (the doum palm, *Hyphaene crinata*) and the *mchezime* (fever tree, *Acacia xanthophloea*). In certain areas *tsanya* woodland (*Colophospermum mopane*) predominates. (On the vegetation of the Upper Shire, as found in Liwonde National Park, see Dudley and Stead 1976: 21-23).

As with the Shire Highlands, at the end of the 19th century much of the Upper Shire Valley was well wooded, and renowned for the diversity and abundance of its larger mammals. Henry Faulkner, who accompanied the Livingstone Search expedition, journeyed up the Shire to Lake Nyasa in 1867, and recorded his hunting exploits in his book *Elephant Haunts* (1868). He noted the following game mammals on the Middle and Upper Shire: waterbuck, hartebeest, oribi, reedbuck, elephant, buffalo, hippopotomus, kudu, impala and sable. Some 60 years later these mammals were still recorded as common on the Upper Shire, along with eland, bushbuck, and grey duiker. Leopards and lions were also noted as common throughout the area, and crocodiles as plentiful in the Shire River, annually taking a toll of human life (Murray 1932: 160). Throughout the early colonial period, the Upper Shire was famous for its marauding elephants, and one herd in particular, the Mpimbi herd, had a fierce reputation and was considered a public menace (see Morris 1995b). Even in the 1960s when I travelled from Mangochi to Monkey Bay, which was then still well wooded, there was a roadsign which read: 'Beware of Elephants'. The Namwera Hills were also famous for its elephants, as well as for its 'man-eating' lions. Annie Bulala (1991) records that Asian and European planters were welcomed into the Namweras as the opening-up of estates forced lions and elephants out of the area. In 1945, Omer Bapu, one of the planters, was praised by Chief Jalasi for helping people to rid the area of lions. One of the estates was named Paramasimba which in Yao literally means 'there are many lions', because of its adverse association with these predators (1991: 16-17, see also N. Carr 1969: 84-99).

In the past in the region of Phirilongwe Hill and the Bwanji Valley game animals were plentiful. Arthur Dent, who had a tobacco estate near Sharpvale, recorded that in the 1920s kudu, eland, oribi, red duiker, sable, porcupine, pangolin, waterbuck, and buffalo were all common, and that elephants were 'plentiful'. He saw a herd of 130 elephant on Phirilongwe in 1929 (letter to G.D. Hayes, May 21/1/1972).

As elsewhere, game animals have been severely reduced in number during the past half century, though elephant, bushpig, hyena, baboon, civet, klipspringer, grey duiker, vervet and blue monkey, bushbuck, leopard and porcupine are still common in the more remote areas, where there are protected forests (woodland) - such as Mangochi Mountain, and in the Namizimu and Phirilongwe forest reserves. Small numbers of kudu, sable, Sharpe's grysbok, warthog and zebra continue to survive in these wooded locations, though these areas are subject to heavy hunting pressure, both by local people and by European coloureds. Collective hunts (*uzimba*) still take place on these hills, as they do on the Chikala Hills to the south-east of Liwonde. (For a list of the mammals of Mangochi see Dowsett and Hunter 1980.)

Two factors were perhaps responsible for the decline of the larger mammals in the Upper Shire Valley. One was the tremendous increase in human population, especially around Lake Malombe, the lakeshore (Bwanji Valley) and near the Shire. The other was the high level of hunting in the area, for Liwonde, being only some 53 km from the capital Zomba, was a regular hunting ground of European planters and administrators during the colonial period.

The continued survival of the larger ungulates in the Upper Shire is largely due to the establishment of Liwonde as a protected area. Like Phirilongwe, it was declared a controlled shooting area in 1962, and eventually, in 1973, gazetted as a national park. But even then, protection came too late for many species: 'The last buffalo were seen in 1960, the last hartebeest in 1970, the last zebra in 1971, and the last wild dog in 1975' (Hough 1989: 90). Eland and the black rhino, which also existed in the area, had long ago become extinct.

The establishment of Liwonde National Park, was largely due to the initiatives of Chief Liwonde and the game ranger Les Kettle, the idea of a game reserve being first broached at a council of chiefs held at Kasupe (Machinga) in late 1965. Supported by the District Council, the Liwonde area was formally declared a game reserve in 1969. In 1973 it became a national park, and was expanded in 1977 to include a northern area, in order to provide a wildlife corridor through to Mangochi Forest Reserve, which was used by elephants who appeared to spend the rainy season on the slopes of the mountain and came down to the Shire during the dry season. It was formally opened to the public in 1978, and its present size is 548 sq km.

Being easily reached from both Zomba and Lilongwe, and close to a tarred road, and having a varied and high population of the larger mammals, Liwonde National Park is now a favourite tourist resort. It has also been the subject of much wildlife research and monitoring of its mammal population. An early estimate (1989-91) of its mammal population was as follows:

Antbear		Oribi	50
Baboon	400	Otter	
Bushbuck	100	Pangolin	
Bushpig		Porcupine	
Civet		Ratel	
Crocodile	300	Reedbuck	50
Grey duiker	100	Sable	800
Elephant	400	Sharpe's grysbok	
Hare		Side-striped jackal	
Hippopotamus	800	Suni	
Hyena	160	Vervet Monkey	500
Impala	600	Warthog	300
Klipspringer	115	Warthog	410
Kudu	300	Waterbuck	1300
Leopard	10	Warthog	410
Lion	30	Waterbuck	1300

NB: Animals listed without numbers indicates that they are present and usually common and thus not counted.

Source: Stead & Dudley 1977, Hough 1989, Simons 1989, Simons & Chirambo 1991

Liwonde National Park is a great tourist attraction, and an important wildlife sanctuary. There is always a good chance of seeing hippopotami and elephants, even though the elephants in Liwonde have a reputation for being unduly aggressive - in 1987 an Italian priest was killed in the park by an elephant. The park also supports one of the largest populations of waterbuck in Malawi, as well as around 800 sable - one of the greatest concentrations of this antelope to be found anywhere in Africa. But as a game sanctuary the park is beset with almost intractable problems, which have long been the subject of discussion within the DNPW. These problems are threefold:

The first is that given the high human population in the areas surrounding the park, and the acute pressures on land, much encroachment has taken place in the park. By 1987 over 1,000 people were living within the park boundaries, and in 1988 a further 10 sq km were lost to local villagers. Given the fact that there is no buffer zone, and the park is relatively small, this loss of land to cultivation is serious.

Secondly, throughout its existence Liwonde park has been subject not only to illegal fishing and the gathering of firewood and thatching materials, but also to extensive hunting (poaching). A considerable amount of hunting takes place within the park, and the evidence suggests that it is on the increase. Elephants are being hunted for their tusks by professional hunters, who are armed with automatic AK 47 guns, and being a law unto themselves, they represent a serious challenge to the game guards. But subsistence hunters from local villages surrounding the park are even more in evidence, and their presence almost ubiquitous. They come into the park, either individually or in small parties, to hunt for (or trap by means of wire snares) impala, sable, kudu and waterbuck. In July 1989, Simons (1990) records, a total of about 150 wire-snares were discovered after intensified patrolling - and many of these were found within only a few kilometers of the scout camp at Makanga - which makes one wonder who is actually engaged in the trapping. Reports of scout patrols (1987-1990) indicate widespread poaching, with the finding of hunting camps, wire snares, dead animals (elephant, hippopotamus, kudu, bushbuck, sable, waterbuck), as well as the encountering of 'armed groups' (WRU 50/4/3). A more recent report, entitled 'Liwonde under pressure', noted that during the period September to November 1994, park personnel collected 5,000 snares, 30 axes, 17 pangas (bush knives), and 6 firearms. The park warden and his staff, it suggests, are to be congratulated on this impressive but 'depressing haul' (WSM Newsletter, January 1995). Enquiries I made among people, especially hunters living in villages adjacent to the park, suggests that although local people accept the validity of the park as a game sanctuary in order that government may derive income from tourists, generally speaking they are not happy (*samakondwera*) with the sanctuary (*nkhalango*: forest). They feel they should be free to enter the park to collect firewood and thatching grass, and to hunt mammals. And there is a general antipathy between local people and the park staff - expressed in the words 'we do not hold together' (*sitimagwirizana*).

The third problem is the extensive damage done to local crops - and to people directly - by the wild mammals that find sanctuary in the park. Wild mammals, of course, are not conscious of park boundaries and thus freely wander into the surrounding cultivations doing extensive damage to such crops as rice and maize. Along the eastern boundary elephants raid the fields, mainly feeding on maize, while at the western boundary, 1 km west of the Shire River, hippopotami do extensive damage. Baboons, monkeys and bushpigs also do a great deal of damage to crops. In a survey of villages surrounding the park, Simons and Chirambo (1991) found that the people most vulnerable to wildlife depredations were small subsistence farmers growing maize, and that many experience, on average, yearly damage of around 10%. Some villagers had lost up to half their expected crop, and two villages on the southern boundary had lost about 30% of the expected maize harvest to wild mammals. Although government hunters each year shot marauding elephants and hippopotomi - between 1989 and 1992, 7 elephants and 215 hippopotomi had been shot - this made little difference to the overall impact of wildlife on local agricultural production. Local protective measures - the erection of watch hides, fire, and shouting and drumming - though taking up a lot of time and energy, were not always effective. In addition, between 1989 and 1992, around 31 people had been killed by wildlife from the park. These involved two deaths by elephant, 12 by hippos, and 17 by crocodiles. Many people also sustained injuries. Many lions had developed the habit of entering village communities, principally to hunt bush pig in the cultivations, and some people had been mauled by them, as well as losing livestock. Wildlife depredations are a perennial problem throughout Malawi and will be discussed more fully in a later chapter, but at Liwonde the juxta position of village communities with a game sanctuary that holds a high density of wildlife species has a special dimension.

Three important challenges are seen as facing the DNPW (Simons 1990). The first is to maintain Liwonde as a viable wildlife sanctuary, and if possible to increase its carrying capacity and its biodiversity. It was felt that a buffer zone, where woodland resources could be taken by local village communities, should be established. In 1985, zebra and buffalo were reintroduced into the park, being translocated from Kasungu National Park. Given the hunting pressure, this did not prove a success. More recently a project to reintroduce the black rhinoceros into the park has been undertaken - given the fears that there are no more rhino to be found in Kasungu National Park or Mwabvi Game Reserve. Plans to reintroduce buffalo, eland, blue wildebeest, zebra and hartebeest are also being discussed, warmly supported by the Wildlife Society of Malawi (Kelly et al 1993: 76-77).

Secondly, the department was anxious to improve tourist facilities within the park, thereby increasing government revenue. Mvuu Camp has thus been upgraded and placed in the hands of a private company, Central African Wilderness Safaris, to ensure high standards of accommodation and comfort, and the staff village has been moved to the western boundary of the park, so as not to unduly disturb the tourists. But the Wildlife Society of Malawi has been concerned that Malawians might not have access to the park, for the cost of tourist accommodation in Malawian terms is exorbitant, and have therefore facilitated the building of a student hostel to enable young Malawians to see and appreciate their wildlife heritage (Kelly et al op cit 74-75).

And finally, the department was keen to establish better relations with the surrounding villages, so that local people got benefits from the park, without endangering its wildlife population. As far as possible local people were to be employed as park staff, and great store was placed on the erection of an electrified game fence, to protect the park, and to prevent wild mammals from encroaching into local village gardens. The fence was completed in 1989, at the cost of some R2 million provided by the South African government. Although the fence was said to be welcomed by local people, in fact the system, based on solar power, was sabotaged by local villagers and the wires ironically utilized in the making of wire snares - thus aggravating the problem of poaching. (For general accounts of Liwonde National Park see Carter 1987: 123-131, Hough 1989: 87-102 and the beautifully illustrated guide by Kelly et al 1993.)

THE CENTRAL PLATEAU

The Central Region of Malawi consists of a plateau area, lying at an altitude of between 800 and 1400 m. Some 120 km from east to west, it stretches from Chimaliro Hills in the north, south to the Dzalanyama range and the Chongoni-Dedza Highlands, a distance of some 220 km. Dedza Moutain has an elevation of 2136 m. The Luangwa Valley/Lake Malawi watershed forms the western boundary of Malawi, but the plateau itself extends some distance into Zambia. Kasungu National Park is situated in the north-west corner. The eastern boundary of the plateau consists of a range of hills, of which the most prominent mountains are, moving from north to south, Chipata (1638 m), Ntchisi (1705 m), Dowa (1698 m) and Nkhoma (1784 m). The mountains offer excellent views of the rift valley escarpment, and the lakeshore plain that stretches from Dwangwa sugar estate south to Chipoka. Nkhotakota Game Reserve is located on the rift valley escarpment, to the north and east of the Chipata Mountain. All the major rivers, Dwangwa, Bua, Lilongwe and Diampwe, rise on the western watershed and flow in a north-easterly direction into Lake Malawi.

Much of the plateau is an undulating plain, and its natural vegetation consists largely of *Brachystegia* woodland, especially on the hills and on the escarpment, with *Acacia/Combretum* woodland being common on the more fertile land between Kasungu and Lilongwe. *Dambo* grassland occurs along the river valleys, often covering extensive areas, and the summits of all the higher mountains are clothed with montane evergreen forest. Apart from the hill areas, which constitute forest reserves, almost all the Central Plateau is now heavily populated and extensively cultivated, tobacco being an important cash crop.

It seems evident that, as in Southern Malawi, the Central Plateau supported a fairly high population of larger mammals in the past - both in terms of species and numbers. David MacPherson, who had a tobacco estate at Namitete, some 50 km from Lilongwe, and who came to the area in 1929, recorded that the Bua/Rusa watershed was a 'magnificent country for game animals'. He wrote, 'The antelope included most "possibles" for the country - eland, kudu, sable, roan, hartebeest, waterbuck, reedbuck, oribi, puku'; and that the area was a favourite hunting ground for Europeans from all over Nyasaland. The country was thus 'full of game', and included a herd of eland two or three hundred strong. Some Europeans took a commercial interest in the eland and using local hunters 'went in for biltong', much to the chagrin of other Europeans who felt it interfered with their 'sport'. At weekends, MacPherson wrote that most European tobacco farmers of the Lilongwe area would be 'out for buck' (1973: 48). The Bua River Valley - *bua* in Chewa means a collective hunt - was described as a 'real game park' and in the late 1920s the game warden Rodney Wood established a hunting lodge for the then governor, Sir Charles Bowring, on the Bua. For a period, the Bua River was a protected area - mainly to protect the puku, which in herds of 30-40 were largely confined to the dambo areas of the Bua and Rusa rivers. There were plenty of hippopotami in the Bua, and occasionally rhinoceroses and buffalo were seen, but they were more plentiful near Ngara Mountain which originally was the location of the administration - the Boma - of the Central Region. Elephants were fairly plentiful, mainly coming over from the Luangwa Valley in the wet season - but even after the establishment of Kasungu Game Reserve in 1922, much poaching of elephant took place, even by MacPherson himself! 'Man-eating' lions were renowned in the region, and, as we shall describe later, one terrorized the people of the Fort Manning (Mchinji) region in the 1930s. Serval, leopard and civet were common, and the occasional cheetah was seen. Hunting dog and caracal were noted, but were rare. Antbear, klipspringer, cane rat, porcupine, otter - both species – Sharpe's grysbok, and zebra were also noted by MacPherson, and buffalo and impala were recorded as being common on the lakeshore near the Chia Lagoon (1973: 48-53).

The hunting trip of Mrs Arthur Colville from Zomba to the Bua River - recorded in her 'Thousand Miles in a Machila' (1911) - also gives a fair indication of the wealth of larger fauna to be found in the Central Region during the early colonial period. At Liwonde a large herd of eland was seen; at Mua Mission buffalo and kudu were wreaking havoc in the gardens; in the forests at the foot of Chongoni Mountain five sable were shot as well as a hartebeest; near the Diampwe River a herd of 50 elephant was encountered, and the author records seeing hartebeest, sable, eland and reedbuck; near the Livulezi River zebra, roan, as well as more eland and elephant were again noted. Thus sable, kudu, elephant, eland, roan, waterbuck, bushbuck, and zebra were all noted as 'plentiful' or 'fairly numerous' (Colville 1911: 38-108).

Such observations - based on recollections - are confirmed by the District Books of Fort Manning (Mchinji), Ngara (Kasungu), and Dowa (1907-1920) which list the following species:

Elephant *	Hippopotamus *	Roan*
Antbear	Hunting dog	Serval
Baboon*	Impala	Sharpe's grysbok*
Black rhino *	Klipspringer	Side-striped jackal
Buffalo	Kudu	Spotted hyena *
Bushbuck*	Leopard	Vervent monkey *
Eland*	Oribi	Warthog
Grey duiker *	Puku*	Waterbuck*
Hartebeest *	Reedbuck*	Zebra *

* indicated as 'numerous', 'common' or 'plentiful'.

Buffaloes, it seems, were not plentiful around the turn of the century, having been decimated by the recent rinderpest epidemic, and puku were common only on the upper reaches of the Bua River.

The black rhino was recorded as being 'fairly numerous' on many of the rivers of the Kasungu district – on Mpelele (near where Kamuzu Academy is now situated at Mtunthama), Kasangadzi, and Mkalalu, all tributaries of the Bua, which flows just north of Ngara Mountain. Because of the association of rhinoceroses with this area, Ngara Mountain and the Nantundu Thicket some 5 km south-east of the mountain, were later (1940) gazetted as game reserves, with a total area of 49 sq km. Nantundu Thicket (*msitu*) was reported to be the haunt of at least 30 rhinos, as well as some buffaloes. A local tobacco planter, A. Cole, who lived at Mpali Estate for many years, and who acted as an honarary game warden, reported that the area was heavily infested with tsetse fly when he first came to the country, and that buffalo, rhino, roan, zebra, kudu, sable and waterbuck were all common around Ngara Mountain. However, by the late 1930s, when the reserves were established, the area had already seen a large expansion in the human population, with extensive cultivations, and both 'tsetse fly and game gradually vanished' - Cole later reported to the 1946 Commission of Enquiry into Forest and Game Reserves (MNA/NCF 1/10/1, NCG 1/6/2, NCE 2/12/1, NN 1/6/1).

It has to be recalled that in the early part of the century, human population was relatively low and probably the total population for the plateau area numbered no more than 185,000 people. By the 1930s it had doubled, although Murray's handbook (1932) notes that game was still fairly plentiful in the Kasungu, Mchinji, and Dowa districts, while in the Lilongwe district, owing to the 'vast increase' in settlement and cultivation due to the success of the tobacco industry, game was annually diminishing, and there were only a few 'remnant' populations of eland, kudu, waterbuck, roan, sable, hartebeest and reedbuck still left (1932: 239).

Since then, with increasing population - that of the Central Region is now approaching two million people - the larger game mammals have largely disappeared. But the forest reserves of Chimaliro, Mchinji, Dzalanyama, Chongoni, Thuma, Kongwe and Ntchisi still collectively carry a small population of larger antelopes - kudu, sable, Sharpe's grysbok, bushbuck, reedbuck, klipspringer, red forest duiker, and grey duiker - as well as such mammals as antbear, porcupine, blue monkey, serval, civet, hare, bushpig and side-striped jackal. But in all these areas - though protected forests - intensive hunting takes place by both Europeans and local people, as well as extensive trapping. In the Dzalanyama Hills, and on both Chongoni and

Ntchisi mountains I found game-pits (*mbuna*), spring traps and wire snares to be common. When at Dzalanyama - the name means 'ash-heap of the game-animal' - I learned (in 1991) from one of the forest guards that a group of Europeans had come by car from Lilongwe one night - the distance is only 50 km - and with the help of local hunters and lamps, hunted and killed several sable which are still to be found at the headwaters of the Katete Stream.

Thuma Forest Reserve is also worth mentioning. Situated on the Rift Valley escarpment between Lilongwe and Salima, it was proclaimed a reserve in 1926. It covers an area of 16 sq km, mainly of *Brachystegia* woodland. Being a remote area, with no roads in the reserve, it remains a haven of wildlife, with around 50 elephant, 50 buffalo, as well as a small number of kudu, eland, bushbuck, lion and warthog. Elephant in the reserve were considered by Peter Blignaut to be fairly tame. In 1990 the poaching of elephant became a serious problem. A local hunter, armed with a high powered rifle, and aided and abetted, it appears, by high-ranking army officers, shot many elephant - some 13 pairs of tusks being found in his house. This led to an outcry in the local press, and calls for the reserve to be given full status as a game reserve, manned by trained game guards (lecture on Thuma, Peter Blignaut, Lilongwe: 8 September 1993).

Within the Central Plateau two game sanctuaries have been established, the Nkhotakota Game Reserve, which covers an area of wild country on the Rift Valley escarpment to the east of Kasungu, and the Kasungu National Park, some 25 km to the west of the town. I shall discuss each in turn.

Nkhotakota Game Reserve

Nkhotakota Game Reserve (now called Nkhotakota Wildlife Reserve) is the largest game sanctuary in Malawi and covers a spectacular area of hills and river-valleys that is rarely visited by tourists. Its present size is some 1800 sq km, and it is bisected by both the Bua River and the main dirt road that runs from Lilongwe to Nkhotakota on the lakeshore. Most of the reserve is covered with a closed *Brachystegia* woodland, with *Terminalia* woodland in the drier parts, and montane evergreen forest on the summit of Chipata Mountain. In the past - Nkhotakota town being an important trading centre - a major trade route undoubtedly passed through the reserve, and there is evidence of earlier settlement and cultivation within the reserve.

In the early colonial period the Nkhotakota district was renowned for its wildlife, and game animals were to be found in fair numbers. These included elephant, buffalo, hippopotamus, reedbuck, waterbuck, kudu, zebra, impala, hartebeest, warthog, bushpig and eland - as well as roan and rhinoceros (Marimba District Book 1907-1930 NCK 3/9/5, Murray 1932: 228). In 1935 the Nkhotakota area was gazetted as a forest reserve, and two years later the provincial commissioner for the Central Region, A.G.O. Hodgson, broached the idea of making the escarpment area to the west of Nkhotakota town a game reserve. The reason for this was that the area could form a sanctuary into which elephants could then be driven - for marauding elephants caused extensive damage to crops along the lakeshore. It would also protect rhinoceros, roan, eland, and other game to be found in the area. It was thus formally gazetted in March 1938, with an area of 878 sq km (MNA/S1/260/37). G.D. Hayes' suggestion (1978: 21), that Nkhotakota Game Reserve was the 'oldest' wildlife reserve still in existence is not true - Mwabvi (Thangadzi), Lengwe and Kasungu sanctuaries were all gazetted earlier. In 1954 the boundaries of the reserve were extended, and people then living within the reserve resettled.

A good indication of the mammalian fauna to be found in Nkhotakota Game Reserve around this time is to be found in B.L. Mitchell's account of a day spent in the reserve in 1953. He noted several herds of zebra and hartebeest, a small herd of elephant, 2 bushbuck, warthog, Sharpe's grysbok, grey duiker, 3 elephant bulls, as well as the fresh spoor of rhinoceros and buffalo - all in a 12 mile walk (Mitchell 1953: 106-8). The popular writings of Guy Muldoon (1955, 1957), which recorded his hunting adventures while working for the agricultural department at Mwera Hill, and later as game control officer at Nkhotokota, also indicates the wealth of mammalian life to be found on the escarpment hills between the Dwangwa and Lilongwe rivers less than half a century ago. Sable and eland were then common around Ntchisi Mountain, and Muldoon described Nyasaland as 'so full of wild life that it might rate one of nature's outstanding animal paradises' (1955: 181). As game control officer for Nkhotakota, Muldoon's task can best be described in his own words; for besides administering the game reserve, 'My duties included the destruction of baboons and bushpigs that raided the fields and gardens of the villagers, the elimination of man-eating lion and leopard, and the control of rogue elephant, buffalo or hippo that threatened human life or subsistence' (op. cit. 61).

As Muldoon reckoned that over 2000 elephants were then to be found in Nkhotokota Game Reserve (73), and as Nkhotakota lakeshore was fertile land with a high human population, his main task seems to have been to drive back the marauding elephants into the reserve. His writings give graphic accounts of his hunting exploits: shooting the man-eating leopards and lions around Mwera Hill and Ntchisi Mountain; destroying bushpig and baboons: in the 'baboon war', as Muldoon describes it, he killed 13 thousand baboons in two years (op. cit. 149); hunting the hippos that raided the village gardens; and hunting elephants in the Upper Shire and Ntcheu districts (1957). Muldoon, with the help of five experienced African hunters, even attempted to drive the famous Mpimbi elephant herd, which had been regarded as a public danger since 1914, into the Majete non-shooting area - but without success (1957: 14-26).

Since those halcyon days when wildlife was seemingly so abundant - and highly detrimental to local subsistence - game animals have seriously declined in numbers. When I visited Ntchisi there was little evidence of elephant, sable or eland which were so common in Muldoon's day. But Nkhotakota Game Reserve itself still carries a wide variety of larger mammals. With regard to its wildlife population, two surveys may be noted: that of the Department of Game, Fish and Tsetse Control for 1959-62, and one more recent (1989).

TABLE SIX
Nkhotakota Game Reserve
Average Numbers of Game Seen per 10 Patrol Days (1959-62)

	1959	1960	1961	1962
Buffalo	12.50	13.60	20.60	29.07
Bushbuck			0.07	4.92
Bushpig			0.72	11.77
Eland	5.42	6.67	11.50	18.7
Elephant	15.90	19.30	23.30	34.0
Grey duiker				3.85
Hartebeest	3.42	3.35	6.52	10.95
Hippopotamus	0.02			
Klipspringer				2.20
Kudu	0.80	1.37	4.12	7.75
Leopard	-	seen	-	seen
Lion	0.03	0.10	0.70	0.35
Reedbuck	0.45	0.10	0.30	3.65
Rhinoceros	0.36	3.00	0.25	1.10
Sable	2.49	4.15	4.85	7.67
Sharpe's grysbok				0.87
Warthog	0.32		0.62	8.27
Waterbuck	2.42	2.62	6.00	8.07
Wilddog			0.17	
Zebra	4.81	5.40	8.50	12.12

Source: Annual Reports of the Department of Game,
Fish and Tsetse Control 1959-62

These figures appear to show a rise in the number of game animals, but these figures are based on the counts of game guards, and the 1962 figures may reflect simply better supervision of the reserve.

The game population of Nkhotakota reserve in 1989 was estimated as follows:

Elephant	400	Mongoose spp.	
Baboon		Red forest duiker	
Blue monkey		Reedbuck	50
Bushbuck	400	Roan	250
Bushpig	200	Sable	500
Cape clawless otter		Sharpe's grysbok	
Civet		Side striped jackal	
Eland	150	Spotted hyena	
Grey duiker	200	Vervet monkey	
Hartebeest	25	Warthog	600
Klipspringer		Waterbuck	50
Kudu	100	Zebra	100
Lion			

NB Animals listed without numbers indicates that they are present and usually common and thus not counted.

Source: Simons 1989

Both the rhinoceros and wild dog are now perhaps extinct in the area. As with Liwonde and Majete reserves, Nkhotakota Game Reserve is subject to much illegal activity, and poaching is rampant within the reserve. Richard Bell on a *ulendo* (20-26th October 1980), noted 2 poachers with muzzle-loading guns, 18 pitfall traps, and the remains of 6 poacher's campfires, one with three bushbuck skins. The reserve, he noted, had the dubious distinction of having, perhaps, the highest level of illegal activity in Malawi. This hunting pressure is reflected in the very low level of wildlife (biomass) density - estimated at 680 kg/sq km (Simons 1989: 62, WRU 50/3/9). But although compared with Liwonde National Park, the larger mammals are not conspicuous - although I saw plenty of warthog, kudu, klipspringer and elephant when I camped near Chipata Mountain - the reserve is important as a conservation area, and has a unique scenic and ecological appeal (see Hough 1989: 135-144).

Kasungu National Park

After Nyika, Kasungu is the largest wildlife sanctuary in Malawi, with an area of 2316 sq. km. Its vegetation is typically that of the Kasungu plain, *Brachystegia* woodland covering the undulating landscape, with open grassy marshland (*dambo*) in the river valleys. The latter, which seasonally become flooded, comprise about 20% of the park. The mean annual rainfall is around 78 cm.

Although during the colonial period the Kasungu district as a whole supported a wealth of wildlife (according to the Ngara District Book of 1907 elephant, buffalo, eland, sable, roan, hartebeest, kudu, reedbuck and zebra were all found in comparatively large members where there was suitable habitat {MNA/NCG 1/6/2}), the area now occupied by Kasungu National Park was in the early decades of the century a settled region. It held a fairly large human population, and this had probably been the case for several centuries, for while most of the park consists of poor sandy soils, there are fertile valleys in many areas and ample water. Richard Bell estimated that in the 1870s the population of what is now the park might have been about 10 thousand people (1983: 3/7).

In the hills to the west - Miondwe and Solonje - there are rock paintings that indicate the early presence of 'stone-age' hunter-gatherers and throughout the park there is evidence of iron-smelting kilns and early village communities. Remains of fortified villages, built to resist Ngoni invaders at the

Male sable antelope

Source: Archives of the Society of Malawi

end of the 19th century, may still be seen today in many parts of the park. Kasungu, as a game sanctuary, owes its existence to the tsetse fly and to the outbreak of sleeping sickness among villagers in the West Kasungu district which occurred in 1922. Some seven cases were definitely diagnosed by the local medical officer in August 1922, and the 'endemic centre' and focus of the infection was seen to be among villagers on the Lingadzi River, at the heart of the present game sanctuary. It was therefore decided by the provisional commissioner, W. Kirby Green, in consultation with the Resident at Kasungu, and a local and rather vocal missionary, Dr George Prentice, that the best means of dealing with this epidemic would be to evacuate the people from the area. This entailed the movement of some 50 villages, comprising 150 huts - a sizeable population of over 2000 people - and their resettlement in the East, in the Dwangwa Valley north of Kasungu Hill, near Kasungu Hill itself, and on the Lingadzi River near Ngara Hill. The area from which they were evacuated was to be declared a forest reserve, and no shooting of game was to be allowed within its boundaries - it being felt that any hunting within this reserve would scatter the game and 'spread the fly'. But the country to the south and east of the game reserve was declared a 'free-shooting area' and both Europeans and Africans were to be encouraged to shoot all the wild game they could find.

This idea of containing both the game and the tsetse fly in an ecological enclave came from the activities of the eccentric Austrian nobleman, Count Marian Steblecki. This ardent hunter, who lived on an estate near Dedza, also had a large estate of some 16 thousand acres in the (other) Lingadzi valley, 40 km north of Salima. Steblecki declared his estate a private game sanctuary, in which only he himself was allowed to hunt. No other person was allowed to hunt there, and local Africans were not even allowed to enter the estate - anyone trespassing, as MacPherson recalled, was reported to the Dowa *boma* 'by his henchmen' (1973: 52). The theory was that while his estate was 'full of game and swarms with fly', outside the estate the tsetse fly should no longer be found and cattle could move freely. Kirby Green applied this notion to the outbreak of sleeping sickness in the Lingadzi (Kasungu) area. Thus in 1923 this area was declared the Fort Alston Forest (Game) Reserve to contain the fly and to protect wildlife; while outside the reserve was declared a 'free-shooting' zone. Some questioned the logic of this proposal, but there is no doubt that while at that time the upper reaches of the Dwangwa and Lingadzi rivers contained very little game, outside the reserve, especially on the Rusa and Bua rivers, game animals were plentiful, and shot indiscriminately and in great numbers. One European hunter, Mr H.R. Cox, who had a hunting camp at the junction of the Rusa and Bua rivers

(Kasera's village), reckoned he had shot in two years of 'free-shooting' (1922-1924), some 800 head of game - mainly to supply Kasungu Mission with dried meat. The policy of having a free-shooting area did not drive game animals into the reserve, as was expected, it simply reduced their numbers. And although the larger mammals at that period - roan, zebra, hartebeest, eland and buffalo - were still fairly common, many noted that the number of game animals found in the reserve was not much different from that in unprotected areas (MNA/S1/1951/22).

Although subsistence hunting undoubtedly continued to take place within the Fort Alston Forest Reserve, as the *Brachystegia* woodland began to regenerate, so game animals too began to increase in number, and to re-establish themselves - particularly buffalo and elephant. With the epidemic of sleeping sickness under control - although tsetse fly was still found throughout much of the country - local people began making requests, through their chiefs, to return to their former villages within the reserve. In 1930 the status of the reserve was changed to that of a 'game reserve', for as the Chief Conservation of Forests, J.B. Clements wrote in a memorandum (February 1930), though of some importance in the conservation of local water supplies, 'the quality of its forests are very poor and practically of no value from a commercial point of view' (MNA/51/1951/22).

From 1932 to 1934 the Kasungu (Fort Alston) Game Reserve was the subject of a great deal of debate, both locally and at the national level. Both Chief Chulu and Chief Mwase Kasungu made requests for their people to return to their former haunts, and to resettle near Ng'ombe Rume Hill, and near the Lisitu and Lingadzi rivers. Much of the reserve was known as 'Chulu's Country' - Chulu being one of the original Chewa chiefs. Given that within its boundaries the reserve had some of the most fertile land in the district, and that it was definitely suitable land for tobacco production, one European tobacco farmer from the Mbabzi Estate, near Lilongwe, A.F. Barron, applied to the government to buy a block of land some 2-3000 acres in extent within the reserve.

But having abolished the old Central Angoniland Game Reserve in 1930 - the reserve, established in 1906, covered an area of land at the headwaters of the Diampwe River in the Dedza district, which had been heavily settled in the last two decades and had lost much of its game - and having made commitments both to the Colonial Office and to the Society for the Protection of the Fauna of the Empire, the colonial government resisted the pressure of both local people and the European planters who wanted to move into the reserve. Thus, although it was acknowledged that the establishment of Fort Alston Game Reserve was 'not by design but by accident incidental to the

1922 outbreak of sleeping sickness' (as the Resident at Kasungu R.H. Keppel-Compton put it), it was declared, nevertheless, to be a reserve that was to be presumed 'inviolate' and which would ultimately be made into a national park. This was the sentiment of the provisional commissioner A.G.O. Hodgson, whose opinion seems to have carried the day. But it is of interest to note that W.E. Jennings the Kasungu DC who visited the reserve in January 1934, actually saw little game though plenty of fresh spoors and dung of elephant, rhino, buffalo, sable, kudu, hartebeest and zebra. He also noted signs of 'considerable unauthorized hunting' (MNA/SI/1951/22, NC/1/10/2).

Between 1923 and 1965 Fort Alston Game Reserve was effectively, as Richard Bell put it, a 'no-man's land', with few staff, hardly any roads, and with little serious enforcement of the wildlife legislation. As one early game warden said, 'The effect of making it a game reserve is to make it completely safe for the poachers, since law abiding people are deterred from entering' (Bell 1983: 3/8). Although there is little data available, it is evident that during this period the wildlife in the park, in spite of considerable poaching which has continued unabated throughout the colonial and post-colonial period, gradually increased in number. In 1970 buffalo were estimated at 300, and elephant at 1200, having increased from an original herd of about 100 in 1920 (op. cit. 9). At the end of the colonial period the larger mammals to be found in the reserve are shown in Table Seven.

After the Second World War petitions were made by Chief Mwase to the Director of the Department of Game, Fish and Tsetse Control H.J. Borley for his people to be allowed to resettle within the reserve. A meeting of village headmen in 1949 complained of the great shortage of food and of crop depredations. Now that there were no people inhabiting the area, one person complained, wild animals had become plentiful. In 1950, during the rainy season, some 16 elephant, 7 roam, 3 baboon, 2 waterbuck and a hartebeest were shot in crop protection exercises by two game guards. The administration was sympathetic towards the pleas for resettlement, and a few villages reoccupied the south-eastern part of the reserve, but otherwise the reserve was preserved intact (MNA/NCG/1/3/1).

From about 1966, Kasungu reserve was developed as a conservation area. An infrastructure of roads was constructed, and in 1970 Lifupa Lodge was opened, the same year as the sanctuary was given national park status.

Along with Liwonde, Kasungu National Park is one of the finest of the game sanctuaries in terms of variety of different mammals seen. It supports a large population of elephant and buffalo, and there are also good chances of seeing sable, hartebeest, zebra and eland, as well as two species

TABLE SEVEN
Kasungu Game Reserve
Average Numbers of Game Seen per 10 Patrol Days (1959-62)

	1959	1960	1961	1962	No. of animals seen, Oct. 1959
Buffalo	43.29	13.35	16.82	29.3	56
Bushbuck	-	0.37	0.10	1.12	1
Bushpig	-	0.37	0.85	4.6	-
Eland	4.58	6.07	7.25	20.0	42
Elephant	18.27	23.75	40.72	59.47	67
Grey duiker	-	-	0.10	1.37	6
Hartebeest	6.04	5.92	7.37	13.7	40
Hippopotamus	0.10	seen	seen	12.37	-
Klipspringer	-	-	-	-	1
Kudu	1.60	4.27	3.9	5.5	10
Leopard	-	seen	seen	0.17	-
Lion	0.16	0.30	0.15	0.67	3
Oribi	0.08	0.12	0.52	0.95	15
Reedbuck	1.65	2.27	2.05	4.67	34
Rhinoceros	0.54	0.90	0.77	4.07	-
Roan	3.10	6.35	07.3	10.2	17
Sable	4.22	3.65	6.5	10.97	1
Sharpe's grysbok	-	-	seen	0.42	3
Warthog	1.24	0.67	1.93	5.35	-
Waterbuck	1.12	0.92	2.25	2.22	34
Wilddog	-	-	-	0.27	-
Zebra	4.29	6.45	8.00	13.27	9

Source: Annual Reports of the Department of Game,
Fish and Tsetse Control 1959-62

that were not mentioned in the early records of the game department: impala and puku. The black rhino was once found in the park, and it was estimated (1983) that there were around 20 animals present. Recent poaching, has, it seems, sadly reduced this number of black rhino, and it may now be extinct in Kasungu. The most recent figures for the population of the larger mammals are estimated as follows:

Antbear		Lion	40
Baboon		Oribi	30
Black rhinoceros	3?		
Pangolin			
Buffalo	1000	Porcupine	
Bushbaby		Puku	75
Bushbuck	100	Ratel	
Bushpig	500	Reedbuck	600
Cane rat		Roan	400
Cheetah	occasionally seen	Sable	400
Civet		Serval	20
Eland	300	Sharpe's grysbok	
Elephant	500	Side-striped jackal	50
Grey duiker	500	Skipspringer	40
Hare		Spotted hyena	70
Hartebeest	500	Vervet money	
Hippopotamus	30	Warthog	800
Impala	100	Waterbuck	10
Klipspringer	100	Wild dog	50
Kudu	300	Zebra	400
Leopard	25		

NB Animals listed without numbers indicates that they are present and usually common and thus not counted.

Source: Simons 1989, Harry S. Munthali, personal communication March 1991. All these figures are estimates only.

In an important survey of the larger mammals of the park, Richard Bell noted that apart from impala, kudu, rhino and bushbuck, all of which are scarce, there are few browsing ungulates in the *Brachystegia* woodland, and the commoner herbivores - roan, sable, hartebeest, reedbuck, oribi, and puku - all tend to be selective grazers (1983: 2, 3 - see Table Eight).

Waterbuck were once common on the lower Lingadzi *dambo*, with about 100 animals in this area (1980); but with extensive cultivations being opened up on land adjacent to the park, the waterbuck were exposed to disturbance and poaching, and their numbers are now significantly reduced. Harry Munthali suggested to me that there were about ten animals remaining within the park.

TABLE EIGHT
The Herbivores

Selective	Grazers Non-Selective	Mixed Feeders	Browsers
	Elephant	Elephant	Elephant
			Black rhino
	Hippopotamus		
	Zebra		
	Buffalo		
	Eland	Eland	Eland
			Kudu
Impala		Impala	Impala
			Bushbuck
			Duiker
			Grysbok
			Steinbuck
Roan			
Sable			
Hartebeest			
Waterbuck			
Reedbuck			
Puku			
Oribi			
Warthog			
Bushpig		Bushpig	Bushpig

NB Animals listed below dotted line are ruminants
Source: Bell 1983/2; 3

As with Liwonde and many other of the game sanctuaries in Malawi, Kasungu National Park is confronted with four problems: intensive poaching; encroachment; depredations from mammals raiding crops in areas adjacent to the park; and the very negative, indeed hostile, attitude of local people towards the conservation area.

Hippopotamus
Source: Archives of the Society of Malawi.

Throughout its history Kasungu reserve has been subject to poaching activities, mainly subsistence hunting by hunters from surrounding villages, particularly from Chulu village. People of this village, as we have noted, originally lived in the park area. Such poaching probably had a limited effect on the mammal population, and some mammals, including the elephant, actually increased in number inspite of intensive hunting by local people. However during the 1970s elephant poaching rose to what has been described as 'epidemic' proportions, not only in Malawi, but throughout Africa. This was because the price of ivory rose from K5 per kilo in 1970 to K50 per kilo in 1975. Because of this, in the period 1978-1981, the elephant population in Kasungu was drastically reduced in numbers from around 1200 (in 1970) to around 800 (1983). Moreover, while in an earlier period the elephants were scattered throughout the park as a result of the intensive poaching, their numbers became concentrated in a triangle of land near Lifupa Lodge. This concentration had an important effect on the vegetation, leading to the development of a 'coppice' *Brachystegia* woodland. It also led to increasing crop damage on lands adjacent to the south-eastern boundary of the park.

Faced with this crisis, in April 1982 an intensive anti-poaching campaign was launched, directed with thoroughness and enthusiasm by the first Malawian game warden of Kasungu, Matthew Matemba. In 1981 it was estimated that at least 50 elephant had been killed in the park by poachers, both for ivory and meat.

The poachers came mainly from the villages in the Chulu area, and used muzzle-loading guns (*mfuti za gogodera*), either old 'Tower' muskets of 19th century vintage or modern imitations made locally from odd piping. These contraptions are extremely dangerous, and one famous hunter, Langton Chinseo Phiri, lost first a thumb, then his left hand in hunting accidents. Skilled in bushcraft he would, in stalking black rhino, imitate the call of another rhino to draw the animal close before shooting. The high price of rhino horn resulted in the intensification of the hunting of this species in Malawi at around the same time.

Gathering local information on the poachers, and setting up clandestine deals, Matemba and his rangers mounted a successful anti-poaching operation, and over 200 poachers were arrested in or around Kasungu National Park, along with some 30 muzzle-loading guns. Both subsistence hunting and the poaching of elephant continues to be a problem - but it is in many ways being held in check - and the elephant population is now estimated to be around 500. (On the anti-poaching campaign in Kasungu see WRU 1/2/30/0, Bell 1983: 3/9-12, Bosman and Hall-Martin 1986: 90-95).

Given its history, encroachment in Kasungu is perhaps less of a problem than one might expect, but it is still a problem, and in 1988 some 9.3 sq km had been illegally cultivated or settled.

With respect to crop depradation at Kasungu this, too, is a major concern, particularly on the eastern boundary. During the 1980s 20 or 30 elephants a year on average were shot in order to protect crops. But importantly, some 90% of all crop protection shooting occurs in a 30 km sector of boundary near the Lingadzi River, where, as Bell put it 'high human and elephant densities meet' (Bell 1981: 85). Thus, to alleviate the problem, the DNPW initiated two strategies: the creation of a buffer zone between the park boundaries and the local villages, whose land was extensively cultivated with such subsistence crops as maize and groundnuts, as well as with tobacco, whereby game drives were used to keep the larger mammals within the reserve; and the construction of a solar-powered electric fence for some 45 km along the south-eastern boundary. This was installed in 1982, and unlike the one at Liwonde, it was intact when I visited Kasungu in 1991.

In a survey of the impact of wildlife as pests around the Kasungu National Park, it was found that maize suffered most from mammal depredation - losses being around 10% of the crop, and that the main pest was the bushpig. Neither vervet monkey nor baboons were considered a serious problem by local farmers, as these animals were diurnal and the crops could be more easily protected by day. The baboon was the only mammal recorded eating tobacco leaves. Importantly, of course, bushpig, vervet monkey and baboon were not obstructed by the electric fence. Although local people complained about the elephant, crop damage from these mammals was negligible - and tended to be local. Bushpig, Deodatus and Lipiya (1990) concluded, was by far the greater problem and the loss of maize due to their depradations ran into many thousands of Kwacha each year.

People living close to Kasungu National Park derive very little benefits from the park itself, and this is the case with all the wildlife sanctuaries. Yet at the same time the conservation area effects them in a negative way. They are not allowed to hunt in the area, or collect firewood, medicines or thatching grass. With Kasungu you have the added problem that people feel that they ought to be allowed to return to their former village sites and to settle within the reserve. Not surprisingly, there is much antipathy by local villagers towards Kasungu as a nature sanctuary. The DNPW has long been aware of this problem. One way of easing the problem has been to allow local people to participate in the utilization of certain resources, such as in the collection of honey, or edible caterpillars under supervision. But until some way is found of channelling income derived from tourism within the park directly towards local communities, antipathy by these communities towards wildlife conservation is likely to remain an intractable problem. It will certainly not be achieved by placing park tourism into private hands (for useful accounts of Kasungu National Park see Carter 1987: 52-67, Hough 1989: 51-69).

THE VIPHYA AND NYIKA PLATEAUS

North of the Chimaliro Hills lies the Mzimba Plain, situated at an altitude of between 1000 and 1350 m. Ecologically continuous with the Central Plateau, the area was covered originally with *Brachystegia* woodland, the undulating country interspersed with broad 'dambos', and with rocky hills. Mt Hora (1717 m), some 35 km north of Mzimba, is one of the more famous of these hills. To the north and east of the Mzimba plain lie two important and extensive highland areas, the Viphya Plateau and the Nyika Plateau, both of which have (or had) rolling montane grasslands, with, in sheltered localities, remnant patches of montane evergreen forest. Much of the Mzimba plain and the Henga Valley north-east of Rumphi is now heavily populated and extensively cultivated, although *Brachystegia* woodland is still to be found on the hills. To the west of Rumphi is the Vwaza Marsh Game Reserve (now called Vwaza Marsh Wildlife Reserve).

Around the turn of the century it is evident that larger mammals were plentiful in the Northern Region, particularly after the rinderpest epidemic of 1893 and the spread of tsetse fly in the early decades of the century. Human population was relatively low and scattered - much less than in the Central and Southern Regions. The population of the Mombera (Mzimba) district, for instance, was estimated (in 1931) to be around 106 thousand people (Murray 1932: 214). As the Ngoni had settled in the area there were many cattle to be found, and although the herds were decimated by the rinderpest epidemic they soon recovered. Their estimated number in the Mzimba district in 1930 was 31,500. The Mombera District Book (1907) records that, although the larger mammals were generally scarce over much of the district, in the Henga Valley, there were 'immense herds' of game to be encountered - reedbuck, waterbuck, zebra, and eland - as well as kudu, buffalo, warthog, hippopotamus, klipspringer, hartebeest, roan, bushbuck, and bushpig. Elephant, hyenas and leopard were described as 'fairly numerous'. Apart from roan and eland, and a small herd of elephant, the Viphya Plateau was noted as containing little game, although klipspringer were common on the rocky hills. The District Book makes it clear that where there was a dense human population, game animals tended to be scarce (MNA/NNM 1/24/2).

I shall discuss the present status of larger mammals in the Northern Region in relation to three localities where they are still found in some numbers - the Viphya Plateau, the Vwaza Marsh Game Reserve, and the Nyika National Park.

Zebra on Nyika Plateau
Source: Archives of the Society of Malawi

The Viphya Plateau

The Viphya Plateau (also known as Viphya Mountains) forms almost the backbone of Malawi between the Chimaliro Hills near Katete and Rumphi. It is a highland area, plateau-like in many parts, standing at an elevation of between 1500 and 1800 m. During the colonial period these highlands were considered a wild, largely uninhabited area. The main road from Mzimba to Chinteche passed through the Viphya, and being open country - in those days extensive montane grassland - game animals, particularly the rather tame reedbuck, were easily shot from the road. Although never a game paradise, reedbuck was found in considerable numbers on the Viphya, and there were also moderate herds of zebra and eland. Near Kaningina Mt, where a forest reserve had been established on the escarpment between the north and south Viphya, buffalo, roan and sable were also found in scattered herds. Bushbuck and red forest duiker were also noted. As the reedbuck, eland and zebra on the Viphya Plateau were proving such an easy target to European hunters - as well as being regularly hunted by local people from the Chintheche area - during the 1930s the idea emerged among some colonial administrators of forming a game reserve on the Viphya. Among the most enthusiastic was the young DC at Chintheche, 'Bill' Rangeley. He was then less than 30 years of age. In March 1938 part of the Southern Viphya, north-east of Wozi Hill Forest Reserve, was declared a game reserve, with an area of around 130 sq km Rangeley visualized the whole of the Viphya as a national park, not merely as a small and isolated game reserve, for it had some of the finest scenery in the country, and there were patches, he wrote, of magnificent forest. He felt that, with protection, the larger mammals on the Viphya would return to their former numbers, for game there had been severely depleted by the rinderpest epidemic and by · unrestricted hunting. As a national park, 'well-stocked' with game animals, the Viphya, he wrote, would have considerable value as a health and tourist resort. He was adamant that the wild dog, which 'harry the game from end to end of the Viphya', should be exterminated, and this could only be done by employing a reliable full-time game guard (MNA/NN/1/11/2).

Rangeley's vision of a national park was not to be fulfilled, for in 1964 the Viphya Project was launched, and in the subsequent decade the rolling hills of the South Viphya were extensively reforested with fast growing exotic timber species, principally pines and eucalpytus species. Fortunately, the larger fragments of evergreen forest and some 'dambos' were left intact, and these areas are still rich in wildlife.

Just prior to the reforestation of the Viphya, accomplished with funding from the Commonwealth Development Corporation (CDC), the highland area of the Viphya was still well populated with larger mammals. This is indicated in a letter to G.D. Hayes from S.G. Williams, who was stationed at Mbowe Estate, south of Mzuzu. In spite of local people and the CDC encroaching more and more upon the Viphya each year, and the establishment of Mzuzu town in the saddle between the North and South Viphya ranges, Williams wrote that game was still 'fairly plentiful' on the Viphya. And he records reedbuck (in pairs), roan (singly or in small parties), bushbuck, as well as herds of eland, bushpig and buffalo. He, like Rangeley 20 years before, suggests to G.D. Hayes that the area ought to be made into a national park (WSM letter S.G. Williams to G.D. Hayes February 1ˢᵗ 1950).

Such a variety of game animals on the Viphya is confirmed by the records of the Department of Game, Fish and Tsetse Control for 1959, as detailed below.

TABLE NINE
The Viphya Plateau
Average Numbers of Game Seen per 10 Patrol Days (1959)

	Luwawa	Chikangawa
Buffalo	-	0.68
Bushbuck	2.02	3.33
Bushpig	-	4.34
Eland	6.91	1.42
Elephant	-	0.17
Grey duiker	8.87	0.23
Klipspringer	0.03	-
Kudu	-	0.06
Leopard	-	0.19
Lion	0.22	0.26
Reedbuck	26.92	5.8
Roan	3.43	3.49
Sable	0.14	-
Sharpe's grysbok	0.23	-
Warthog	1.89	0.70
Waterbuck	-	0.13
Zebra	2.81	-

Source: Annual Report of the Department of Game, Fish and Tsetse Control 1959

From these records it is evident that woodland species like kudu and sable were uncommon on the Viphya, while grazers associated with the montane grassland - zebra, reedbuck, roan and eland - were abundant in areas free of hunting pressures. It is precisely these latter four species that have been most effected by the pine plantations on the Viphya which have eradicated much of the grassland (see Phillips 1980).

In a wildlife survey of the South Viphya Plateau in 1969, Archie Mossman stressed that its wildlife population had been severely depressed both by heavy poaching and by the habitat changes caused by the extensive pine plantations. By African standards the ungulate species list for the Viphya is now impoverished, and although eland, roan, zebra and sable were seen by game guards in the period March to April 1969, only bushpig, reedbuck, grey duiker, red forest duiker, and monkeys seemed common. He noted that only the reedbuck seemed to be holding its own, no doubt due to its liking for *dambo* areas (1969: 56-58).

There is still a surprising amount of wild mammals on the Viphya, in spite of the pines and the extensive hunting that still takes place. George Welsh, who was chief forester on the Viphya from 1969-1972, recorded leopard, lion, ratel, civet, bushpig, reedbuck and serval, as well as noting that a pack of wild dog had been seen in 1970. Two staff members had been killed by lions while working on the plateau, and he recalled also a lion being snared by local hunters, who had utilized cut telephone wire to make the snares (G. Welsh personal communication April 1992). When I stayed near Kasitu Dam in August 1978, I saw many red forest duiker, bushbuck, blue monkey and reedbuck, as well as a civet, and zebra, roan, and eland may well survive in secluded areas of the plateau.

Vwaza Marsh Game Reserve

Vwaza Marsh Game Reserve is situated south-west of the Nyika Plateau, some 30 km west of Rumphi. It has a varied landscape, and is rich in wetland areas, deriving its name from the extensive marshland in the north of the reserve. In the south-eastern corner there is a smaller area of marsh around Lake Kazuni, and the Luwewe River, which runs from north to south through the middle of the reserve, also has floodplain grassland. Most of the reserve, which has a present size of 986 sq km, is covered with *Brachystegia* woodland, with open *Combretum/Pterocarpus* woodland in the more fertile areas. Riparian evergreen thickets and areas of *Tsanya* woodland are also found.

It is probable that the area that now constitutes the reserve was sparsely populated by humans in the past, particularly along the South Rukuru River, which forms the southern boundary of the reserve. On Phopo Hill near Lake Kazuni, there is evidence of iron-age settlement dating back to the 3rd century AD. The reserve owes its existence to H.B. Wilson of Blantyre who visited Lake Kazuni in 1933. He was very struck by its scenic appeal, and the fact that the small lake had abundant wildfowl, and about 20 hippos which could always be seen there. He suggested to the administration that it should be made into a game reserve, as a hippo and wildfowl sanctuary. As the hippo did a great deal of damage to the gardens of the local people, and as the South Rukuru River was an important source of water in what was otherwise an arid district, the DC Mzimba was reluctant to make the Lake Kazuni area into a wildfowl and hippo sanctuary - whatever its tourist appeal. (A new road had recently been made through to the Njakwa Gorge making access possible.) He noted also that there was a considerable amount of game in the Vwaza Marsh area, 40 km to the north, chiefly of roan and buffalo. The Vwaza Marsh, it is worth mentioning, like montane evergreen forests elsewhere in Malawi, was held in some awe by local people, in being associated with the spirits. If people were killed while venturing into the marsh this was interpreted as due to the fact that they had been 'taken by the spirits' (C. Kapalala in Boeder 1982: 56-57, MNA/NC/1/10/2). Given the reluctance on the part of the local administration it was not until 1941 that Lake Kazuni was declared a game reserve, with an area of 205 sq km.

At the end of the Second World War the status of the reserve at Lake Kazuni again became the subject of debate. Local people living near the lake and near the Vwaza Marsh complained about crop depredation by elephant, buffalo, hippo, and even by rhinoceros, and thus expressed hostility towards the reserve. The provincial commissioner at Mzimba, Cecil Barker, suggested that land near Lake Kazuni was required for rice production, and that the presence of a large number of protected hippos was detrimental to such a scheme (MNA/NN/1/6/1). It was hardly surprising, then, that the Commission of Enquiry into Forest and Game Reserves, which met in 1946, recommended in its report that the Lake Kazuni Reserve be de-gazetted. The reserve area, it concluded, was in no way different from the surrounding country, which was equally infested with tsetse fly and wild animals, and noted that the 'whole area is entirely unsuitable as a site for a game reserve.' It was pointed out that, from a European hunter's point of view, Lake Kazuni, though an attractive spot, was hardly likely to attract tourists if no duck shooting was allowed (MNA/NN 1/6/1)!

The government, however, did not follow the commission's recommendations, and in 1956 the Vwaza Marsh area was declared a controlled hunting area, although the ordinance did not specifically restrict human settlement.

That it became a conservation area was very largely due to the efforts of Chief Katumbi, who was the 'moving spirit' behind the idea. He became honorary game warden for the area. As a result of this protection, buffalo, eland and roan soon increased in number, and both sable and elephant were noted, as well as rhino. In the Report of Department of Game, Fish and Tsetse Control (1958) the chief was publically congratulated for his efforts in game conservation. In 1977 the area was finally gazetted as a game reserve, and people living within the park were resettled elsewhere. About 2000 people were involved. The area they had cultivated quickly regenerated into *Brachystegia* woodland.

Some indication of the larger mammals to be found in the Vwaza Marsh Game Reserve - as a non-shooting area - at the end of the colonial period is expressed in the following table:

TABLE TEN
Vwaza Marsh Game Reserve
Average Numbers of Game Seen per 10 Patrol Days (1961-62)

	1961	1962
Buffalo	10.9	39.6
Bushbuck	3.15	9.95
Bushpig	1.85	8.15
Eland	42.8	40.35
Elephant	20.45	32.3
Grey duiker	9.3	14.8
Hartebeest	9.0	8.6
Hippopotamus	1.05	2.32
Impala	-	1.92
Kudu	-	4.42
Leopard	-	0.08
Lion	-	0.32
Reedbuck	11.60	22.6
Roan	32.2	45.5
Sable	3.5	5.62
Sharpe's grysbok	8.1	5.6
Warthog	2.2	14.23
Waterbuck	-	0.32
Zebra	0.50	2.25

Source: Annual Report of the Department of Game,
Fish and Tsetse Control 1961-62

It is of interest that on these patrols no puku, klipspringer or rhinoceros were observed.

In an important ecological survey of Vwaza Marsh Game Reserve, Thomas McShane (1985) estimated the population of the larger mammals to be as follows:

Buffalo	900	Lion	15
Bushbuck	700	Puku	15
Bushpig	700	Reedbuck	300
Eland	75	Roan	700
Elephant	250	Sable	20
Grey duiker	1000	Sharpe's grysbok	1000
Hartebeest	700	Spotted hyena	common
Hippo	100	Warthog	1500
Impala	600	Waterbuck	2
Klipspringer	150	Wild dog	two sightings
Kudu	500	Zebra	250
Leopard	26		

With regard to the smaller mammals the following have been recorded:

Antbear	Porcupine
Bush baby	Ratel
Bush squirrel	Serval
Cane rat	Side-striped jackal
Clawless otter	Sun squirrel
Covet	Vervet monkey
Genet	Wild cat
Hare - both species	Yellow baboon
Mongoose spp.	Yellow-spotted hyrax
Night ape	

Source: McShane & McShane-Caluzi 1988: 46-49

The last black rhino was sighted in 1969.

As with the other wildlife sanctuaries the Vwaza Marsh Game Reserve is faced with several key issues with regard to its maintainance as a conservation area. The first is a high level of poaching, even though the density of human population in the adjacent areas is perhaps less than that in other parts of Malawi. But as many local people lived in the reserve prior to its proclamation as a wild life sanctuary, there have not only been petitions for a re-alignment of the reserves boundaries, but also much illegal hunting has taken place in the reserve. In the years 1984-85 patrols reported 10 dead elephant, 61 other dead mammals, 30 hunting camps, 112 snares or traps, 90 gunshots and 36 groups of intruders - 14 of whom were armed. Between 1982 and 1985, McShane estimated that with regard to the mortality of the larger mammals 256 animals had been killed by poachers, including 66 elephant, 69 buffalo, 13 roan, 10 kudu, 23 hartebeest, 32 warthog, 4 reedbuck and 3 zebras. All this indicates a very high level of illegal hunting. Much of this hunting was carried out by a relatively small number of recognized hunters and much of it was geared to local subsistence. Because of the low numbers and the fact that they were easily recognized, most of these hunters were easy targets, McShane contends, for investigation activities.

A second management problem, as elsewhere, is crop depredation. Elephant damage, in particular, is a major problem along the south-eastern boundary near Lake Kasuni. When I camped there in May 1991, I counted 78 elephant crossing the South Rukuru River at dusk, moving outside the reserve. I asked the game guard where they were going - and he answered me quite literally, 'to the people's gardens to feed on the maize'. This they did, in spite of efforts by the guards, with flares and shots fired into the air, to drive them back into the reserve. The elephants returned at daybreak, moving back into the *Brachystegia* woodland of the conservation area. In other parts of the reserve it is the bushpig which is the main cause of crop damage, accounting for over 80% of the depredation. Baboons were also a problem in some areas.

McShane emphasized the crucial role that elephant played in the ecology of Vwaza Marsh - in being the prime tourist attraction, in the damage it caused to local crops outside the reserve, in its impact on the local vegetation, and the fact that it was very heavily poached for ivory.

Concluding his survey, McShane noted that the continual requests by local people to resettle within the reserve, and the high level of poaching and other minor offences such as the collecting of various foods and materials - all of which, of course, forms part of the local subsistence economy - suggested to McShane that the DNPW had not been very successful in influencing public opinion, with regard, that is, to the value of Vwaza Marsh as a protected area.

It is with regard to Vwaza Marsh Game Reserve that the idea of trophy hunting was first introduced into Malawi. 'Sport hunting' or 'safari hunting' - primarily by wealthy Europeans or Americans - was seen by members of the DNPW as essentially positive, in that it could make a substantial financial contribution to the management of the reserves. Rules and regulations for safari hunting were drawn up (1986), and these emphasized that the hunting should be conducted according to certain ethical standards: ie no shooting from a vehicle, or hunting at night by means of a lamp. Quotas and fees were set, for example:

Quota		Licence Fee (US$)
Elephant	3	2,000
Buffalo	3	600
Hippopotamus	3	600
Leopard	3	1,000
Roan	3	500
Hartebeest	3	200
Zebra	3	250
Kudu	3	300

Source: WRU 50/2/0

It was recognized, however, that as wildlife population of the reserve was generally low, due mainly to widespread and intensive illegal (mainly subsistence) hunting, that quotas for safari hunting would also have to be kept low, if wildlife numbers were to be sustained. It was also recognized that local people would also tend, as John Hough put it, 'to be rather upset when they are prevented from hunting but they can see foreigners doing it' (1989: 130). It seems hardly fair to allow rich foreigners to shoot the larger mammals for 'sport', while hunting for 'subsistence' purposes is proscribed. 'Safari' hunting, though it may assist the central government in terms of foreign exchange and the private safari companies that organize such hunting tourism, is highly unlikely to benefit the local communities adjacent to the reserve. The existence of the reserve already has such a negative impact on local communities, through lack of hunting rights, inability to utilize forest resources within the reserve, and crop depredation, so 'safari' hunting is likely to aggravate this problem. (For general information on Vwaza Marsh Game Reserve see Carter 1987: 68-80, Hough 1989: 125-134).

Nyika National Park

Nyika is an extensive plateau area covering over 2000 sq km, and has been described by romantically-inclined writers as 'remote and awesome.' It was visited by Laurens van der Post in 1949 who thought it had a 'King Solomon's Mines, a Queen of Sheba touch about it' (1952: 177), but the well-known Jungian traveller conveyed little information about either the plateau or its wildlife. The plateau has an elevation of between 1950 and 2400 m, and is bounded on all sides by steep scarps, those to the north-east forming a part of the Rift Valley escarpment. Livingstonia Mission is to the east of the plateau, overlooking Lake Malawi. To the north are the highland areas of the Mafinga and Misuku hills. The distinctive feature of the plateau is its undulating topography, consisting of extensive rolling grasslands interspersed with patches of evergreen forest. The foothills are covered with *Brachystegia* woodland, with protea scrub at the mid-altitudes. The annual rainfall on the plateau is around 120 cm. The plateau is often covered in cloud and mist, and although it has a bracing climate to Europeans, local people treat the Nyika with a sense of awe and reverence. Ever since the time of Cullen Young, Lake Kaulime on the plateau has been known and renowned as a rain-shrine, and as a place where the spirits take the form of a huge snake. Hector Banda graphically told me in April 1991 that local people believe that anyone venturing near the lake may find themselves lost, or simply disappear. I discuss the nature of such rain-shrines in a companion volume (Morris 2000: 191-195).

The Nyika Plateau has been described as a 'wilderness' area, but there is evidence to show that the area has been occupied and utilized by humans for thousands of years. Rock paintings, such as those at Fingira Rock Shelter, indicate that hunter-gatherers frequented the plateau some 3000 years ago, and there is plenty of evidence of stone-age occupation (Sandelowsky & Robinson 1968). Throughout the centuries it is probable that the Nyika Plateau was the venue for hunting excursions - both for individual hunters and for communal hunts (*uzimba, chisokori*) - and, when the idea of creating a game reserve on Nyika was first mooted in 1938, there was a village community already located on the plateau, at Chisanga. Although Nyika has long been largely uninhabited, it has never been a pristine wilderness, untouched by humans. Arthur Loveridge recalled how utterly surprised and disconcerted he was to discover, early one morning on the plateau when out hunting zebra, an old man and two women trekking across the landscape - believing the plateau to be completely uninhabited! The old man was carrying his belongings in an eland skin (Loveridge 1954: 113-114).

Misuku Hills, Nyika Plateau
Source: Archives of the Society of Malawi

When discussions about the future of the Nyika Plateau became prominent in the late 1930s, Lord Delaware was then looking into the possibilities of European settlement on the plateau, and the development of sheep husbandry - the area was already renowned for its herds of roan, eland and zebra. But because of continuous hunting pressure from people living on the fringes of the plateau - the Phoka often hunted communally using nets - there was a feeling among many administrators (such as the DC at Mzimba H.C. Foulger) that unless protection was afforded them, the remaining herds of ungulates would soon be completely 'wiped out' (MNA/NN1/11/2).

The idea of making the Nyika into a wildlife reserve goes back to the beginning of the century, when John McClounie, a forester based at Zomba, crossed the plateau in 1902. He published an account of his journey in *The Geographical Journal* the following year, and was clearly impressed by the number of roan and zebra he saw, though he does not mention eland. Around Mpanda Hill (2017 m) in the north, he came across a small plateau which he thought a 'veritable game reserve', for here he saw plenty of warthog, rhinoceros, buffalo and zebra, as well as smaller antelopes. He not only recognized the Nyika Plateau as a potential health resort, but suggested that it should be made into a game reserve. Frank Dorward hints that McClounie may well be considered the 'true originator' of the Nyika National Park (1993: 2).

Although there had been discussions about creating a game reserve on the Nyika in the late 1930s, it was not until 1952 that the plateau was declared a non-shooting area. It was then that much started to happen. Between 1950 and 1951 a road was constructed up to the Nyika, organized and supervised by that 'remarkable person' - as 'Bob' Dewar describes him (1993: 10) – 'Bill' Rangeley, who was then the DC Mzimba. In that same year (1951) the CDC began to establish pine plantations near Chelinda (Chilinda), with the view to developing a pulpwood scheme. Eventually around 500 ha of pine plantations, mainly *Pinus patula*, were established. The scheme however was soon abandoned, the CDC later concentrating their efforts on the South Viphya.

The writings of the foresters who worked on the Nyika at this time give some indication of its wildlife in the early 1950s. John Cater, for instance, writes that there was not 'a great deal of game on the Nyika', but what there was could be easily observed, and on two days he counted 72 eland, 85 roan, 113 zebra, 4 warthog, 3 red forest duiker and 7 reedbuck. He estimated that there were probably then (1954) about 350 eland, 200 zebra and 150 roan on the whole plateau. Reedbucks were noted as 'scarce' - and only a few hartebeest, oribi (?) and buffalo seen. Although one remnant forest patch has the name *zovo-chipolo* (*zovo yachipolwe*: 'the elephant of Chipolwe'), elephants were only infrequently seen. Cater also notes serval, leopard and jackal, but mentions seeing only one hyena.

In reflecting on the rather depleted status of the larger antelopes - particularly of young roan and eland - Cater notes two factors. One is the habit of the antelopes to migrate in the winter months (June-August), moving down from the plateau to the *Brachystegia* woodland on the escarpment, where they are more liable to poaching. He mentions the Phoka custom of hunting game on Nyika by means of nets, and game drives. Secondly, the presence of wild dogs on the plateau, which are 'often seen' (1954: 6-8, reprinted in 1993), was also a problem. In 1954 the Annual Report of the Department of Game, Fish and Tsetse Control noted heavy depredations by wild dog on the Nyika. Although in those days eland, roan and zebra seem to have been present on the plateau in fair numbers,

THE BRITISH SOUTH AFRICA COMPANY.

Notice No. I of 1899.

NOTICE

It is hereby notified that the District known as the MWERU MARSH is proclaimed A GAME RESERVE and the Boundaries of this Reserve are as follows:—

Starting at the point where the boundaries of the British South Africa Company and the Congo Free State meet at the North of Lake Mweru the boundary shall run along the coast of Lake Mweru to the Kalungwisi River and thence along that river to Kasenjere's Village and thence by a line passing through Msama's, Abdallah's, and Mkula's Towns to the boundary of the Congo Free State and shall follow that boundary Westwards to the point of starting.

(Sgd) ROBERT CODRINGTON,

Deputy Administrator.

Blantyre

1st March, 1899.

British Central Africa Gazette, 15/09/1896

reedbuck were uncommon, and Frank Dorward, who was a forester on Nyika from 1955-57, recalls that Rangeley once asked him if he had seen any reedbuck, fearing they had become extinct (Dorward 1993: 20).

By 1957 the game population of the Nyika seems to have built up considerably following the prohibition of hunting five years before, although as the foresters attached to the CDC at Chelinda departed, so poaching again began to reach 'serious proportions' (Annual Report of the Department of Game, Fish and Tsetse Control 1957). But the general picture of the larger game animals to be found on the Nyika Plateau grassland at this time is indicated in the following table.

TABLE ELEVEN
Nyika Plateau
Average Numbers of Game Seen per 10 Patrol Days (1959- 62)

	1959	1960	1961	1962
Buffalo	-	-	0.05	0.25
Bushbuck	0.55	3.40	4.70	2.20
Bushpig	0.34	10.50	9.50	10.10
Cheetah	-	-	-	seen
Eland	59.20	137.20	81.80	142.40
Elephant	47.00	0.05	-	-
Grey duiker	2.50	5.50	7.70	11.00
Hartebeest		0.20	seen	0.10
Klipspringer	0.05	0.13	0.13	seen
Leopard	0.03	0.22	0.17	0.05
Lion	0.27	0.77	0.72	0.20
Reedbuck	05.60	18.50	21.40	37.10
Roan	30.80	61.40	45.20	42.80
Sable		-	1.10	-
Warthog	1.95	5.80	4.70	7.20
Waterbuck	-	-	-	seen
Wild dog	0.05	-	-	
Zebra	25.30	68.60	52.30	105.70

Source: Annual Reports of the Department of Game,
Fish and Tsetse Control 1959-62

Throughout the 1950s, after visiting the Nyika on a filming expedition with Arthur Westrop, that 'undefatigable' secretary of the Nyasaland Fauna Preservation Society, G.D. Hayes, made efforts to persuade the government to proclaim the plateau a national park - even confronting the then Colonial Secretary (Westrop 1968: 398-99, Dorward 1993: 28). But it was not until 1965, following independence, that Nyika was formally declared a national park, with an area of 940 sq km. It was originally named Malawi National Park, but in 1969 the name was changed to Nyika National Park. Visitors' chalets were built at Chelinda, and in 1977, mainly through the vigour and enthusiasm of Myles Turner, the regional game warden, the park boundary was extended to include all the plateau escarpments, especially those in the south and north-east. This increased the area of the park to its present size of 3134 sq km. Two reasons were emphasized for this extension: the need to protect the catchment areas of the four major rivers that originate on the plateau; and the importance of protecting those mammals, particularly eland, roan and zebra, which move from the plateau down to the woodlands during the dry season - and in the past were subject to much harassment from poachers. Extension of the park boundary involved the re-settlement of several villages (Johnson 1995: 11).

Over the years the wildlife of the Nyika Plateau has been the subject of a good deal of research, on its population and distribution (Wye College Report 1972, Dyer 1986), and on the effects of fire on wildlife grazing patterns (Lemon 1968). What is significant, with respect to the larger mammals, is the present abundance of the reedbuck. In 1950 it was estimated that there were less than 20 reedbuck in the park; now it is thought they number around 4,000. Kudu and hartebeest are rarely seen on the plateau, being found mainly in the woodlands in the northern extension. There are still occasional sight records of cheetah and wild dog, although the latter species is not mentioned at all in a checklist by Johnson in 1995.

Elephant	75	Lion	15
Baboon		Mongoose spp.	
Blue duiker		Porcupine	
Blue monkey		Puku	
Buffalo		Ratel	
Bushbuck	100	Red forest duiker	
Bushpig	200	Reedbuck	4000
Cheetah		Roan	500
Civet		Serval	
Eland	2000 (800)	Sharpe's grysbok	
Grey duiker	350	Side-striped jackal	
Hartebeest		Spotted hyena	
Klipspringer		Vervet monkey	
Kudu		Warthog	300
Leopard	100	Zebra	500

NB Animals listed without numbers indicates that they are present and usually common and thus not counted.
Source: Simons 1989, Johnson 1995

As with other conservation areas throughout Malawi, whether forest reserves or game sanctuaries, one of the major problems on Nyika is the prevalence of illegal hunting, although this is not mentioned as a problem by either Carter or Hough. In the past, communal hunts, using either fire or nets, often took place on the plateau, especially in the dry season, and in spite of the patrols of game guards, hunting still takes place - motivated by either 'empty stomachs' or 'empty purses' as one wildlife officer put it (Mkandawire 1983). Given its relative isolation, and the low population of humans in some areas in the north, poaching is probably less of a problem, when compared. with Kasungu and Liwonde wildlife sanctuaries. Even so, there is still a lot of illegal hunting, particularly on the periphery of the park, in the woodlands of the south and the north-west. In 1988-89, 15 eland, 2 elephant, 2 reedbuck, 4 duiker, 2 roan, 1 bushpig and 1 warthog were reported as being killed by illegal hunters, and Michael Dyer noted a high incidence of hunting in those areas of the park that were least patrolled (WRU 50/1/0). In recent years the Nyika has become a popular venue for wilderness treks, often on horseback. On one such trip one of the horses was shot by a local poacher. It was presumed that the poacher resented the intrusion of the trekkers in 'his territory', and particularly the interference with his traps. This particular trekker had taken upon himself to dismantle all the wire snares that he found.

Another important problem on the Nyika is the conservation of the evergreen forest tracks, which were apparently much more extensive on the plateau in the past. These forests are the haunts of the blue and the red forest duiker, and checkered elephant shrew, the blue monkey, as well as the rather local species the black and red squirrel (*Paraxerus lucifer*). To conserve the forests, firebreaks are burned each year in the early dry season. A third of the plateau grassland is also burned each year in the early part of the dry season - a policy recommended by Paul Lemon (1968: 81). This prescribed early burning not only helps to protect the forests, but avoids the destructive impact of the fires that inevitably occur in the later part of the dry season - often caused by local hunters - as well as providing fresh forage for the larger grazing animals. (For general accounts of Nyika see Carter 1987: 36-48, Hough 1989 29-50 and Johnson 1995).

TABLE TWELVE
Larger Mammals of Malawi

	Nsanje Mwabvi Game Reserve	Lengwe National Park	Majete Game Reserve	Shire Highlands	Upper Shire Valley/Phiri Longwe Mountain	Liwonde National Park	Nkhota-kota Game Reserve	Kasungu National Park	Viphya Mountain	Vwaza Game Reserve	Nyika National Park
Antbear	O	O						O		O	
Banded Mongoose	O	X		O		O				O	
Black rhino	?					?	?				
Blue monkey	X	X		O			O		X		O
Blue duiker							?				
Buffalo	X	X	O				O	X	O	X	O
Bush squirrel	X	X	O	O	X	X	O	O			
Bushbaby	X	O	O	O		O					
Bushbuck	X	X	X	X	X	X	X	X	X	X	X
Bushpig	X	X	X	O	X	X	X	X		X	X
Cane rat	X	O	O	O			O			O	
Caracal		O		?							
Cheetah								O			O
Civet	O	O	O	O	O	O	O	O	O	O	O
Eland		O					O	O		O	X
Elephant			O		X	X	X	X	O	X	O
Four-toed elephant shrew	X			O	O	X		O		O	
Genet	X	O	O	O	O	O	O	O		X	O
Giant rat	X			X							
Grey duiker	X	X	X	X	X	X	X	X	X	X	X
Hare	X	X		O	O	X	O	O		O	O
Hartebeest			O				O	O			X
Hedgehog	O			X				O			
Hippopotamus			X			X	O	O		X	
Impala	X	X	O			X		O		O	
Klipspringer	X		X	O	O		X	O	O	O	O
Kudu	X	X	X		O	X	O	X		X	O
Leopard	O	X	X	O	X	O	X	O	O	O	X
Lion	O		O		X	O	O	O	O	O	O
Nyala	X	X									
Oribi							O		O		
Otter				O		O	X	O		O	O
Pangolin	O	O						O		O	
Porcupine	O	O	X	O	O	O	O	O		O	O
Puku								λ		O	
Ratel	O		O	O		O	O	O		O	O
Red forest duiker				O			O		X		O
Reedbuck	O	X	O	O	O	O	O	X	O	X	X
Roan							O	X	O	O	X
Sable	X	O	O		O	X	O	O	X	O	O
Serval	O	O		O				O			O
Sharpe's Grysbok	O	X	O		X	O	O	O	O	O	O
Side-striped jackal	X	O	X	O	O	O	O	X	O	O	O
Slender mongoose	O	X			O		O			O	
Spotted hyena	O	X	X	O	O	O	O	O		X	X
Sun squirrel	O	X		O			O			O	
Suni	X	X	O								
Vervet monkey	X	X	X	X	X	X	X	X	X	X	O
Warthog	X	X	X		X	X	X	X	O	X	O
Waterbuck	O	O	X			X	O	X		O	
Wild cat	O	O		O						O	O
Wild dog	O		O					O		O	O
Yellow baboon	X	X	X	X	X	X	X	X	X	X	O
Zebra	X	?	O		O		X	O	O	O	X
Zorilla				O							

X: Widespread; O: Occasional

CHAPTER THREE

A SHORT HISTORY OF WILDLIFE CONSERVATION IN MALAWI

THE EARLY COLONIAL PERIOD

R ecent histiography has shown that in the early part of the 19th century southern Malawi was a well-populated region, particularly along the lakeshore and in the Lower Shire Valley. The area was the focus of developed trade routes, a complex agricultural system which used dry season cultivation in low-lying areas (*dimba*) and where iron-working was a flourishing industry, to be commented upon favourably by Livingstone (1865: 536). While iron production was mainly in the highlands, there was a developed cotton economy in the Lower Shire Valley (Mandala 1990: 36-63). By the end of the century, however, the increasing ravages of the slave trade after 1840, the advent of the militaristic Ngoni, and the incursion of Yao traders into the Shire Highlands, all adversely affected population distribution and disrupted the economy of the area. This led many people to take refuge in such places as high on the mountains of Zomba and Mulanje, or on Chisi Island in Lake Chilwa. In his travels near Lake Chilwa towards the end of the century, the Scottish divine Henry Drummond reported that the region was 'almost unihabited' and that 'nowhere else in Africa did I see such splendid herds of the larger animals as here' (1889: 30-32). Zebra were particularly abundant, and he went on to describe Central Africa as 'the finest hunting country in the world', where elephant, buffalo, eland, lion, leopard, zebra, hippopotamus, rhinoceros and 'endless species' of antelope were all to be found (106, cf. McCracken 1987: 67). He even mentions the giraffe, although it is doubtful if this species is an indigenous species to Malawi.

Elias Mandala attributes this abundance of wildlife - in the Lower Shire at least - to the Mang'anja's loss of control over nature, resulting from the devastation and desolation caused by the slave trade, coupled with the chaos and instability that followed the famine (*chaola*) of 1862-63, when the rains failed over two seasons (1990: 74-78). Around the turn of the century, beginning with Johnston's administration of 1891, further disruption to the local economy and to the land was caused by the alienation of vast tracts of land to European settlers and companies. Almost 4 million acres, representing 15% of the land was granted in freehold to Europeans, and this included much of the land of the Shire Highlands (Pachai 1978: 11-47). Vaughan writes perceptively on the social effects of these socio-economic changes and on the perceptions of both the colonial officials and local Africans to these changes. She makes some speculative remarks regarding local conservation measures with regard to game animals, mentioning totemic beliefs and the control of chiefs over the exploitation of ivory, and writes that the 'breakdown in game preservation techniques may well have been accelerated by the European laws which took the control of game away from the chiefs'. In the first three decades of the 20th century, as game increased and tsetse fly spread, the European contention that wildlife was in danger must have seemed hollow to local Africans, who were fundamentally concerned with their own livelihood during a period of famine and disease, for in the early decades of the century there were serious outbreaks of infectious diseases, as well as of famine. European game policies, she feels, must have appeared to the Africans as hypocritical in extreme (1978: 8).

It must be noted, however, that the term 'conservation mania' when applied to the policies of the early colonial administration in Malawi is something of a misnomer with respect to wildlife. The administration was not concerned with 'conservation', a term which was used only in relation to soil. The concept of conservation in its wider ecological sense was not in fact articulated until the middle decades of the present century. What the colonial government was concerned with was a much more limited conception - that of game preservation. And for Europeans at the turn of the century 'game' had a more restricted meaning even than the cognate term in Chewa *nyama*: it applied only to the larger mammals, the hunting of which was considered 'sport'. Following, it seems, the perspectives of Kjekshus (1977) and Vail (1977), Vaughan's contention that the government had a policy of 'carving out game reserves in populous areas' (9) is a misleading exaggeration. For what the early game regulations of British Central Africa (1897) was in essence concerned with, was to restrict the hunting of larger game animals only to Europeans, who alone could afford the game licences. Only two 'game reserves' were in fact specified in the first game ordinance: the Elephant Marsh near Chiromo, and Lake Chilwa - both popular duck shooting areas for Europeans - as they still are. Neither of these was initially a 'reserve' in the true sense, for those possessing the appropriate licences could freely hunt there. The animal species specified in the 1897 game schedule were all ungulates (elephant, blue wildebeest, rhinoceros, zebra, buffalo, eland, warthog, bushpig and around 19 species of antelope). Several species not in fact found in Malawi - giraffe, sitatunga, tsessebe and lechwe - were also listed on the schedule - although at that period 'British Central Africa' was still a fairly undefined area and included part of Eastern Zambia.

According to the Game Regulations, a £25 licence enabled a person to shoot all the 28 species specified, including elephant, rhino, blue wildebeest and giraffe, in any part of the protectorate. A £3 licence excluded these four species. Outside of the private estates and the two game reserves a person was free to 'kill, hunt or capture' any wild beast - which included the carnivores and smaller mammals like the porcupine, baboon, monkey and pangolin, which were not considered 'game'. There were severe penalties for those who contravened the regulations, that is, hunted the larger game animals - the ungulates - without a licence. The regulations therefore were essentially concerned with restricting the hunting of game animals - particularly the elephant, which was the prime economic resource - to the European population. It was not in the least concerned with the 'conservation' of animal life, as Vaughan suggests. Needless to say, such regulations found little support or sympathy among the African com-

Sable Antelope killed on a hunting expedition
By Mr Gordon, Archives of the Society of Malawi

munities in Malawi, who felt that their basic rights and freedoms were being denied them - as indeed they were.

The game regulations of 1902 elaborated upon the earlier schedule and specified the number of animals that could be killed or hunted. Elephant, buffalo and eland were placed under a special schedule, and could only be killed under a special licence, along with three species of mammals that were thought to be particularly rare, but which in fact have never been recorded from Malawi - the mountain zebra, wild ass and white-tailed gnu. Under the £25 licence, elephant (2), rhinoceros (2) and blue wildebeest (6) could be hunted and killed, while the schedule for the 'B' licence (costing £4) covered besides the many ungulates, carnivores like the serval, cheetah and jackal, as well as some birds like the egret and maribou stork. Under the 'B' licence a person was entitled to hunt or kill a range of ungulates and other mammals, totalling in all, around 100 game animals per year. With a view of 'preserving' game from indiscriminate slaughter, two areas were set aside as 'game reserves' - the Elephant Marsh and the 'Central Angoniland Reserve' which consisted of an area south of the Dedza-Lilongwe road, covering essentially the Dzalanyama range of hills. Carnivores such as lion, leopard, hyena, mongoose and others were not protected by the game laws, and could be shot or killed anywhere within the protectorate, even within a game reserve. By means of a gun licence, the colonial authorities attempted to keep a strict control over firearms. The possession of high-power rifles and the importation of ammunition was kept strictly in the hands of Europeans. Shotguns and muzzle-loaders were allowed to local chiefs and hunters, primarily for the protection of crops rather than for hunting.

The game ordinance of 1911 essentially followed the same pattern. Elephant and rhino (and a number of birds) could only be hunted and killed by special licence, but the protectorate 'B' licence of £2 (£10 for visitors) entitled a person to hunt or kill the following:

Antbear	2
Blue wildebeest	6
Buffalo	6
Egret	10
Eland	6
Hippopotamus	4
Kudu	6
Monkeys	6
Other antelopes	30
Roan	6
Sable	6
Warthog	10
Zebra	6

A total of 104 specimens of wildlife could thus be legitimately killed during the year. At the discretion of the District Resident a special licence could be granted to local Africans for a fee of £1, and permission granted to kill animals that were damaging crops or molesting people. But in essence what the game regulations entailed was to restrict the hunting of game animals to Europeans, and it seems, looking at the lists of those who took out a 'B' licence, that this included missionaries, as well as planters and administrators. Significantly, only one game reserve was specified in the 1911 ordinance - the Central Angoniland Game Reserve. Both Lake Chilwa and the Elephant Marsh had by then been descheduled. Contrary to what Vaughan argues, in the early decades of this century there were no game reserves at all in areas where there was a high human population - the Shire Highlands and the Lower Shire Valley. Nor were Europeans concerned to 'conserve' the depleting numbers of larger game animals. Murray (1922: 198) made the significant comment that game was still plentiful in Nyasaland except in those areas populated by Europeans. What the game regulations were all about, as said, was to preserve game animals - specifically the prototype *nyama* (kudu, eland, sable, roan and bushbuck) - for the exclusive use and enjoyment of Europeans. The opposition of the planter community to the government policy of 'game protection' (sic) was not because, as Vaughan suggests (1978: 10), they came from a social class less concerned with hunting - many planters had their origins in the British upper classes and were avid hunters - but as we shall see, because they felt that they should have unrestricted access to game animals on their estates. Like the English aristocracy, they deemed such animals to be their property, their 'preserve' and resented having to pay the government a licence fee.

These issues came to a head in the 1920s when the government, prompted by Rodney Wood (who was a well-known planter, with an estate at Thyolo, as well as a keen naturalist) announced its intention to revise and update the 1911 game ordinance. This created a furore, with opposition stemming from both the planters and the missionaries who, for very different reasons, formed a united front against the administration.

The 1926 game ordinance was not so very different from that of 1911, but there were important changes of emphasis. The protectorate licence had gone up from £2 to £5 but the number of animals that could be hunted or killed under the schedule was only slightly reduced. It allowed the person to hunt or kill four of the following species: hippopotamus, buffalo, eland, hartebeest, roan, sable, kudu, waterbuck, impala, puku, reedbuck, and not more than 30 of the smaller antelopes - oribi, duiker, suni and klipspringer - as well as two monkeys. This made a total of 80 animals. Elephant, blue wildebeest and again, the giraffe, could only be hunted under special licence, and both antbear and warthog had been taken off the schedule and could be freely hunted. One contemporary remarked that they were 'no longer protected' but of course neither of these animals was earlier 'protected'; they were simply hunted under licence. The game laws in fact could in no sense be seen as conservation, although of course they limited hunting: what they essentially did was to make the hunting of large mammals the 'preserve' of Europeans. But unlike the earlier schedules no hunting was allowed in game reserves without a special licence. There was, however, provision for a special native's licence. At £1 it could be issued to local hunters at the discretion of the District Resident. Four game reserves in which animals were given full protection were now recognized; the Lengwe and Tangadzi reserves in the Lower Shire - both to protect the declining numbers of nyala, which were established through the initiative of Rodney Wood; Chidiampiri Game Reserve in Lake Chilwa (to protect the island's python population) and Kasungu Game Reserve. The latter reserve, as we have discussed, had been established quite fortuitously in 1922, when, during an outbreak of sleeping sickness people had been moved out of the Lingadzi and Dwanga valleys (McCracken 1987: 66). The 1926 game ordinance specifically forbade, without the written permission of the District Resident, the hunting of game by means of nets, traps, snares, poison and pitfalls, or any such appliances, and it expressly forbade the use of fire and dogs for the purposes of hunting game. The ordinance thus outlawed all the traditional methods of hunting animals for food, and of protecting crops from the depredations of wildlife, and there were stringent penalties for anyone contravening the Act. In 1926 there were 22 convictions under the game ordinance, and one such case in the Kachindamoto area, whereby a man was sentenced to six months hard labour for netting six bushbuck, was even discussed in the British House of Commons. Apparently, the skins of six bushbuck had been found in the man's house along with nets and he freely admitted that he had netted the bushbuck in order to protect his gardens. The district magistrate at Dedza later reduced the man's sentence to five weeks imprisonment with hard labour.

During 1926 there was mounting opposition to this game ordinance, spearheaded by R.S. Hynde, the editor of the weekly newspaper *Nyasaland Times*. Missionaries associated with the Dutch Reform Church were particularly hostile to the new bill, which was then going through the legislative council, and so various meetings were held and letters of protest addressed to Dr Alexander Hetherwick, a fellow missionary and a member of the select committee on the new game ordinance. Opposition to the ordinance was focussed around the following premises:

1. That there was abundant proof that big game and tsetse go together.
2. That the tsetse had caused the loss of many herds of cattle, sheep and goats belonging to local people.
3. That the destruction of game means the destruction of tsetse.
4. That the government protection of game cruelly hits Africans in respect to their gardens and grain stores.
5. Game animals and carnivores go together, and thus the lives of many Africans were being unnecessarily sacrificed every year.
6. That the progress of the country was retarded by the protection of big game animals.

Game animals, the missionaries suggested, were described by the local people as *zoweta za boma* - the domestic livestock of the government. The Rev MacAlpine of Bandawe described the game ordinance as 'preposterous' while the respected Dr Laws thought it 'utterly absurd' and suggested that the bill should be thrown out entirely. It would be better for the country, he thought, if game animals were completely exterminated. Personally, wrote the Rev J.A. Dickinson of the Nyasa Mission, Cholo (Thyolo), 'I do not see that a sentimental policy which preserves animals at the expense of the populace can be justified.' Another missionary from Ekwendeni suggested that if the advocates of game protection knew the conditions of the people in the Northern Region they would pass a people's protection ordinance. Scores of missionaries wrote to Dr Hetherwick expressing their views and their opposition to the game ordinance. The main suggestions centred on the following concerns:

1. They highlighted the extensive damage to gardens and crops done each year by wildlife, particularly the depredations of elephants, eland, bushpig and baboons. 'Not a single garden is left intact in the whole district', wrote one missionary from Neno, and during the planting season people stayed in their gardens day and night. 'In several villages we do not find a soul; everyone is watching the maize gardens'. People ask for guns to chase away the bushpig and baboons but, he concluded, 'naturally we refuse. In parts of the Dowa District a more enlightened administrator, A.G.O. Hodgson suggested almost 50% of the maize crop each year was destroyed by

elephant. Given the restrictions on firearms and on traditional methods of hunting, local people had no means of combating the marauding elephants, and the depredation of their gardens by bush-pig at night, and baboons during the day. This led to severe food shortages in many areas.

2. The missionaries also stressed the heavy toll on human life (and on livestock) exacted by carnivores, particularly the leopard and lion. 'During my eight years at Mchinji', wrote the Rev Van Heerden, 'I do not remember a single year in which there were no man-eating lions in one or other part of the district'. The Commissioner for the Northern Province, based at Nkhata Bay, admitted that in some districts lions killed on average 50 persons annually. In the Ngara district, south of Kasungu, villages had to be stockaded as protection against lions, and in many parts of the protectorate nobody walked along the highways at night, and this included the main Zomba to Blantyre road.

3. The missionaries stressed the fact that the restrictions of the traditional methods of hunting had a deleterious effect on the health of Africans, many of whom were severely undernourished. 'The ordinance specifically forbids', wrote one missionary, 'just those ways in which Africans can kill game, viz. the pit, nets and hunting with dogs. This practically forbids them from obtaining meat, apart from the occasional goat' and meat he felt was necessary for a healthy diet.

4. In their protests the missionaries highlighted what they felt was a strong association between game and the presence of tsetse fly - which had led to the loss of livestock through the disease nagana, and to the recent outbreaks of sleeping sickness in many parts of the protectorate. The Rev Stewart of Ekwendeni stressed that after the rinderpest outbreak in the Mzimba District in 1893 - which had virtually wiped out the buffalo and eland population - tsetse fly had entirely disappeared from the region. But, two decades later, with the increase and spread of game, the tsetse fly had returned to its old haunts.

The general feeling of many missionaries therefore was that legislation should go in for the furthering of the destruction rather than the protection of game animals. But, in spite of their opposition, the 1926 game ordinance was passed by the legislative council and became law. As it did so, a petition against the ordinance was drawn up by the Nyasaland Chamber of

Agriculture and Commerce, largely it seems under the instigations of R.S. Hynde and was signed by 203 Europeans - mostly planters and missionaries. The petition against the Game Ordinance 1926 argued that the ordinance was directly and fundamentally opposed to the interests of both Europeans and Africans, and should, therefore, be disallowed. The bill, it suggested, turned the whole protectorate into a game reserve, for no game animals could be hunted or killed except under licence, whether on land occupied by Africans or on private estates. It denied, the petition stated, Africans their ancestral rights, namely to kill game animals for food, and prohibited their traditional methods of hunting, and was equally unjust in that the government protected game but would not pay compensation for damage done to property. The petition reiterated many of the themes and complaints that had been voiced against the ordinance by the missionaries, namely that the game animals caused much destruction to food crops, that lions caused much loss of life and terrorized whole neighbourhoods and that the tsetse fly, harboured by game, killed many cattle and threatened the lives of people with the dreaded sleeping sickness. The petition concluded by affirming the views expressed at a conference of the federated missions held in Blantyre in October 1926, namely that the proposed game ordinance, with its emphasis on the preservation of game, failed to take into account:

1. The toll of human life from lions, leopards and buffalo.
2. The fact that the game laws were based on class distinctions. The game laws, it noted, were based not only on class privilege, but led to racial animosity, because Africans 'cannot see why they are not allowed to kill game which Europeans, on payment of a licence, are at liberty to do'.
3. That the preservation of game was contrary to the agricultural development of the country.

The administration stood its ground and refused to make any alteration affecting the main principles of the game ordinance, and significantly, at meetings in early 1927, both the Nyasaland Planters' Association and the Cholo Planters' Association refused to support the petition. It became apparent that although the missionaries and the planters seemed united in opposing the bill, their reasons for doing so were very different. Rodney Wood, who was widely respected as a knowledgeable naturalist, and who was a close friend of the governor, Sir Charles Bowring, and was a planter himself, explicitly voiced the real reasons behind the opposition of the planters to the game bill, namely, that they wanted free shooting and resented the increase of the protectorate licence to £5. Like landed aristocrats elsewhere, the planters resented government's interference into what they felt was their private domain. Thus the real source of the planters' grievance against the ordinance was the explicit disallowance of ownership of all the game on private (freehold) land. As the governor himself noted, the rights of the planters over their land were jealously guarded, and they greatly resented the attempt by government to interfere with their attitude towards the question of game preservation on their estates. Rodney Wood, who seems to have been the main inspiration behind the ordinance - which, he reflected, expressed the views of all 'real sportsmen' - even suggested to the government an amendment to the game ordinance to placate the settlers. It suggested that any person without a game licence 'could hunt any game on freehold land of which he is the owner or occupier'.

But the views of the missionaries and planters were not that dissimilar, for among both communities there were enthusiastic hunters - a 'butcher' minority as Wood called them - who felt they should be free to shoot everything in sight. One observer remarked that it was the missionaries who were the most bloodthirsty with regard to the extermination of game and every living thing, and it was noted that many members of the Dutch Reform Church Mission, who were the most vocal in the opposition to the bill, were of Afrikaaner background and avid hunters. 'They belong to a tradition', remarked the governor, 'which has led to the wholesale slaughter of game in their own country, mainly for the purposes of making biltong'.

Nor were the missionaries so very different from the planters when it came to the social implications of the petition. Their defence of the rights of Africans to hunt animals by traditional methods, and to protect their crops against elephants, bushpigs and baboons implied that they should be free to trap and snare animals, to organize communal hunts with dogs and fire, and to acquire and use firearms. Yet most of the planters, and some of the missionaries, recoiled from these suggestions. Thus, when the government issued a limited supply of firearms to local Africans for the protection of their lives and property, there was a storm of protest from the European community on the grounds that this put public safety at risk and one of the main reasons the Cholo Planters' Association rejected the petition was that it seemed to suggest that Africans should be free to hunt without restrictions and this, they surmised, would inevitably lead to the wholesale destruction of game on their estates.

There were those missionaries who genuinely upheld what they felt were the rights and interests of the African communities, but the overwhelming number of Europeans came to support the game ordinance, the essence of which was not to 'protect' game animals but rather to 'preserve' them for the exclusive use of European 'sportsmen' - whether missionary, planter, administrator or a visiting big-game hunter.

The government made two reasoned arguments in defence of the game ordinance against the missionaries and such 'anti-game enthusiasts' as R.S. Hynde.

First, it argued that much of their protest was misplaced, for with regard to garden damage the worst offenders were bushpig, monkey and baboon, none of which were 'game' within the meaning of the ordinance. Neither were the marauding lions and leopards - which were also not protected by the game laws - outside game reserves. The ruthless destruction of game in regions where carnivora abound would only aggravate the problem, and lead, the government felt, to the increase in the numbers of cattle-raiding and man-eating lions. Under the regulations of the new ordinance Africans were in fact permitted to shoot or otherwise destroy game, or any other animals, which in any way molested or damaged their life or property.

Second, on the advice of such people as Rodney Wood, the government entomologist Dr Lamborn and the eminent authority on tsetse fly at that time, Major E.E. Austin of the British Museum, the government refused to accept the fact that the widespread extermination of game would necessarily lead to the elimination of testse fly. On the contrary, it held that an ill-considered attack on game animals would lead to the dispersal of the tsetse into fly-free areas, with the resultant loss of livestock.

Needless to say, throughout the period under review, Africans continued to employ their traditional methods of hunting game - as they still do today - and voiced their grievances against the game ordinance. But the government could do little to control the former, and there was, it is worth recalling, an amusing incident when the governor was visiting the Bua River in great pomp and style only to observe a large and noisy communal hunt (*uzimba*) taking place on a wooded hillside a short distance away - much to the embarrassment of his retinue which included Rodney Wood. But to grievances against the ordinance, expressed by Africans through their local chiefs, the administration, it seems, was unwilling to give much serious attention.

The early game ordinances were primarily concerned not with conservation but with establishing hunting privileges for a European elite - and the majority of planters, government officials, and missionaries considered themselves 'sportsmen' and took out a hunting licence. Hunting game animals was a favourite pastime, and the *ulendo* an institution, and their memoirs often include a chapter of their hunting experiences. Thus the well-known missionary, the Rev Donald Fraser (1923: 65-66), could look back nostagically to a time when, on holiday in the Mzimba District, he had killed klipspringer, bushbuck, reedbuck, duiker, zebra, roan, sable, eland, warthog and bushpig. But the 1926 game ordinance, under the influence of Rodney Wood whose own biography reflects an important change in social attitude, also came to articulate for the first time the need to conserve animals not as sporting game for an elite, but so that they might be seen and enjoyed by future generations. (On the 1926 game ordinance, from which the above is extracted, see 51/558/23 MNA/S1/1721/23).

Rodney Wood, in a letter to the Governor, perhaps summed up the attitude of the more enlightened Europeans towards the game ordinance when he wrote, 'I feel now that no broad-minded person who has any love of sport at all, and I might add any decency in the matter, can have any objection to the new ordinance. Long may it remain law, and I hope it will be possible to enforce it adequately. I hope too that no one in authority in England will take any notice of the "butcher" minority and the commercial "get rich quicks" who have no sporting instincts or love of nature whatsoever.'

Wood expressed little sympathy, however, for the crop depredations in local gardens, feeling such reports were exaggerated (2 June 1927, MNA/S1/1721A/23).

The main outcome of the 1926 game ordinance was to establish three game sanctuaries - Lengwe, Taugadzi and Kasungu - which offered complete protection for the wildlife within their boundaries, and to make hunting outside these reserves the exclusive right of Europeans who alone could afford the game licences. All traditional methods of securing meat, whether by trapping or hunting, were proscribed. Subsistence hunting by local people was thus deemed illegal. But Wood was also hostile to commercial hunting by Europeans - which seems to have flourished in the early part of the century, and judging from the records, was still being practised in the 1920s - especially the hunting of eland (RCW to Edwin Glover, September 1929 MNA/GFT 1/3/1). But there were also some Europeans who felt that the best thing that could happen to the country, with respect to its development, was the complete eradication of the larger mammals. Dr Laws was clearly of this opinion, and one planter from Ntcheu remarked that 'big game must be forced to retreat before the plough and the sooner the better'. Another European - a missionary from Mangochi - stressed that if the game ordinance were strictly enforced this would inevitably lead to an increase in game and thus aggravate the problem of crop depredation. As it also forbade subsistence hunting by dogs, he felt that ordinance to be a 'horrible injustice' to local people. Like other missionaries he also took the view that game protection would worsen the problem of tsetse fly (MNA/S1/664/26, S1/1721A/23).

In 1928 a member of the Game Protection Department in Tanganyika (Tanzania), F.D. Arundell, drafted for the government a report that looked specifically at the problem of crop depredation, particularly by baboons and elephants, and at the issue of 'game' more generally. Among his recommendations were the following: that where lions and leopards were not troublesome they should be left alone, as they are the best allies against the depredations of bushpig and monkeys; that the meat of any animal shot by crop protection guards should go mainly to the owner of the garden where the depredation took place; that the Central Angoniland Reserve was constantly disturbed, and was neither suitable as a game sanctuary nor as a reserve for elephants (the reserve in fact was abolished in 1930); that a small game department should be created, a part of its essential duties being the protection of local agriculture from depredation.

The latter suggestion was taken up by the Governor Charles Bowring who was already thinking along these lines, and in 1929 Rodney Wood was appointed Game Warden for the Protectorate (MNA/S1/1161/28). The choice could hardly have been better, for Rodney Wood was a keen and knowledgeable naturalist - as I can recall when I met him in 1960 at Magombe Estate - and being a local planter was held in high regard by the majority of the European population. Although an enthusiastic hunter in the early years, he was very concerned at the depletion of the larger mammals, and was a strong advocate of wildlife conservation. One of the first things he did as game warden was to formally declare Chidiampiri (the name means 'to eat the puff adder') Island, in Lake Chilwa, a game reserve. The small island was uninhabited, covered in dense bush, and was used by local people as a rain shrine, and was reputed to be 'swarming' with pythons. It was estimated that there were at least 200 pythons on the island, which has an area of 2.6 sq km. It was reported that one European, while out duck shooting on Lake Chilwa, bagged 17 duck and 2 geese in one day and had shot 8 python. Noting that local belief associates the python with the rain-spirits (this is fully discussed in Morris, *Animals and Ancestors* 2000: 197-99), Wood was determined to protect the pythons. In 1930 Chidiampiri was proclaimed a game reserve. By 1934, when the DC Zomba made a journey to the island on foot - for Lake Chilwa was then almost dry - he reported that the pythons had left the island, and only saw one python (MNA/NN/1/61). When I visited Chidiampiri in February 1991 with John Wilson, a fishing community had long been established on the island, which is rich in phosphates and hence supports a dense vegetation, and much of it was under maize cultivation.

During the two years that Rodney Wood was game warden for the protectorate - he retired from the position in 1931 on the grounds of ill-health and went to recuperate in the Seychelles - he was extremely active. He corresponded constantly with the Governor, Charles Bowring, who appears to have been a close friend, and with the secretary of the Society for the Preservation of the Fauna of the Empire, C.W. Hobley. He was full of ideas and suggestions: on how to improve trout fishing on Zomba plateau; on the need to establish a small wildlife park at Monkey Bay, partly on account of its scenic beauty; maintaining Tangadzi and Lengwe Game Reserves (both proclaimed in 1928) as sanctuaries for the nyala; and on the need to create one large game reserve which would hold all the main game animals of the protectorate, rather than having small scattered reserves. But most of Wood's time was taken up - as he admitted - with his activities as the Tsetse Control Officer. This entailed the attempt to keep game and the tsetse fly within certain prescribed areas through the creation of 'buffer lines'. These limited the movement of game animals, particularly with respect to the region south of Kasungu Game Reserve, which was developing as an important tobacco growing area. Wood, employing local guards, was also heavily involved in crop protection exercises. These entailed the shooting of mammals that were involved in crop depredations: elephant, hippopotamus, bushpig and baboon (for discussion of the crucial issue of crop depredation see Morris 1995b). As the protectorate game warden, Rodney Wood was also to play a central role in the hunting of 'man-eating' lions, particularly the lion that harassed the people of Mchinji district in the villages east of the mission between 1929 and 1930. Around 36 deaths were recorded (MNA/S1/1721A/23).

But there was one issue that always troubled Wood - the continued existence of communal hunts (*uzimba*) by local people. These of course were in direct contravention of the 1926 game ordinance, although such hunts were common throughout the colonial period and in some areas still take place. Wood thought this kind of hunting an 'abominable practice' and made every effort, through pleas and directives to the Governor and to administrative officers, to get the practice not only proscribed, but also eradicated in practice. He was particularly concerned because, as we noted above, on a visit to the Bua River with the Governor Bowring, they had observed a large scale hunt taking place! Though indulged in throughout the protectorate, he wrote that this 'barbarous method of hunting' should not be tolerated. Needless to say, Wood did not succeed in putting an end to the traditional *uzimba* (MNA/NC 1/10/1).

When Rodney Wood resigned as game warden in 1931, he recommended to the government that the post of game warden be abolished, and that the maintenance of the three main game reserves, together with the duties of crop protection, be undertaken by the district administrations. Each of the three game reserves should have two to four game guards under the control of the DC, and three cultivation guards, with some 20 assistants, should be directly employed to deal with elephant control. The provincial commissioner, Wood suggested in a memorandm, should advise the Governor each year on the status of wildlife within his jurisdiction. Measures for the control of tsetse fly, Wood recommended, should be the responsibility of the government medical entomologist, Dr William Lamborn. Honorary game wardens could also be appointed in specific areas, but such interested Europeans were to act in an advisory capacity only. Such measures, Wood argued, would make the post of protectorate game warden unnecessary.

Although conservation bodies in the United Kingdom, specifically the SPFE, had expressed concern at the depletion of game within Nyasaland during the early colonial period, and were clearly troubled by Wood's resignation and the demise of the embryonic game department, they were assured by Wood that the situation in the country was fairly positive. Wood was confident, and 'happy' in the Lower Shire reserves, and felt that the district administrations could adequately deal with the problem of crop depredation and the enforcement of game regulations.

In 1933 there was an international conference on the protection of the fauna and flora of Africa held in London. The outcome was a good deal of debate regarding the possibilities of creating national parks within the colonial territories. Within such proposed parks hunting would be strictly controlled and licensed, and there would be prohibitions on certain forms of hunting, namely: the use of nets, fire or dogs - all employed of course in local subsistence hunting. Although the Governor Harold Kittermaster was later to contemplate the idea of creating national parks on the Nyika, Zomba and Malosa plateaus, it was a suggestion never taken up during the colonial period. In 1933 a revision was made of the game ordinance, which allowed the hunting of game by local people at times of famine, and also scheduled two new game reserves, the Ngara and the Nantundu reserves south of Lilongwe (MNA/GFT 1/3/1).

THE POST-WAR YEARS

From 1931 until the end of the Second World War game conservation in Nyasaland was handled by the district administrations, and was to remain at a virtual standstill. Game guards were employed by these administrations mainly to protect crops, especially against the ravages of hippopotamus and elephant, often attempting to drive the latter back into the forest reserves or game sanctuaries. The game reserves themselves, like Kasungu, remained, as we have discussed earlier, largely a 'no man's land'. They had few staff, and there was little serious effort to enforce the wildlife legislation. They were frequented only by the occasional poacher, or by people travelling across the country.

At the end of the war, in 1945, the government, under the guidance of the labour government in the United Kingdom, resolved to look into the whole matter of forest and game reserves. It therefore appointed a commission, under the chairmanship of a local planter, Malcolm Barrow, with the government entomologist, Colin Smee acting as secretary. Surprisingly, neither W.H.J. Rangley nor Rodney Wood - two of the most knowledgeable men with respect to local culture - were appointed to the commission, which consisted of a small select group of Europeans. It included the three provincial commissioners. The commission held public meetings in Blantyre and Lilongwe, and invited suggestions, written opinions and reports from all DCs and any interested parties. It consulted with C.W. Benson, an experienced ormithologist who was then DC Blantyre, H.J. Borley the DC at Dowa and who was later to head the new game department, with H.S. 'Peter' Selous who was the son of the famous big-game hunter and the DC at Fort Johnston, as well as with W.H.J. Rangeley, then DC Nkhotakota. The commission also consulted senior members of the forestry department: P. Topham, R.G.M.Willan, W.E. Lewis and J.B. Clements, and of the agricultural department: E. Lawrence, R.W. Kettlewell and APS Forbes. Many of these men had spent many years in the country and were conversant with the problems of rural areas. The important contributions these men made to the early development of the country have often been overlooked by historians. Significantly, there was little representation of local African opinion.

The report of the Commission on Forest and Game Reserves was presented to the Governor Edmund Richards in June 1946. It consisted of three parts dealing with, respectively, forest reserves, game reserves, and game preservation and control.

The forest reserves in Nyasaland had been mainly created in the period 1922-1930. Some 49 forest reserves had been gazetted varying in size from 230 acres (White Rock Reserve, Fort Johnston {Mangochi}) to 800 sq miles (2072 sq km) (Fort Alston, Kasungu, the latter being gazetted as both a forest and as a game reserve). The total area designated as forest reserves was then 2,651 sq miles, representing about 7.09% of the protectorate land area. An important motivation in the creation of forest reserves was the need to protect catchment areas, and hillslopes liable to erosion. Although it was widely held that no hunting was allowed in forest reserves, this in fact was not the case, provided that permission to hunt was obtained from the forest authorities. The chief conservator of forests J.B. Clements emphatically reported to the commission that 'It is not part of forest policy to foster game in the forest reserves; rather the reverse. The incidence of large numbers of game is prejudicial to the regeneration of forests and to sound management'. He thus saw the conservation of mammals and forest husbandry to be antithetical endeavours. The commission in its report concluded the need of legal provision for four types of protected forest areas: forest reserves, village forest areas (in 1945 over 500 villages had such village forests under the jurisdiction of the village headman), protected hill slopes, and the riparian tracts along stream banks. The latter protection, it noted, was extremely unpopular among local people, who valued such land for gardens (*dimba*). The report argued, however, that propaganda should be initiated to inform local people of the value of protected forest areas, concluding that the conservation of forest areas was essential for the welfare of the indigenous population of the protectorate.

With regard to the game reserves, the commission noted that eight had been gazetted since 1928, namely:

	Year gazetted	Size/sq miles	(sq km)
Thangadzi	1928	9	(23)
Lengwe	1928	50	(130)
Chidiampiri	1930	1	(2.6)
Kasungu	1930	800	(2,072)
Nkhotakota	1938	339	(878)
Ngara/Nantundu	1940	19	(49)
Viphya	1938	50	(130)
Lake Kazuni	1941	79	(205)

This made a total of 1347 sq miles (3489 sq km), respresenting 3.66% of the total land area. In outlining the history of the game reserves (as Appendix E to the report) the commission reflected on the fact that these reserves had been haphazardly created over a period of years, either with the vague idea that they may have tourist potential, or to cope with some local problem. None of the reserves were 'planned' and there was no co-ordinated scheme. Many of the reserves, it suggested, were too small to function properly as true game sanctuaries, and they were 'dotted' about the country. With regard to both the Viphya and Lake Kazuni reserves, it argued that these reserves interfered either with people's welfare, or with future development. It further considered that there was no area of the country which could be developed into a national park 'worthy of the name' - in retrospect, a very limited vision. The commission therefore rec-ommended that four reserves - Chidiampiri, Ngara/Nantundu, Viphya and Lake Kazuni - should be abolished, mostly on the grounds that the game that they contained was no greater than that of surrounding areas, and that the important mammals found in these reserves - zebra and rhino specifi-cally - were protected under the game ordinance, as the hunting of these animals was strictly controlled. The commission thus recommended retaining only four game reserves: Thangadzi Stream, Lengwe, Kasungu and Nkhotakota. It noted that with Kasungu the local game guards were both inadequate in number and lacking in proper supervision, while with Nkhotakota, though a suitable area, it required very efficient patrolling on the lakeside to prevent marauding animals, specifically elephants, from leaving the reserve and entering the cultivated areas.

With regard to game preservation and control outside of the reserves, the commission suggested that in many areas there had been an increase in the population of game animals. This increase and dispersal had led in 1939 to the suspension of game licences in the Kasungu and Nkhotakota districts as game had become so troublesome in damaging crops. (This was contrary to the impression that G.D. Hayes had in 1945!) Enquiries indicated that in each district there were from 12 to 30 game guards who were engaged in patrolling the reserves or crop protection, and around two hunters who specialized in the hunting of elephants. Guy Muldoon, who later worked for the game department, gave a good account of these local elephant hunters in his memoirs (1957). There was clearly a feeling around - and this was expressed by W.H.J. Rangeley and other DCs - that outside of the game reserves, the numbers of game animals should be severely curtailed, or even eradicated. Rangeley, for example recommend-ed, that all hippopotamus and waterbuck along the lakeshore should be exterminated, and others recommended the eradication of elephants in all areas close to human cultivation. The commission recognized that crop protection was an important function of government which needed to be maintained, and that damage to crops was a constant source of complaint by local people. It thus suggested a revision of the game ordinance so as to include a specific category of 'vermin', and that this should include monkey, baboon, bushpig, warthog and porcupine.

In order that the game reserves would function effectively, and that damage to local crops by the above vermin, and by marauding game animals leaving the reserves, would be kept under strict control, the commission recommended that the formation of a Department of Game, Fish and Tsetse control was 'absolutely essential'. It suggested that this department should have an officer-in-charge, an entomologist responsible for tsetse fly, and four European game rangers, under whose supervision there would be employed around 144 game control guards and 800 porters, as well as 4 clerks. The game rangers were to earn £40 per month (which is what I earned as a young tea planter in Thyolo in 1958), while the game guards were to be paid around £3, porters 18 shillings a month. The guards were to be armed with .404 Vicker's Rifles. The report of the commission concluded by suggesting that for the first few years of the new department, 'it will be necessary to reduce considerably the number of game animals in all areas', in addition to the routine protection of crops. The organized reduction of game was to be done by all staff in the 'off season'. There thus seemed to be a clear policy of protecting the larger mammals within the four specified reserves, but eradicating all game outside of these sanctuaries, which took on the form of enclaves of wildlife (on the 1946 Commission see MNA/NN 1/6/1).

From 1949, when it was finally formed, until 1962 the Department of Game, Fish and Tsetse Control flourished - if that is the right word, for it was always understaffed and underfunded with regard to its dual functions vis-à-vis game (i.e that of game conservation and crop protection). Yet it is clear from the beginning that crop protection, rather than game conservation, was given priority in terms of the department's game responsibilities. As its 1949 report acknowledged, 'Since the main reason for the formation of the game side of the organization was the protection of crops, emphasis has to date been laid on game and vermin control rather than on game conservation'. Indeed the game rangers were initially described as 'game control officers'. The Director of the Department of Game, Fish and Tsetse Control from 1949 to 1962 was H.J. Borley and he had under him the Tsetse Entromologist B.L. Mitchell, who wrote a number of interesting articles on wildlife (1946, 1950), and between three to four European game rangers. Among the latter were Guy Muldoon, O.J. Carey, E.T. Llewellyn, C.W. Brown, and L.T. Kettle.

From the reports of the department it is evident that although game conservation and the upkeep and supervision of the game reserves were important concerns, the main emphasis in the work of the department was on crop protection. This involved deploying game control guards or local hunters to protect local crops, and this in turn involved the shooting - or netting or poisoning - of the troublesome or marauding animals. Table Thirteen indicates the animals killed on crop protection exercises during the years 1948-1961.

During these 14 years the total numbers of animals killed in the protection of crops were as follows:

Baboon	78,712
Buffalo	562
Bushpig	3,405
Carnivora (lion, leopard)	560
Elephant	852
Hippopotamus	1048
Roan, eland and kudu	1362
Other antelope	660
Waterbuck	220

Added to this are the 'vermin' (mainly baboon and bushpig) killed for bounty by private effort, amounting to 204 thousand animals. The baboons and bushpig were mainly shot, but they were also netted and poisoned. Such crop protection activities were focussed on the districts of Nkhotakota, especially along the fertile lakeshore, Kasungu, Dowa, Chikwawa, Chinteche and Fort Johnston (Mangochi). It is clear that the department followed the suggestions of the commission, and in the early years (1948-1952)

Roan antelope

TABLE THIRTEEN
Staff Employed and Animals Killed in Crop Protection Activities 1948-61

	1948	1949	1950	1951	1952	1953	1954	1955	1956	1957	1958	1959	1960	1961
Average number of armed hunters each month	92	51	51	49	41	31	30	25	21	22	24	26	28	26
Animals killed														
Elephant	68	79	28	56	125	63	110	20	25	45	59	50	57	67
Hippo	77	106	103	105	33	58	48	137	74	62	60	64	48	73
Buffalo	300	63	55	45	6	19	31	32	9	1	-	-	3	-
Waterbuck			163	33	18	4	1	-	-	1	-	-	-	-
Roan, eland, kudu		1077	187	46	32	13	-	4	3	-	-	-	-	-
Other antelope		357	72	55	58	62	31	18	2	-	1	2	-	2
Baboon	8567	13928	16626	18471	7777	3908	5027	1666	963	829	171	284	320	175
Bushpig	988	613	751	184	150	175	230	184	50	31	19	11	14	5
Carnivore	90	79	76	83	64	40	26	19	-	24	18	8	11	22
Beasts killed per man employed	121	145	191	346	158	107	137	83	65	-	-	-	-	-

Source: Annual Reports of the Department of Game, Fish and Tsetse Control 1949-61

made a concerted effort to eradicate all game animals that were causing crop depredations outside of the reserves. By 1955 buffalo, roan, eland, kudu and other antelopes had ceased to be a problem, and hippo had been drastically reduced in numbers. The number of bushpig and baboon killed in these crop protection exercises is quite staggering - 286 thousand - yet surprisingly these mammals still survive, and are frequent in some areas, even close to human habitations. The hippo, however, is virtually extinct along much of the lakeshore where it was once plentiful. On average 150 animals were killed each year per game control guard employed. The sale of the game meat shot went mainly to local treasuries. There was also an effective crocodile 'destruction scheme' carried out on the lake, and large numbers of crocodiles were killed, often using poison baits. The poison used was potassium cyanide, but the reptiles usually went under the reeds and were lost - and although great numbers were killed this way, the practice was eventually discontinued, as the skin of the crocodile has commercial value (see Potous 1956, who records his experiences as a 'crocodile hunter' during the colonial period).

The game rangers in the department were also involved in the hunting of 'man-eating' carnivora, especially lion and leopard. Such activities are graphically illustrated in the books of one game ranger Guy Muldoon (1955, 1957).

In the early years of the department little effort was devoted to game conservation - crop protection was the order of the day and this involved the killing of hundreds of elephant as well as the destruction of the 'vermin': bushpig and baboon. But by degrees efforts were made to re-establish the sanctity of the game reserves, although it was recognized that all the main reserves - Lengwe, Kasungu and Nkhotakota - were being 'heavily poached'. Nevertheless, nyala were on the increase in Lengwe, and in 1952 the Nyika grassland and the area around Majete Hill were both declared to be non-hunting areas. A rough jeep track was made to the Lifupa River, in the interior of Kasungu Game Reserve, and zebra, hartebeest and rhino were reported as being seen by waterholes. In 1953 a new game ordinance was enacted. Thus, by degrees, increasing attention within the department was being paid to the conservation aspects, and a number of the prosecutions were made in an effort to curb poaching in the reserves. The demarcation of the boundaries of all the reserves was clarified, and the game rangers spent a good deal of time on conservation work during the dry season. In spite of the recommendations of the commission, Lake Kazuni Reserve was not abolished, and in 1956, largely through the initiative of Chief Katumbi, a controlled shooting area was declared around the Vwaza Marsh. At the same time, Mwabvi Game Reserve was fairly well established, with rhino, nyala and buffalo all recorded. Kasungu, it was noted, carried a fair elephant population, 'which shows no sign of declining'. In 1959 electric fences were tried out for the first time - to protect the rice lands near Lake Malombe from the depredations of hippo. These efforts, however, did not prove a success. By 1960 observation camps had been established in Mwabvi, Kasungu (Lifupa) nd Nkhotokota (Chipata) reserves, and the department made efforts to establish sponsored visits by local secondary school children to these reserves. These proved to be a great success. Over the years the number of game licences taken out seems to have declined. Controlled burning was established on the Nyika Plateau (Reports of Department of Game, Fish and Tsetse Control 1949-62).

The above outlines some of the main efforts undertaken by the department in the years between 1948-1962, with respect to game conservation. Poaching throughout the period continued unabated, and as independence approached, it was increasingly difficult to obtain any convictions. Throughout the period, whether with regard to 'propaganda' in favour of wildlife conservation or in relation to controlled burning on the Nyika, the department was clearly hampered by a lack of funds. But thinking within the department is perhaps best expressed in the following extract, 'In general it seems increasingly clear that the long term future of wild life conservation in Nyasaland lies in concentrating on selected areas, where there is little or no human competition for the use of the land, rather than in relying on measures of general application' (1956: 34).

The 1953 game ordinance followed the pattern of the earlier ordinances. It deemed that no person should hunt on private land without permission of the owner, or in a game reserve or controlled area. Outside of these domains 'no person shall hunt any game unless he holds a valid licence authorizing him to do so' (11) and contravention of these rules constituted an offence. This effectively made subsistence hunting by local people illegal. Some animals could only be hunted under a special governor's licence, and these included any animals in a game reserve: giraffe, zebra, blue wildebeest, puku, colobus monkey, cheetah, nyala and rhinoceros. (It seems that the department was still unaware that there were no giraffe to be found in the country and that the blue wilderbeest had long been extinct on the Phalombe Plain). A full licence allowed a person to shoot any number of waterbuck, grey duiker and buffalo, and the following number of other game:

Bushbuck	2
Eland	2
Hartebeest	2
Hippopotamus	4
Impala	2
Kudu	2
Leopard	2
Lion	2
Reedbuck	6
Roan	3
Sable	2

In addition, the licence permitted up to '20 head' of such smaller antelopes as blue duiker, Sharpe's grysbok, klipspringer, suni, oribi and red duiker to be shot. There was a special elephants' licence. Licences were to be granted by DCs. Any person carrying out trade in trophies (i.e. elephant tusks, or the horns or skins of game animals) had to be in possession of a permit. It was not deemed an offence to kill any animal in defence of human life, or in the defence of property. Four game reserves were scheduled in the ordinance: Kasungu, Lengwe, Nkhotokota and Mwabvi.

For reasons it is difficult to ascertain, in 1963 the Department of Game, Fish and Tsetse Control was disbanded, and matters relating to game conservation and crop protection came under the jurisdiction of the new Department of Forestry. After independence it was re-constituted (in 1973) as the Department of National Parks and Wildlife (DNPW). (For studies of hunting and game preservation elsewhere in Africa see Graham 1973: 35-121, Anderson and Grove 1978, Mutwira 1989, Steinhart 1989).

G.D. HAYES AND THE NYASALAND FAUNA PRESERVATION SOCIETY (NFPS)

The interest in game conservation that was evoked by the 1946 Commission, led indirectly to the formation of the Nyasaland Fauna Preservation Society (NFPS). This was mainly the 'brain-child' of George Dudley Hayes, known to all his friends as 'G.D'. Born at Ramsgate in 1904 he first came to Nyasaland in 1925 to join the A.L. Bruce estates at

Magomero as a tobacco planter - having already had some farming experience in Sussex. While working at Magomero, Hayes would spend his weekends hunting antelope on the Phalombe Plain, and at Matope on the River Shire. During 1931 he worked on the road project linking Balaka with Mangochi, and was given licence to hunt marauding elephants in the area of Phirilongwe Mountain. In 1935 he jointed the Agricultural Department at Chikwawa in the Lower Shire, and spent much of his time in what is now Lengwe National Park. But hunting elephant evoked a transformation in Hayes' attitude to wildlife, and like Rodney Wood he became a 'penitent butcher' and an ardent conservator and defender of wildlife. In 1939 he became honorary game warden for Lengwe Game Reserve, which in those days had plenty of elephant, eland and zebra - none of which are found in the park today (Hunter 1978: 70). In 1940 Hayes joined the King's African Rifles on war service. He was invalidated out and sent to England but he returned to Nyasaland in 1945. The situation he found, with regard to wildlife, greatly disturbed him, for game animals that were once commonly seen in the Lower Shire, or on the road to Matope, or north of Lilongwe, had largely disappeared. Moreover, he discovered, at the time of the 1946 Commission, that the general government policy was one of 'extermination' - the eradication of all larger mammals outside of game reserves. Such eradication was deemed necessary both in terms of crop protection and in terms of controlling tsetse fly. All this troubled 'G.D', and in September 1945, he wrote to Colin Smee, the secretary of the newly formed commission. He had been particularly troubled by a letter to the *Nyasaland Times* which was entitled 'game must go'. The letter emphatically argued that conservationists were starry-eyed idealists, and that there was no room in Nyasaland for both agriculture and the larger game animals, so the latter had to be eradicated. Hayes wrote to Smee, 'In a territory such as Nyasaland where there are extensive areas of land quite useless for agricultural purposes, it should be possible to find and set aside two or three in which the fauna of the country can be preserved. Also, considering how opinion differs among experts on the subject, it is felt that any destruction of game as an anti-tsetse measure would be a most dangerous expedient to adopt'.

He went on to suggest that if such reserves could be found 'suitable for animals but unsuitable for settled agriculture, and properly supervised, they would be as many as a territory the size of Nyasaland could reasonably afford'. In the letter he makes a strong plea that Lengwe Game Reserve be such a reserve, even though poaching at that time went on relatively unchecked. He suggested the area be put under the control of a game warden and adequately staffed, that all unauthorized hunting be stopped immediately, that garden protection be undertaken in neighbouring areas, and that all meat obtained in such protection activities be given to the people whose crops had been damaged. He indicated that Lengwe reserve had tourist potential, and could become a minor 'Kruger National Park' (MNₐ\/NSB 3/6/1). In the event, as we have seen, the commission report recommended the formation of four game reserves.

Feeling the need for a formal group to act as a wildlife lobby, G.D. Hayes contacted the Fauna Preservation Society in London. Thus it was that the first meeting of the NFPS was held in Limbe Country Club on 1ˢᵗ August 1947. Five people were present, all local planters and friends of 'G.D.': E.C. Peterkins, L.J. Rumsey, S. Tweedie and J. Reid-Henry. Hayes was elected secretary-treasurer. At the meeting it was agreed that the society should 'do all in its powers to further the preservation of wild animals in the protectorate in properly controlled game reserves where it is feasible to do this without detriment to human progress' (WSM/GDH papers). As G.D. Hayes was later to point out, the 'preservation' of wildlife was a rather radical proposal at that time, for it was firmly believed by many Europeans that the existence of wild animals in the protectorate was incompatible with 'progress', and that an 'extermination policy' was at the forefront in the minds of many administrators. It was agreed at the first meeting of the NFPS that the annual subscription would be twenty-one shillings and sixpence.

Some ten years after its formation the membership of the NFPS reached the 60 mark, and such membership consisted mainly of members of the European planting community, although such government officers as W.H.J. Rangeley, R.G.M. Willan, W.D. Lewis and C. Haskard were keen supporters. There were no African members, but when in 1952 H.W. Bwanausi applied for membership it was unanimously agreed that the society should be open to all people who fully understood the aims and functions of the society. In 1959 the society formally drafted a constitution. The objectives of the society were fourfold:

a) To foster by every means in its power the preservation of wildlife in Nyasaland.
b) To educate public opinion on questions of wildlife conservation.
c) To encourage and promote national parks and game reserves wherever this can be done without conflict with sound principles of land use.
d) To co-operate with similar bodies in other territories.

Membership was open to all those of any race having the objectives of the society at heart.

During the first few decades of its existence the NFPS, through its secretary G.D. Hayes, made a substantial and enduring contribution to wildlife conservation in the country. Although the society was often highly critical of the Department of Game, Fish and Tsetse Control, believing that it was more concerned with the protection of agriculture against the depredation of wild game, rather than being for the protection of wildlife, it nevertheless worked in close co-operation with the department. Its director H.J. Borley often attended meetings of the society. And it is true to say that almost all government initiatives with regard to wildlife conservation had their genesis in proposals that were first broached by the Fauna Society. I knew G.D. Hayes well between 1959 and 1965, and camped with him at Mwabvi, and I had the distinct impression that at that time Hayes was the NFPS; certainly he was its inspiration and driving force. For over 30 years, as we earlier noted, he worked enthusiastically and tirelessly to promote the conservation of wildlife in the country (for tributes to Hayes see Hunter 1978, Schwarz 1982). Even at the first formal meeting of the society in November 1947, representation was made to the government

Donation of plane to NFPS from the German government
By Mr Gordon, Archives of the Society of Malawi

concerning the status of puku on the Bua River, the declaration of a bird sanctuary at Mangochi, the setting up of a game department so that the destruction of game animals could be kept to a minimum compatible with crop protection, and the preservation of such predators as leopard and lion, in order to check the numbers of bushpig and baboon. In subsequent years the NFPS, or 'G.D.' personally, were instrumental in encouraging the government to establish Majete and the Nyika as controlled, no-shooting areas (in 1952), in enlarging Mwabvi Game Reserve in order to ensure the conservation of the rhinoceros, in providing honorary game wardens and even game guards' wages, for the government was badly under-resourced, and in persuading the government to give klipspringer full protection (Hunter 1978: 73).

Hayes was always at the centre of controversies wherever the issue of wildlife was concerned. In 1951 a letter appeared in *The Nyasaland Times* that was severely critical of the newly formed Department of Game, Fish and Tsetse Control. It complained about the 'indiscriminate granting of shotguns to Africans on the very poor excuse that they are for garden protection' - which it was alleged was leading to the complete destruction of the country's fauna - and of the incompetence of the department in dealing with 'man-eating' predators. Springing to the defence of the department, Hayes wrote, 'No one wants protection for the fauna more than we do but the African is entitled to have his crops protected and no less so because the "butchers" are inadequately controlled.' He went on to argue both of the need for game guards to protect crops and of the control of illegal shotguns. The department was, Hayes insisted, attempting to deal with harmful lions and leopards, but it lacked sufficient trained personnel. What was really needed, he wrote, was a game department, as opposed to a mere game control department. While defending the department, Hayes was always critical that its emphasis was on control rather than on game conservation or 'preservation' as it was termed in those days. The shift towards conservation within the department between the years 1948 and 1962 was partly due to the influence and pressures extended by 'G.D.' and the NFPS. In 1958, G.D. Hayes wrote an assessment of the wildlife situation in Nyasaland under the title 'The problem and what is needed'. He pointed out that Nyasaland was a relatively small country, and had a population that was approaching 3 million people, the majority of whom were engaged in agriculture. In such circumstances for 'fauna preservation' to have any success it 'must be confined largely to game reserves and National Parks'. He highlighted two problems: inadequate staffing within the game department and uncontrolled hunting (poaching) within the reserves. Hayes felt that the Department of Game, Fish and Tsetse Control had a dual function: the management of the game reserves and crop protection. Yet 'there are but three European game control officers for the whole protectorate. This would be hopelessly inadequate if these officers confined themselves to crop protection but they are also expected to act as game wardens with the result that they are unable to do justice to either office'.

With regard to poaching within the reserves, much of this, Hayes suggested, went undetected, and was probably more common in the Kasungu and Nkhotakota reserves than elsewhere. But to make matters worse, many magistrates took a very lenient view of offences against the game laws, which mainly involved subsistence hunting. A group of Africans were caught hunting with nets in the Thyolo district. When the department brought a charge of illegal hunting against them they were fined five shillings (5/-) each. Hayes noted, 'no one would suggest that the maximum penalty of £100 should be imposed in a case of this nature but the 5/- fines merely caused mirth among the accused'. With regard to 'what is needed' Hayes suggested that the government's attitude towards wildlife had to change, and it should pay more than lipservice to the undertaking it had given to preserve wildlife, that there should be a substantial increase of staff in the Department of Game, Fish and Tsetse Control in order to manage the reserves adequately, with a special emphasis on wildlife conservation as opposed to crop protection, that the game laws should be adequately enforced, that a great deal more could be done by schools to inculcate nature conservation and to impress upon students the aesthetic and economic value of wildlife, that more publicity should be devoted to conservation efforts, and that all reserves should have guarantees of permanency, and the Nyika should be declared a national park (WSM/GD Hayes papers).

It is worth noting that the secretary of the Fauna Preservation Society in London C.C. Boyle visited Nyasaland in June the previous year (1957), as the guest of G.D. Hayes. This reflected the progress in game conservation that had been made in the protectorate over the decade. Hayes took Boyle on trips to Lengwe and the Nyika, as well as visiting Chief Katumbi and the government Chief Secretary. Hayes took the opportunity to press the view that the Nyika should be made into a national park, and that some provision needed to be made for water in Lengwe. The Chief Secretary was sympathetic to both proposals, but non-commital (Oryx 1957: 217-223).

At the time of independence there was another crisis, and had not Hayes and the Fauna Society intervened in the positive way that it did, it is

more than likely that Lengwe National Park would never have been created, and the nyala in the Chikwawa district would now be extinct. In his
tribute to 'G.D', Nigel Hunter makes this clear. In 1964, on the eve of independence, the government had plans, on the recommendation of the
Forestry Department, to abolish Lengwe Game Reserve. It aimed to trans-
fer the 15 nyala, which were thought to be present there, to Mwabvi
reserve. Given his long associations with the area and with the nyala,
Hayes was 'aghast', and hurried to London to consult with well-known conservationists. On his return he visited Lengwe with Les Kettle, who
worked for the Forestry Department and was a keen conservationist, and
as we have noted, he was later to be an important influence in the creation
of Liwonde as a game sanctuary. The two men saw a fair amount of game
and counted 25 nyala while watching at one waterhole. With a large sugar
development project being established nearby at Nchalo, Hayes realised
that something had to be done immediately or the nyala at Lengwe would
be lost. He wrote a report to government, which then reversed its decision
to abolish the reserve. But as cultivations in the Shire and Mwanza valleys,
which had opened up in the years after the Second World War, had cut off
the nyala's access to permanent water, it was imperative that something
should be done about the water supplies in the reserve. The existing waterholes normally went dry about the end of August. Largely through Hayes'
direct involvement and enthusiasm, and on the direct orders of Dr Banda,
who had just taken over as head of state, a borehole was sunk in the
reserve, and the water then piped to the waterhole.

So satisfactory had been the 1964 experience, as Hayes records, that the
government decided to go ahead in developing Lengwe as a game sanctuary. In 1965, under the supervision of Hayes and Kettle, who was the game
ranger in charge of the reserve, a 'hide' was built near the waterhole - a
'hide' that is now famous. In 1966 a tourist rest camp was constructed, and
a decade later the fauna society provided a hostel for student accommodation in order to help educational programmes. Hayes wrote a little article
on these events entitled, 'How Independence Saved an African Reserve'
(1967). Hayes himself and members of the NFPS were continually involved
in the creation of Lengwe as a reserve, providing both support and finance.
The satisfaction in all this, as Nigel Hunter writes, is that in 1970 Lengwe,
along with Kasungu, was gazetted a national park (Hunter 1978: 74).

It was largely through G.D. Hayes that a close and relatively harmo-
nious relationship existed between the NFPS, which was largely supported by ex-patriots, and the Department of Game, Fish and Tsetse Control,
and later the DNPW.

Male and female nyalas and warthog

Archives of the Society of Malawi

During the 1970s Hayes wrote a series of papers and articles on the history of wildlife conservation in Malawi, and on the aims and history of the NFPS. Hayes was always adamant that wildlife preservation did not simply involve the preservation of the larger game animals in reserves simply for the aesthetic enjoyment of tourists, but was a much wider conception. By 'wildlife' it was meant not just elephants and antelopes, but all living things within a particular environment, and he emphasized that from the outset the aims of the NFPS were educational 'to educate public opinion on questions of wildlife conservation'. It just so happened, with a policy of 'wildlife destruction' being articulated by government officials, and with the game department's emphasis on control rather on conservation, that the early efforts of the society were necessarily focussed on establishing viable game sanctuaries. It is difficult to appreciate, he recalled, that many people in the past believed that the wildlife in Africa was on its way out, that the existence of the larger mammals was incompatible with agricultural development, and there were even some types 'who refused to appreciate or accept that wildlife was worth conserving anyway'. The correspondence relating to the 1926 game ordinance make it clear that there were many Europeans who felt that the best thing that could happen for the protectorate was the complete eradication of its wildlife, especially elephant.

153

There was also the prevalent notion among many Europeans that the demise of the 'once teeming wildlife of Africa' was due to African people. With their irrational, cruel and destructive methods of capturing game animals through trapping and the communal hunt (*uzimba*), the fauna of Nyasaland had largely disappeared - or so it was felt. Hayes himself was critical of the 'cruel method' of hunting by the use of fire, (1972: 22) and in the NFPS newsletter of June 1960 there is a long account by T.W. Bradshaw of one such game drive (*kauni*). Carrying torches at night and involving about 30 men and boys Bradshaw highlights the irrationality of the hunt and the 'barbaric instincts' of local people with regard to such wildlife destruction (WSM/G.D. Hayes papers).

But Hayes was not happy with this one-sided picture and emphasized two issues. The first was that it was unfair and untrue that local people were to blame for the decline of Nyasaland's fauna since the time of Livingstone. He wrote, 'It is customary to lay the blame for the pathetic deterioration in the numbers of all species of wild animals in Malawi over the last hundred years or so at the door of the indigenous inhabitants but it is, I suggest, very doubtful if this accusation will stand up to a careful analysis of the available evidence' (1972: 22). He indicates that when early travellers first arrived in the country they found it 'teeming with game', even though communal hunts and game drives were undoubtedly common in the pre-colonial period. What he emphasizes, however, at least in his published articles, is not the enormous destructive impact that European hunters had on the wildlife of the protectorate - which I highlight elsewhere in the study - but the destruction of the wildlife habitats, that was a consequence of the steep rise in the human population and the opening up of land for cultivation. In his account of his confrontation with a lion one evening on his way to Mangochi in 1932, Hayes notes that the newly-made road from Balaka to Mangochi was thickly wooded and devoid of villages for long stretches (1972: 25). For Hayes, it was the destruction of habitat not local hunting methods that was mainly responsible for the eradication of much of Malawi's ungulate fauna. Added to this was the fact that firearms were introduced by Arab slave traders throughout the 19th century, and later by the British, and the impact of these must have been enormous. But in his unpublished papers, Hayes is much more critical of European hunting. He wrote, 'any honest assessment of the reasons for the terrible destruction of Africa's wildlife cannot do other than lay the blame squarely on the doorstep of the European immigrants' and that the 'wasteful hunting methods' of local people were not a crucial factor in the demise of the wildlife.

The second issue relates to the fact that Hayes was keen to emphasize that within the local culture there were customs and beliefs that implied a conservation ethic. Always open to new ideas, Hayes carried on a long correspondence with Father Matthew Schoffeelers and Kings Phiri, whose studies of Mang'anja and Chewa cultural history are important, enquiring about local attitudes to wildlife. What he learned from them, he incorporated into his writings. He thus suggested that local people, through their patterns of social life and cultural beliefs were not insensitive to the preservation of their environment, particularly the wildlife, from which they derived their livelihood. Hayes noted the following, even if rather briefly and schematically. He said that that the communal hunts and game drives, though to Europeans 'shockingly wasteful of wildlife', were not disorderly affairs. They took place only at long intervals, and were highly organized, with a person in charge, (*mwini liwamba wa uzimba*), and were hedged with customary rules and ritual prohibitions, and involved the use of special charms. He went on to say that: there existed professional hunting fraternities or guilds, which controlled hunting activities, and which were largely under the jurisdiction of local chiefs, who often had considerable powers, both secular and religious; that given the close association between animals and spirits of the ancestors, and the strong belief in the mystical power of an animal to harm (*chirope*) - a belief almost universal throughout Africa - the hunting and killing of wild mammals was never wanton or wasteful; that totemic beliefs associated with clan membership, and religious beliefs, often involved ritual prohibitions on the eating of certain mammal species. He noted that the Yao Muslims of Mangochi were forbidden from eating pork in their religion and thus in the 1930s the district was literally full of warthog and bushpig; that there were ritual prohibitions on the hunting and killing of wildlife within a sacred forest, that is, in graveyards (*manda*), especially those associated with local chiefs, and the rain shrines (Hayes 1972: 23-24). (These aspects of Malawian culture are more fully discussed in other publications {Morris 1998, 2000}.)

At the annual general meeting of the NFPS in 1962, the chair, R.G.M. Willan made an important address. Willan was then the Chief Conservator of Forests. He is the 'Peter Quillan' of Laurens van der Post's travel book, wherein he is described as a 'big, strong, open-air fellow who enjoyed his work, (and) who loved the country' (1952: 98). At the meeting Willan suggested that an important function of the NFPS was to constantly remind the government of its responsibilities to the people of the country. Although viable game reserves had been established, which held a great diversity of wildlife, public and government consciousness of their value, he remarked, had not yet been aroused. There was therefore the need for the society to engage more in educational matters, and to stimulate an awareness of the value and importance of wildlife among all sections of the public - the young as well as those in government circles. In the decades that followed, the NFPS was increasingly engaged in supporting and more often than not financing various educational projects, such as the formation of wildlife clubs, the building of student hostels in the wildlife sanctuaries, and sponsoring the guided visits of Malawian children to the reserves and national parks - all of which proved to be a great success. These projects were often organized through local branches of the NFPS and involved close co-operation with the DNPW. In 1975 the society founded a wildlife journal, *Nyala*, appropriately named, given the long association of the society with the protection of this antelope. The journal is still flourishing after 20 years, its editor for most of this period being Cornell Dudley. It is an important source of information and research material relating to all aspects of Malawi's wildlife. In 1989 the NFPS - which had described itself as the National Fauna Preservation Society since independence - officially changed its name to the Wildlife Society of Malawi. The new name served to reflect more closely the activities of the society.

In the closing years of his life G.D. Hayes produced the first guide to *Malawi's National Parks and Game Reserves* (1978) which contained his early essay on wildlife conservation, as well as useful information on the sanctuaries, and on the larger mammals of Malawi. A decade later John Hough (1989), acknowledging 'G.D.'s' 'inspiration', published an extended, up-dated version, but significantly by-passed any reflections on the local culture or on local people's conceptions of wildlife - which had interested Hayes. In addition, Hayes was also working on a book to be entitled *African Animal Tracks and Tracking*. It was to be an illustrated field guide to the signs, droppings and tracks of all the larger mammals of Malawi. It was never completed, and since his death in 1981, there have been many books on this topic (Walker 1981 being one of the first).

THE POST-COLONIAL ERA

When the Department of Game, Fish and Tsetse Control was disbanded in 1962, the work of crop protection and game conservation came under the auspices of the Forestry Department, as the Department of Forestry and Game. A decade later, in 1973, the Department of National Parks and Wildlife (DNPW) was established and a new era of conservation began. At its inception it had around 100 personnel (Clarke 1983: 10). Already in 1963 the government had shown an awareness of the wider aspects of wildlife conservation and had issued a Wild Life Policy Statement which read, 'It is the policy of the Malawi government to afford all the protection in its power to game animals and wildlife in general in so far as such protection does not conflict with planned development of other essential national resources. In affording protection to game and wildlife the government has in mind the value of this national resource as a tourist attraction, as a possible source of food and as a scientific and educational asset of national importance.

It is the intention of the government to afford protection to wildlife in all existing game reserves and forest reserves by means of enforcing restriction of hunting and the prevention of disturbance of the natural habitat. In other areas it is the intention to control the hunting of animals, birds and other forms of wildlife through restriction by licence both of hunting and of trade in game meat and trophies through the provisions of the game ordinance.

The government intends to encourage the fullest public support for its wildlife policy through education in wildlife conservation and by general publicity to stimulate the interest of the people of Malawi in the importance of wild life as a national asset and to obtain the willing co-operation of the people in all wild life conservation programmes' (Hayes 1972: 29-30).

Although not acknowledging that the wildlife of the country had an intrinsic value, this statement nevertheless recognized the importance of the fauna and flora as national assets. Following suggestions laid down by the NFPS it accepted that the government should play a leading role in environmental education, and seek the active co-operation of people in its wildlife conservation programmes. The policy was a far cry from the earlier focus on crop protection. Nevertheless, the government still recognized the crucial importance of protecting gardens from the depredations of wild animals, particularly hippopotamus and elephant. This was seen as crucial near the wildlife sanctuaries - Nkhotakota, Kasungu and Liwonde in particular. In 1975 a crop protection unit was established by the DNPW.

It consisted of a senior game ranger, two game rangers and about 30 hunter scouts plus ancillary staff. That same year Myles Turner joined the department as Regional Game Warden for the Northern Region. Turner was highly experienced in wildlife management having previously been

Game ranger
Archives of the Society of Malawi

warden of the Serengeti National Park. Recognizing the importance of establishing a research programme, so that policy decisions within the department could be based on sound evidence and adequate knowledge, the DNPW further established a Wildlife Research Unit at Kasungu National Park. In 1977 Richard Bell joined the department as senior research biologist, and over the next decade Bell and his colleagues initiated and carried through a substantial amount of important research on many aspects of wildlife ecology and management (Bell 1981, Bell and Jachmann 1984, Jachmann 1984, 1986).

By 1973, four important national parks - Nyika, Kasungu, Lengwe and Liwonde - had been established, totalling an area of 6,885 sq km. This constituted around 7% of the total land area of the country. By the end of the decade tourist facilities had been established in each of these parks. Together with the four game reserves - Vwaza was declared a game reserve in 1977, and Majete, Mwabvi and Nkhotakota had long been proclaimed sanctuaries for wildlife - these constituted a further 3614 sq km (4%). Therefore Malawi, as Hayes admitted, probably had as many wildlife sanctuaries as the country could afford. The emphasis thus was put by both the DNPW and the NFPS in developing these sanctuaries, and in putting increasing energy and resources into environmental education.

In 1971 a new Game Act was proclaimed (Laws of Malawi Chapter 66: 3). It followed the pattern of the earlier game ordinances, and the following were its main provisions:

- No hunting was allowed on private land without permission of the owner, or in controlled hunting areas or game reserves.
- No person could hunt without possession of a valid licence, and the national licence, costing £10, allowed a person to shoot 1 male bushbuck, 2 warthog, and 5 grey duiker - a far cry from the earlier schedules, which included a long list of ungulates that could be shot. The same licence applicable only for a district cost £2.
- Special permission had to be obtained to hunt the following: blue duiker, buffalo, female bushbuck, cheetah, colobus monkey, eland, elephant, hartebeest, hippo, impala, klipspringer, kudu, leopard, lion, suni, nyala, oribi, puku, reedbuck, red duiker, rhinoceros, roan, sable, Sharpe's grysbok, waterbuck, wildebeest, zebra and blue monkey.
- No person could carry on trade in trophies or manufactured articles from trophies for sale unless in possession of a permit.
- The 'games rules' specified that the following were illegal: hunting after dark; possession of gin traps, hunting by means of a vehicle, or with the use of dogs or fire; and, without the permission of a game control officer, hunting by means of poison, nets, traps, snares or pitfall. The use of the latter was allowed only if used on, or adjacent to cultivated land.

As with the earlier game ordinances, the new laws of Malawi made all forms of traditional hunting illegal, and specifically outlawed the use of fire or dogs in hunting.

The National Parks Act of 1973 (Laws of Malawi, Chapter 66: 7) provided for the declaration and management of the parks. It states that the reasons for having national parks is 'for the purpose of the propagation, protection, conservation and study therein of animals in their natural habitat, vegetation and objects and places of geological, ethnological, archaeological, historical, scientific and educational interest, for the benefit and enjoyment of the inhabitants of Malawi and of visitors thereto' (3: 1).

The act gives all animals in a national park full protection from hunting and from any kind of disturbance, and though it has a humanistic emphasis, it highlights the fact that the parks are primarily for the benefit and enjoyment of Malawian people - not rich tourists. Moreover, the importance of the national parks is not simply the larger fauna, or even the biotic community, but includes phenomena of historical importance. Three parks are specified in the National Parks Act - Nyika, Kasungu and Lengwe. Liwonde was declared a national park in 1973.

The game reserves - Nkhotakota, Mwabvi, Vwaza and Majete - are incorporated into the Game Act, and no rationale is given for their existence. In legal terms the main difference between the reserves and the national parks are that all animals are protected in national parks but only the vertebrates in the reserves, and that trespass is an offence in national parks. This, of course, excludes local people from free access through the park (Clarke 1983).

Besides the important work being done in the research field, a shift of emphasis was also indicated around 1980. Game wardens became wildlife management officers, and there was an increasing emphasis on environmental education. This took three forms: the creation of environmental education centres, with officers to staff them, the sponsored visits of many Malawian children to the national parks, and the formation of wildlife clubs. In these endeavours there was a very close co-operation between the department, and the NFPS, who initiated many of the projects, and sought funding from the Beit Trust and the World Wildlife Fund to support them.

One of the most important of these projects was the creation of an environmental education centre and a nature sanctuary right in the middle of Lilongwe City - which is quite unique. An area of just over 700 hectares, along the banks of the Lingadzi River in the centre of the city between the 'old' town and capital city, the sanctuary consists primarily of a rich *Acacia/Combretum* woodland. It harbours bushbuck, grey duiker, a few introduced blue duiker, as well as a variety of smaller mammals such as genet, porcupine, bushbaby, civet, and the occasional otter or serval. There are crocodiles in the river, and a profusion of bird species. Besides being an environmental education centre, the sanctuary itself is a delightful wildlife oasis in a busy and growing city.

As part of the increasing emphasis on environmental education, much publicity was given to Malawian wildlife and environmental issues through regular columns in local newspapers and journals. Such environmental articles written by Sam Chire (*tchire*, woodland) and Nanchengwa (hammerkop) were readable, informative and highly popular, and later published by NFPS in book form. The NFPS also sought, through the DNPW, to make environmental concerns more evident in development projects, and stressed the crucial importance of rural afforestation. Even in the 1940s G.D. Hayes, when a member of the Thyolo National Resources Board, had made a strong plea for the need, not only to protect stream banks, but for afforestation programmes, given the growing population around Blantyre - Limbe (MNA/NSE 1/3/2). The 1946 Game and Forest Commission also drew attention to the urgent need for such afforestation. The lack of urgency by governments and local authorities has led to the present crisis, where forested hills - often reserves such as Ndirande Mountain - are being completely denuded of tree cover. This includes the loss of precious montane evergreen forest.

Environmental centres were also established at Mzuzu, at Michiru Mountain conservation area near Blantyre, and at Lake Malawi National Park in Mangochi district.

A second important aspect of environmental education was the building of student hostels at all the major wildlife sanctuaries - Lengwe, Liwonde, Kasungu and Nyika - and the organization of sponsored educational visits by local school children. Briefings are carried out before the trip, and normally there are follow-up activities organized within the school later. As said, these visits have proved to be a great success, for many Malawian children have never encountered in their normal life such larger mammals as elephant, kudu, impala and warthog. Also, given the fact that the national parks and game reserves are utilized almost exclusively by foreign tourists - for the cost of visiting the parks is beyond the reach of ordinary Malawians - these visits have an important social as well as educational significance. It may be noted that the park entry fee for a Malawian in 1995 was K12, and that to stay in a chalet cost between K60 and K95, while the basic wage for an ordinary Malawian worker was around only K10. Ordinary membership of the Wildlife Society of Malawi was then K50 (without publications), that of a Wildlife Club K5.

Warthog
Archives of the Society of Malawi.

Wildlife Clubs have also proved to be a great success. The first club was formed in 1977, and within a decade there were almost 200 clubs scattered throughout the country, around 60 of these being in secondary schools. There were also village wildlife clubs. The emblem of the wildlife clubs is the tortoise (*kamba*), which, as we shall see, is a key figure in Malawian folklore. Though slow, the tortoise is always portrayed as a thoughtful creature, considering all possibilities before acting and so making no mistakes. A booklet was produced by the NFPS entitled *How to Start a Wildlife Club*, and there was and still is a regular newsletter (*Kamba*) and a magazine, *Nantchengwa*.

Although many of these wildlife clubs visit the game sanctuaries - I accompanied several and enjoyed the experience tremendously - this is not their raison d'etre. For clubs are also involved in such activities as discussions, film shows, and working on local conservation projects, or the creation of nature trails.

These clubs continue to play an important role helping to ensure that the wildlife of the country survives, and that, through increasing awareness, the quality of the environment in Malawi is sustained. This is of crucial importance for the well-being and aesthetic enjoyment of future generations - as one local reporter wrote (*Daily Times* 4 June 1985).

As in 1946, in the early 1980s the government, through the DNPW, decided to take stock of the situation regarding wildlife conservation. A master plan was thus drafted for the national parks and for wildlife management more generally (Clarke 1983). A brief discussion may be devoted to this plan.

The government recognised, it suggested, that wildlife is a complex of renewable 'natural resources' that has both a positive and a negative relationship to human needs. By 'wildlife', it was meant all biotic species, and it was acknowledged that all parts of an eco-system are inter-related, so no plant or animal could ever be considered in isolation. It suggested that it was the intention of government to manage these 'resources', this term indicating that the underlying ethos of the plan was anthropocentric, in a professional and scientific way for the benefit of humans, particularly the people of Malawi. It further recognized that the actual and potential benefits of wildlife are various and many - and includes aesthetic, scientific, cultural and recreational values. The plan confirms that wildlife 'can make contributions to the welfare and productivity of other forms of land use, such as agriculture, ranching and forestry. Wildlife can enhance environmental quality, and act as a resevoir of genetic diversity; and it can provide utilitarian benefits such as food, hides, timber, and revenue from utilization' (1983: 34). Some of the benefits are long-term and enduring - recreational value, watershed protection, and genetic diversity; some are not quantifiable - those relating to the scientific, cultural, aesthetic and educational values of wildlife, of larger mammals in particular. The plan therefore makes a strong plea that wildlife sanctuaries should not be seen simply in commodity terms, and must be recognised as a 'public service' subsidised by the state. It contends, 'They will rarely raise revenue sufficient to cover the total costs of having and managing them. It should not be expected of them that they be money making enterprises' (8.6.4).

The notion that wildlife sanctuaries 'must pay for themselves', the plan suggests, should have little place in defining management policies for the national parks. And it goes on to argue that a key recommendation of the plan is that the department 'should eschew arguments that use revenue earned as a mainstay of its case for having protected areas, and that the more important values of parks and reserves should be actively emphasized and given wider publicity' (10.2.2).

While simplistic monetary arguments are used to justify the existence of wildlife sanctuaries, the more enduring values of protected areas and wildlife will tend to be lost on government, and it may be easy for someone to argue that a greater economic return might be derived from putting a given area of land under maize, cotton or tobacco, rather than having it as a wildlife reserve. Such a case has certainly been put forward for Kasungu, and John Kandawire also argued for the de-gazetting of Mwabvi reserve on similar grounds. The problem is that the current world economic system, capitalism, and the ideology expressed by such agencies as the World Bank, does indeed put a crucial emphasis on monetary return - profit - rather than on long-term human needs. Nevertheless, the plan puts an important emphasis on the more 'enduring values' that can be derived from conservation areas and their wildlife, namely as reservoirs of genetic diversity, for their potential in furthering educational, scientific and recreative values, and for their beneficial effects on land husbandry and fisheries management - particularly in ensuring water conservation.

In its guidelines, the plan therefore suggested the following reasons for maintaining and managing protected - conservation - areas:

- to preserve selected examples of Malawi's biotic communities;
- to protect areas of aesthetic beauty and of special interest;
- to preserve rare, endangered or endemic species of wild animals and plants;
- to assist in maintaining water supplies through catchment conservation, thus benefitting agriculture and fish conservation;
- to provide facilities for the advancement of scientific knowledge;

163

- to provide facilities of the public use and enjoyment of the 'resources' within the protected areas.

The last two reasons must not be prejudicial to the overall project of conserving biotic community and its wildlife.

The plan recognized the need for a specific government department to implement the state's park and wildlife policy, and five principles were proposed as being essential to its management programme:
- management by a professional agency, staffed by trained and experienced officers;
- adequate funding, so that it may achieve its objectives in a professional and competent manner;
- a strategy that recognizes the importance of research studies and monitoring programmes;
- a positive approach in encouraging public understanding and appreciation of wildlife and participation in the implementation of the department's conservation programmes;
- a commitment to international co-operation with agencies involved in conservation and in controlling the illegal trade in wildlife products. (3.7).

The plan recognized that much wildlife lived outside of reserves and national parks, and therefore could not be fully managed by the state. The laws of Malawi put many species under de jure protection - through the Game Act and the Wild Bird Protection Act - but de facto management was all but impossible. The hunting, trapping and snaring of wild mammals, large and small, takes place all over Malawi, and though strictly speaking all this is illegal, it forms an essential part of the local subsistence economy. The question was whether any species outside of a wildlife sanctuary was in fact a 'manageable resource'? The plan suggested that if it was, then de facto management should be introduced, if it could not be 'managed' then legal protection should be withdrawn (4.5.3). Some clarification, it was felt, was needed. The emphasis throughout the plan was on control and management by central government, through the DNPW, seen as a 'state agency'.

The functions of the department were noted as many and various to manage the wildlife sanctuaries and to collect the revenue derived from their use; to conserve certain species of wildlife through the enforcement of the game laws; to control the 'vertebrate pests'; to encourage educational programmes relating to the national parks and wildlife conservation; to issue relevant licences and permits; to encourage and promote research, and to act as the government's adviser in matters relating to conservation areas and wildlife (6.1.1.).

Wildlife management was recognized by the plan as falling under three headings: wildlife conservation; the utilization of wildlife; and the control of wildlife in an effort to reduce the detrimental effects of wildlife on human life and property.

Local subsistence hunting was barely discussed in the plan, but hunting licences taken out between 1978 and 1982 averaged 1031 a year. This brought in an annual revenue of around K4,891. It had however little relationship to the harvesting of wild animals, for the greater part of hunting in Malawi is unlicensed, illegal, and focussed on subsistence (7.2).

The national parks and wildlife reserves, the plan concedes, have little relevance to most Malawians. The majority of people who visit parks are foreign tourists. I made a survey of visitors to two wildlife sanctuaries, Vwaza Game Reserve, and Kasungu National Park, and my analysis confirmed that very few Malawians visit the wildlife sanctuaries, and those that do tend to be government officials. Of people staying at Lifupa Lodge in Kasungu National Park (1990) 11% of visitors were Malawians, 15% from North America, 8% from South Africa, 3% from other African countries, (Kenya, Zimbabwe, Tanzania), the majority of the remainder coming from Europe (63%) - even though many of these were temporary residents in Malawi. With regard to people staying at the tented camp in Vwaza Game Reserve, near Lake Kazuni, the following figures pertain (1990).

Place of Origin	Number of Visitors
Australia	9
Denmark	2
France	2
Germany	8
Ireland	4
Italy	1
Malawi	26
Netherlands	23
South Africa	28
Tanzania	1
United Kingdom	58
USA	14
Zambia	1
Zimbabwe	2
Total	**179**

Again, only about 14% of visitors were Malawians and of these many were on official duty. Simon Munthali (1990) noted the following figures for visitors to national parks:

	Per cent
Non-resident foreigners	51.0
Resident foreigners	34.0
Malawians	4.4
Officials	10.6
Total	**100.0**

Wildlife-based tourism is actively encouraged by the department wherever this does not conflict with the conservation objectives of the protected areas. And the level of tourism is felt in need of some control to avoid undesirable impacts on the environment and its wildlife, or on the quality of the tourist experience itself. It was acknowledged that there is a need to actively encourage Malawians to visit wildlife sanctuaries. Although income from wildlife-based tourism in 1988-89 was estimated at K163,974 - leaving aside the money spent by tourists outside the parks and reserves - Munthali reiterates the sentiments contained in the 'Master Plan', namely that the generation of revenue from wildlife-based tourism must be a subsidiary objective in the management of conservation areas. He concludes that the 'generation of revenue cannot be a primary factor in justifying the establishment and continued existence of parks and reserves in Malawi' (Munthali 1990: 51).

Although, the plan recognizes, it may be argued that income derived from wildlife tourism may ultimately benefit local people living near wildlife sanctuaries, for these people such benefit seems rather tenuous. What benefits they do tend to enjoy - through hunting or the gathering of woodland products - they do so illegally. Given the degree of 'hostility' shown towards the parks and reserves by local people, the plan argues that it might be feasible to allow or encourage people to use protected areas in the gathering of woodland resources such as poles, firewood and thatching grass, provided such harvesting is controlled and monitored. A key recommendation of the plan is therefore that local people should derive 'greater direct benefits' from the protected areas (10.3). Another recommendation is that large residential complexes - such as exist at Lifupa in Kasungu National Park and at Chelinda on the Nyika - must be phased out, and relocated at the edges of the park.

Another issue dealt with by the plan is the implications of 'island geography', the fact that all wildlife sanctuaries in Malawi have become islands of 'natural' habitat, surrounded by agricultural lands, and with regard to some of the conservation areas like Kasungu and Liwonde, by areas densely populated with people. To cope with this problem the plan suggests active management, keeping protected areas as large as possible, retaining several protected areas so that different wildlife communities are protected, and, at times, population manipulation through the translocation of animals.

Vertebrate pest control, what in the past went under the heading of 'crop protection', has continued to be an important feature of wildlife management within the department. A crop protection unit was established soon after the formation of the DNPW - in 1975. It tended to operate from three centres: Lilongwe, Limbe and Mzuzu. The aim of the unit was essentially to minimize interactions between people and wild mammals that have an adverse impact on human interests. The greatest economic impact is undoubtedly caused by primates and bushpig. During the wet season the wildlife 'control units' tend to deal with elephant and hippopotamus, during the dry season attention is directed towards baboon, vervet monkey and bushpig. Predators that are troublesome, such as lions and leopards and crocodiles, are dealt with when the need arises (12.5).

The number of mammals killed during 'pest control' activities 1977-1982 is indicated in the following table.

TABLE FOURTEEN
Wild Vertebrate Pests Killed in Malawi 1977-82

	1977	1978	1979	1980	1981	1982	Total
Baboon	20	13	23	137	209	256	658
Buffalo	22	16	17	10	13	12	90
Bushbuck	53	-	-	37	11	18	119
Bushpig	13	7	11	20	161	113	325
Elephant	55	68	32	49	40	55	299
Genet	-	-	-	-	1	1	2
Grey duiker	15	-		9	3	3	30
Hippopotamus	132	114	93	70	88	124	621
Hyena	3	3	6	18	14	2	46
Jackal	4	-	1	15	6	12	38
Klipspringer	1	-	-			-	1
Kudu	-	-	-	-	1		1
Leopard	7	-	3	2	4	5	21
Lion	7	8	8	4	14	7	48
Porcupine	5	-	-	-	-	-	5
Red forest duiker	-	-	-	9	-	-	9
Reedbuck	8	-		1	3	2	14
Sharpe's grysbok	3	1	-	-	-	-	4
Vervet monkey	20	-	81	131	561	812	1605
Wildcat	-	-	-	1	1	-	2
Total							**3938**

Average 656 animals killed per year
Source: Clarke 1983: 71

It is noteworthy that many more ungulates were killed in the Northern Region, which has the lowest human population, and that the main mammals involved in crop depredations are still elephant, hippopotamus, baboon, vervet monkey and bushpig. The porcupine also does a good deal of damage and though common in some areas it is strictly noctural and frequents rocky caves. Compared with the earlier period there were many less baboons killed annually. The main 'pests' were troublesome in all three regions.

Some six years after the drafting of the 'master plan' a major project was launched - in 1989 - specifically directed at wildlife management and crop protection. Directed by Patrick Rogers, with Leonard Sefu acting as the project co-ordinator, both having had wide experience in wildlife management, the project was funded by the FAO for a three-year period. The project was designed to strengthen the DNPW's capability in managing conservation areas, and put particular emphasis on the protection of crops and people from wildlife 'pests'. It was particularly aimed at finding ways of reducing the conflict between humans and wildlife, especially in the areas surrounding the national parks - Liwonde and Kasungu specifically. Important research studies were initiated and undertaken, particular in regard to the compilation of a national inventory of the larger mammals, in assessing the verterbrate pest impacts around the Liwonde and Kasungu national parks; and in monitoring the impact of the electric fence constructed on the eastern boundary of Kasungu between 1982 and 1988, particularly as this effected public perceptions and relations (Simons 1989, Deodatus and Lipiya 1990, Simons and Chirambo 1991, Deodatus and Lipiya 1991). We have discussed the impact of vertebrate pests - that is the impact of elephant, hippopotamus, baboon, vervet monkey and bushpig - on local communities elsewhere (Morris 1995b). With regard to the electric fencing at Kasungu, which was extended from 43 to 120 km in 1991, most people interviewed along the north-east boundary of the park welcomed the fence, although there are clearly problems with its maintenance, as significant damage was done to the fencing not only by elephants and buffalo, but also by people (poachers?). It was also evident that an extensive campaign was needed to inform people and to mobilize public support for the fence - whose raison d'etre was to prevent crop depredations, and thus reduce the conflict between wildlife and the people living in the vicinity of the conservation area (Deodatus and Lipiya 1991).

But the project not only conducted important research, but also made substantial practical inputs to the department: in running training courses for game scouts; in facilitating study tours and professional courses in wildlife management for wildlife officers; in rehabilitating the department's radio network and in training personnel in radio operation; in the construction of solar-powered fencing for crop protection; and in undertaking a 'hippo culling exercise'. Hippos in particular were seen as causing extensive damage in rice cultivations, often damaging between 10% and 33% of the crop (Rogers and Jamusana 1989: 12).

What the project indicated in its various publications is that although the substantial benefits of national parks and wildlife conservation was acknowledged in all national policy documents, their economic value far exceeding the cost of managing the protected areas, these benefits were not evident to local people. In terms of the protection of watersheds, the income derived from tourism - which is largely focussed on wildlife, as reservoirs of genetic diversity, as a potential for furthering science and education, as a recreation value, and for the beneficial effects on land husbandry and fisheries management (Nkhotakota reserve is an important spawning ground for lake salmon *mpasa*), - the national parks and the country's wildlife are of inesteemable value. They contribute in very positive ways to the improvement of life in Malawi, quite apart from the fact that wildlife is a part of Malawi's national heritage which is worth keeping for its own sake. Indeed Rogers and Jamusana speak of wildlife as occupying a central place in the 'national psyche' (1989: 13-14). Yet the only 'benefits' of wildlife to local villagers, Rogers's intimates, are:

(a) trampled crops and raided gardens,
(b) denial of access to collect firewood in protected areas,
(c) denial of access to potential agricultural land,
(d) arrest/imprisonment for gathering woodland products or hunting (poaching) - traditional activities which are illegal in the conservation areas.

There may be legitimate and rational grounds for restricting cultivation and hunting within national parks and game reserves, but as Rogers concludes in the Project Resumé (1989), 'If conservation is to succeed in Malawi people must become aware of and convinced by those arguments. They must also reap some benefits from wildlife, and not just bear the costs as they do at present. The benefits of conservation are real and Malawi will be a poorer place, not just spiritually but also economically if conservation fails'.

Thus, without public support the outlook for wildlife in Malawi as in the rest of Africa, looks bleak. The present relationship between wildlife and rural people in Malawi - based as this is on laws inherited from a colonial past - has been described as 'adversarial'. This was acknowledged by the master plan, which suggested two main ways of overcoming the problem: by stressing and publicising the positive and enduring values of national parks and wildlife through environmental education programmes and wider publicity; and by developing and implementing ways in which the local rural population can directly profit from, or where possible participate in, the wildlife management. This has been done to some extent with the introduction of bee-keeping and allowing the gathering of firewood under licence, and in the selling locally of culled meat, as at Lengwe. Rogers and Jamusana suggest that much more should be done in this direction, perhaps in ways similar to the campfire programmes in Zimbabwe. Thus besides educational initiatives, it will increasingly be important to develop ways in which local people can participate fully in wildlife management and in the controlled utilization of the benefits than can be derived from conservation areas and wildlife (Rogers and Jamusana 1989, Mkanda and Yamusara 1990).

What the FAO project also highlighted, in relation to the 'master plan' recommendations, was that the DNPW was seriously understaffed and underfunded. This is still the case, and it is likely to deteriorate given the implications of the structural adjustment programmes imposed on Malawi by the World Bank.

Throughout the 1980s there was close co-operation between the NFPS and the DNPW with respect to the support and implementation of many conservation projects. As in the past, the Wildlife Society was not uncritical of the government department, particularly as the decade witnessed the demise of the country's rhino population - which until 1989 had still existed in small numbers in Kasungu National Park and Mwabvi Game Reserve - and the loss of Majete's elephants. But on the whole co-operation between the two organizations was fruitful, particularly in the field of environmental education and in the translocation of certain mammals. The NFPS indeed continued to flourish throughout the decade, most of its activities organized through local branches at Blantyre, Zomba, Lilongwe and Mzuzu. Membership throughout the period stood at over 600, with about 40 or more affliated wildlife clubs. The society helped in the financing of scout camps and student hostels in the conservation areas, facilitated the visits of school children and wildlife clubs to Lengwe, Nyika and Liwonde National Parks, organized wildlife essay competitions in schools throughout Malawi, as well as being deeply involved in supporting environmental education more generally. *Nyala* continued to flourish as a wildlife journal, and in spite of some contrary opinions, combined the

The signing of a loan agreement between Reserve Bank and World Wild Life Fund. The Governor of the Reserve Bank of Malawi, Mr John Tembo signed the agreement with Sir Peter Scott, Chairman of the World Wild Life Fund at Club Makokola in Mangochi on 2ⁿᵈ August, 1977.

Ministry of Information

publication of important research papers with popular articles and news items. *Nantchengwa* magazine for young people was an on-going publication, and the society published a wide range of books, pamphlets and guides. With eventually around 1600 school-based wildlife clubs in the country, the society obtained funding to publish its newsletter, *Kamba*. As already meantioned, in 1989, given its increasing emphasis on wildlife conservation, rather than simply on the preservation of game animals, the NFPS changed its name to the Wildlife Society of Malawi (now called The Wildlife and Environmental Society of Malawi), and in 1992 established its own headquarters in Limbe. Funded by grants from USAID and from various trusts, the society, after holding an important workshop in Lilongwe in 1991, became an independent NGO, with a full-time executive director. Much of these developments must be credited to Carl Bruessow, who was then Chairman of the society. Like G.D. Hayes he was - is - a 'wildlife enthusiast' and he became the society's first executive director. In recent years the society has expanded its activities even further, employing a number of full-time staff, working on various projects, including a social anthropologist. The society was instrumental in the 'return' of the black rhino to the country, for in 1993 a breeding pair from Kruger National

171

Park were released in Liwonde; in establishing community forestry projects in the Chiradzulu and Chikwawa districts as well as working on various projects in co-operation with rural small-holders. In 1995 it launched a new popular wildlife magazine *Samalani* (*ku-samala*, to protect, to care for). The emphasis of the society is therefore now on encouraging community participation, and as Bruessow suggests, 'It is not a society that is there to benefit its members but rather to generate public support and action towards resolving environmental wildlife concerns' (*Samalani* magazine 1: 6, 1995).

CONTEMPORARY PERSPECTIVES ON WILDLIFE CONSERVATION

Wildlife conservation in Malawi has essentially passed through three distinct phases: an initial phase (1895-1930) of 'game preservation' when the hunting of game animals was the preserve of a European 'sporting' elite; a second phase (1930-1960) when game reserves were established but sport hunting remained an essential concern of government, coupled with a strong emphasis on crop protection and the eradication of the offending mammals; and a final phase when sport hunting declined and viable game sanctuaries were established with a tourist clientele (1960-1990). We are now moving into a fourth phase, with the recognition that wildlife protection geared solely to the generation of foreign exchange and to the aesthetic enjoyment of rich overseas tourists, and to the detriment of the well-being of local people - is highly problematic. It is a strategy that is not conducive to the long-term conservation of wildlife, whose survival is ultimately in the hands of local people.

Many writers have indicated the similarities between the game ordinances implemented by colonial governments and medieval hunting laws in Europe (Graham 1973, MacKenzie 1985). As in medieval times, the game ordinance, devised and enforced by the colonial government in Nyasaland, made all game animals - essentially the larger ungulates - the sole property of the crown, the state. It assumed the 'royal prerogative' to game. Prior to this, of course, local people, as with peasants in Europe, had assumed that wild animals belonged, in the last analysis only to God, and that they were the property of no person. It is a fact of history that humans generally, prior to the rise of state institutions, did not acknowledge or articulate the concept of 'property' and considered all wild mammals, like the air we breathe, to belong to no one until they were captured or killed. The colonial game laws made all wild animals the property of the state, and with its system of game licenses ensured that hunting was the sole privilege of Europeans - as an aristocratic elite. As Graham remarked, 'it is a universal feature of game laws that they never favour the unprivileged' (1973: 40). The colonial rulers thus claimed exclusive ownership of wild mammals, and all subsistence hunting, whether by traps, snares, nets, fire or dogs, was declared illegal - a crime. As in the European context, subsistence hunting was described as 'poaching', and throughout the colonial period Europeans, the majority of whom engaged in hunting as a recreation, gave such subsistence hunting a very bad press. It was described as wasteful, cruel, barbaric and irrational and as being the primary factor in the decline of the larger mammals. Even more enlightened Europeans like Rodney Wood expressed a strong antipathy towards subsistence hunting, and, given the importance of such hunting to the local economy, to some Europeans every African was a potential 'poacher'. The contrast between subsistence hunting of local people, and the 'sport' hunting of Europeans as an aristocratic pursuit (the 'Hunt' as MacKenzie describes it {1988: 13-22}) - is discussed more fully elsewhere (Morris 1998: 118-19). While subsistence hunting can be seen as a 'prelude to eating', sport hunting shifts the focus of the hunt to the act of killing, (Graham 1973: 35), and is highly ritualized; it is misleading however to view subsistence hunting as merely an empirical activity. It too is highly ritualized in the Malawian context.

By the 1920s, with much of game population depleted in Malawi, there was a shift of opinion in the thinking of many Europeans, and a need was felt to preserve game animals. Many of these new conservationists were 'penitent butchers' like Rodney Wood, and in a wider context they include such well-known figures as Frederick Selous, Theodore Roosevelt and Abel Chapman. Harry Johnston, who in 1891 was the first consul-general in Nyasaland, was one of the founding signatories of the Society for the Preservation of the Wild Fauna of the Empire (SPFE) in 1903 (Fitter & Scott 1978: 8). The SPFE was to have an important influence on the administration - indirectly at least - throughout the colonial period. While in the early period the game laws essentially functioned to preserve game for ritualized sport hunting, which focussed on the collecting of trophies and which, to an important degree, served as a ritual of prestige and domination, the establishment of 'game reserves' had a different motivation. Even though, as we have noted, the motivations behind the establishment of 'reserves' in colonial Nyasaland were many and varied and largely geared to human problems and needs. It is worth noting of course that the concepts of 'game reserve', 'park', and even 'forest' all signified, in the past, the hunting preserves of the ruler and the aristocratic elite.

The shift of emphasis towards 'game saving' within specific locales has been interpreted by Alistair Graham in psychoanalytic terms. He suggests that a 'compassion' for wildlife only comes from people who have largely isolated themselves from the hostile influences of wild mammals. Graham sees the agricultural pursuits of humans and the continuing existence of larger game animals as basically incompatible, and notes that the depletion of the latter is unrelated to subsistence hunting, being largely due to increased human population. The motivation to conserve mammals, by people who in their early years were avid hunters, Graham puts down to the 'Mowgli complex'. This is defined as an 'infantile regression', and characterized by 'fantasies' of identification with the animal world. The motivation to conserve wild mammals is therefore seen as a form of animism, 'the direct product psychologically of repressed aggression' (1973: 132). The urge to preserve wilderness areas (wild-deer ness), which he sees purely as a figment of the human imagination ('pristine nature is an illusion' he writes {214}); the close identification with animals to the degree that people are viewed almost in misanthropic terms; the game-viewing tourists who 'chase' animals in cars in a masquerade hunt - all are associated by Graham with the 'Mowgli complex'.

Whatever the hidden motivation that prompts people to conserve wild fauna, the establishment of game reserves at the end of the colonial period went hand-in-hand with crop protection, and a determined effort to control, even to eradicate all larger mammals outside of the reserves. This signified an implicit acknowledgement by the administration that the presence of the larger mammals and human populations, whose subsistence was based on agriculture, did not easily co-exist. Such crop protection activities are still an important aspect of the present government, and thus, with continued population increase in the Lower Shire, riverbank cultivation and efforts to curb human-hippo conflict through such exercises, there are now no longer any hippopotamus between Bangula and the Zambezi (WSM Newsletter, November 1995). G.D. Hayes was adamant that throughout the later colonial period the game department was largely devoted to the eradication of the larger mammals rather than to their preservation (cf. Steinhart 1989: 255-58 on Kenya).

But by 1960 moves were afoot to establish the main game reserves as viable sanctuaries, fully staffed, and equipped with facilities to cater for a growing tourist clientele. How important wildlife is to the tourist industry is reflected in all the tourist brochures that have been produced by the Malawian government and by other tourist agencies since independence. All highlight the aesthetic enjoyment to be derived from wildlife. Although there have been some setbacks, with the depletion of such larger mammals as the elephant, rhinoceros, zebra and hartebeest within some of the reserves, the establishment of wildlife sanctuaries in Malawi has largely been a success story. For Lengwe, Nyika, Kasungu and Liwonde, as we have noted, all contain viable populations of the larger fauna, thus facilitating interesting 'game viewing'. But it must be recognized that although there is a strong advocacy by deep ecologists and wildlife conservationists for 'wilderness' areas, these areas are neither pristine, nor were they conceived to be purely for the benefit of the wildlife inhabitants, rather these sanctuaries were seen as beneficial to humans - for scientific, educational, recreational, even therapeutic purposes, as well as having economic benefits. Equally, what also has to be recognized is that these sanctuaries contribute very little to the well-being of local people - on the contrary, by restricting hunting and the utilization of the woodland for basic subsistence needs and in being a 'reservoir' of wild mammals which cause serious depredations to crops and human life, the sanctuaries cause much harm to local communities living in their vicinity. Small wonder, then, that the majority of rural people in Malawi have an antipathy, even a hostile attitude, towards such wildlife sanctuaries.

A recognition of this state of affairs has led many conservationists to suggest the need for a complete rethinking of wildlife conservation, even a change of attitude towards the African hunter, who as a 'poacher' has been maligned and criticized by wildlife conservationists for over half a century. One of the best accounts of this changing orientation towards conservation is Adams and McShane's *The Myth of Wild Africa* (1992), which is subtitled 'Conservation without illusion'. It is of particular interest because McShane spent four years undertaking wildlife research in Malawi, mainly at Vwaza Marsh reserve, and the study has a short chapter on poaching within this reserve (pp. 122-138, see also Thomson 1986: 167-176).

In recent years Africa, in the Western imagination, has become less of a 'dark continent' than one of the last remaining wilderness areas, and in the popular mind, as depicted by many books and by TV, Africa consists entirely of wide grassy plains filled with wild animals. It is portrayed 'as a glorious Eden for wildlife' which can serve as a kind of refuge from the rigours and stress of industrial and urban life. The 'myth of wild Africa' is seen by Adams and McShane as having its origins in the 19th century, and

175

as being expressed through two images, that of the 'Garden of Eden', a land tamed and subdued to recreate a paradise for humans, and that of the 'wilderness', an untouched, pristine landscape, unsullied by humans. They suggest that these two images reflect two very different attitudes to nature and wildlife. The first was expressed by such conservationists as Gifford Pinchot in the United States, for whom conservation implied the rational development and use of the earth and its resources for the good of humans, essentially it embodied anthropocentric values. The second was expressed by John Muir, the guru, along with Arne Naess, of the deep ecologists, who stressed the inherent values of the 'untouched' wilderness. African people of course, like social ecologists, advocate neither the control and dominion of nature, nor the celebration of the wilderness in its own right, but have always acknowledged the close *interdependence* of humans and its wildlife. The important point, of course, as Graham emphasized, is that Africa has never been a pristine wilderness, anymore in fact than was North America, which was peopled by American Indian communities long before the arrival of Columbus. Humans, on both continents, have long been an integral part of the landscape. Thus, as Adams and McShane write, the myth of Africa as a pristine wilderness, problematic from the onset, was an 'utter fallacy' by the mid 19th century with the advent of the Arab slave traders and European hunters and adventurers (1992: 17).

As with Graham, they stress the antipathetic attitudes of Europeans (missionaries, hunters and administrators alike) towards African hunting, and its contrast with the highly ritualized 'big-game' sport hunting of the Europeans. They conclude, 'The onslaught of white hunters, the imposition of game laws, the creation of parks and reserves and the spread of agriculture gradually reduced the importance of hunting in many African cultures. The key role hunting had played in shaping these cultures, and its continuing relevance in terms of the relationship between Africans and wildlife, was not generally recognized by Europeans' (1992: 31).

Important, however, is the recognition that African people have always lived in close proximity to wildlife, and that mammals are, in a real sense, a crucial part of their heritage. Hunting and the gathering of products from the woodland - firewood, poles, thatching grass, medicine, fungi - play a fundamental role, as I discuss elsewhere, in the everyday life of rural people in Malawi. Although there is a strong pragmatic emphasis in Malawian culture, and in their attitude to wildlife (meat {*nyama*} as in other African cultures carries the same 'meaning' as edible quadruped), this did not entail a Promethean attitude towards animals. In subsistence terms the interaction between humans and wild mammals was more one of equality, entailing a constant struggle by humans to subsist. Even the woodland itself, at an earlier period, was something that people endeavoured not to preserve, but to keep at bay, to fend off encroachment. Indeed, Graham goes so far as to suggest that it goes against human nature 'to give away land to wild animals' (1973: 45) and that Africans constantly, through burning and the cutting back of woodland vegetation, endeavoured to maintain a living space. He writes that for many Africans wild animals mean 'either meat or trouble', a concept that is very difficult for urban dwellers to understand, let alone experience (117). In the pre-colonial context, before the acquisition of muzzle-loading guns, he argues that humans and elephants vied with each other for territory. Ecologically, he suggests, and in terms of social organization, humans and elephants are very similar. Elephants and many communities in East Central Africa, have social groupings that are essentially matricentric, and both humans - as shifting cultivators - and elephants are extremely destructive to the woodland habitat. Even the life cycles of human and elephants are similar, for both have protracted childhoods, and are exceptionally long-lived species (Graham 1973: 97-98).

Graham's account is highly pessimistic, and seemingly critical of all forms of wildlife conservation - at least of the larger mammals. He appears to see no difference between the preservation of mammals for sport hunting and wildlife conservation - both, he feels, are expressions or sublimations of our inherent aggressive instincts. He emphasizes only the destructive aspects of human aggression, suggesting that humans are the most aggressive mammals on earth, while highlighting the distinction between aggression and predation (133). Thus Graham basically argues that 'No nation in history has succeeded in preserving game (i.e. larger mammals) among the people', so there is no reason to expect African countries to be any different (87).

What is also significant is that when game reserves and parks were established in Malawi - as elsewhere in Africa - they largely followed the pattern of the United States national parks, such as Yellowstone and Yosemite. Muir, of course, was instrumental in the creation of Yosemite. In these parks no hunting or any other economic activities were allowed, and the parks were treated as wilderness areas - although, of course, they were nothing of the kind. Dee Brown records that in 1877, five years after the Yellowstone area had been made into the first 'National park' and while the first American tourists were admiring its natural wonders as a 'wilderness', General William Sherman was pursuing several hundred Nez Perce

Indians through the park (Brown 1971; 258, Graham 1973; 195). As we have noted earlier, the creation of many of Malawi's national parks, and thus the establishment of so-called 'wilderness' areas entailed the forceful removal by government - both colonial and post-colonial - of several hundred people who lived in the area. None of these areas were pristine or untouched.

The pattern of national parks first developed in the United States, was later taken up by the International Union for the Conservation of Nature and Natural Resources, based in Switzerland. And it is this pattern that was largely advocated by conservation agencies, and implemented by governments. The result, as one observer put it, has been a 'bizarre situation', in which 'Africans are hired, trained and armed to guard African parks to keep out African people, for the benefit of both the protected animals and the foreigners who come to see them - and of course for the tourist revenue, which goes into government or hotel bank accounts, not to rural people' (Timberlake 1985: 160).

Adams and McShane echo these sentiments, suggesting that the mode of establishing parks in Africa has resulted in a park surrounded by people who were excluded from the planning of the area, do not understand its purpose, receive little or no benefit from the money poured into its creation, and hence do not support its existence' (1992: XV).

They conclude that the notion of 'wilderness' does not apply to the African context, for human and animals have evolved together in the continents diverse eco-systems. They also maintain that African countries have, historically, successfully co-existed with wild animals, although, of course, this has only been the case where human populations have been relatively low and sparsely distributed. But given the current antipathy of local people towards game sanctuaries, in Malawi as elsewhere in Africa, their main contention is that such sanctuaries will eventually be over-run by people in their need for land, unless the national parks serve, or at least are not inimical to, the well-being of local people. Conservation and development thus need to go hand-in-hand, as part of a single process, for 'conservation cannot ignore the needs of human beings, while development that runs roughshord over the environment is doomed' (1992: X1X).

Adams and McShane give a graphic account of the conflict between game scouts and local people living near Lake Kanuri in Vwaza Marsh Game Reserve where an angry mob of local villagers killed two game scouts. They also relate the life and times of one local hunter - poacher - Joshua Nyirenda. Armed with an 1844 Tower musket, a relic of the Arab slave trade, he was arrested with three other men for hunting elephant in the reserve. As a second offence he was fined $500 or five years hard labour. Unable to pay the fine - the annual income for a farm worker in Malawi in 1990 was only $176 - Joshua went to prison. What is of interest about their account - quite unique among conservationists and wildlife officers - is that they sympathise with the hunter's predicament, and acknowledge the crucial importance of subsistence hunting in the local economy and to the very livelihood of men like Nyirenda. The 'poacher' is no longer depicted as a 'villain' - the origins of this term is worth reflecting upon in this present context - and Adams and McShane suggest that conservationsists are gradually coming to realize the 'futility of waging constant war against poachers' (1992: 130).

These authors therefore conclude that a completely 'new approach' is needed towards wildlife conservation, one which ensures that the benefits derived from conservation are directed more towards the needs and well-being of local rural communities. 'Conservation will either contribute to solving the problems of the rural poor who live day to day with wild animals, or those wild animals will disappear' (1992: X1X).

The person who, perhaps, more than anyone else, has been responsible for this changing orientation in conservation, is Richard Bell. Like McShane, Bell spent many years in Malawi as a wildlife research officer. His essay (1987) on 'Conservation with a human face' is, in fact, seminal.

In the contemporary literature and media there are two images of Africa that are widely circulated. One image, emphasized by tourist agencies in particular, depicts Africa, as we have noted, as a garden of Eden or a wilderness area teeming with wildlife and suggestions are made to keep parts of this Africa in its 'pristine' state for the good of future generations. This wilderness concept was well expressed by Bernard Grzimek and Laurens van der Post. Grzimek was an avowed and passionate advocate of African wildlife conservation in the early post-war period. In his classics like *Serengeti Shall Not Die* (1960), which he co-authored with his son Michael, who was tragically killed in a plane crash in 1959, and is patterned significantly like a zebra skin, Grzimek portrayed the African plains as a wilderness. It was 'eternal' nature, with great herds of wild animals, untouched by humans. This Africa was 'dying' - and so much of Africa, he tells us, was already dead - but small parts of Africa, like the Serengeti, must be retained in its 'awe-filled past glory'. He argued that a national park, to be effective, must be a 'primordial wilderness' and that no humans, certainly not Africans, should be allowed to live within its boundaries. That there were any wild animals at all in the Serengeti was largely because the Masai people who lived in the area had changed its landscape

179

and co-existed with the larger mammals for several centuries. But this was lost on Grzimek. He was utterly opposed to granting grazing rights to the Masai, and failed to see that the idea of striking a balance between wildlife and human needs 'was a constructive and creative approach' to wildlife conservation (Adams and McShane 1992: XV1, 50-53, Collett 1987). Laurens van der Post, that bête noire of many anthropologists, had an equally romantic idea of Africa as a 'wilderness'. He had spent much time, he writes, in the 'wilderness', having been born in South Africa. 'Wilderness' for van der Post was a 'way to truth', it was an 'instrument' for enabling urban people, who are 'estranged from nature', to recover their 'lost capacity for religious experience' as well as to regain contact with their 'natural selves', the 'hunter side' of our being - to which we need to 'return' (in Martin and Inglis 1984: 12-14).

This expresses a nostalgia for a past that never existed, for as we noted earlier, the notion that Africa was a pristine wilderness is a 'myth'. As with deep ecologists in the United States (cf. McKibben 1990), neither Grzimek nor van der Post recognized the existence of local people in their search for a 'lost harmony' with nature. Africans are effaced in their 'wilderness vision'. Unfortunately, much of conservation has been directed towards sustaining this image of Africa as a yet 'unspoilt Eden' (Anderson and Grove 1987: 4).

The other image of Africa is quite different. It depicts Africa as in crisis - both politically and ecologically. The image we thus have of Africa, as portrayed through the media, is one where political violence and repression, famine, civil wars, and ecological degradation are ubiquitous, and for some political analysts and conservationists the situation is hopeless. Nowhere on the continent, one political commentator, wrote, is there a 'flicker of hope'. Although Africa does indeed have its problems - like the rest of the world - Patrick Chabal (1992) has countered, as far as politics is concerned, this is a biased and highly prejudiced image. Richard Bell has attempted to do the same with regard to the alleged ecological crisis.

Africa, according to many commentators is facing 'environmental bankruptcy'. It is 'dying' through ill-advised attempts to modernize itself, and such development has led to famine, soil erosion, desertification, and ecological degradation. Africa is held to be in 'crisis', and on the brink of ecological collapse (Timberlake 1985). Again, although Africa does have serious ecological problems that need to be addressed, Bell suggests that this scenario is overdrawn and misleading. Bell points out that although the human population in Africa is indeed increasing rapidly, the continent has still not reached its ecological carrying capacity, and that surveys have indicated that a considerable area of usable land is available. When Europeans encountered Africa at the outset of the colonial period, they encountered a human population probably smaller than it had been since the iron-age revolution some two millenia earlier, due to the slave trade, the introduction of diseases, and the rinderpest pan-endemic which raged through the continent in the 1890s. As human and livestock populations were reduced to a low ebb, Bell writes, so wildlife and its habitats expanded - a situation that was perpetrated by much of the colonial conservation legislation (1987: 89). As regards to famines, when these are not related to droughts, then Bell suggests, they are invariably associated with civil disturbances or are related to political and economic rather than to ecological issues. With respect to the availability of land, Bell points out that although Malawi is the fifth most densely populated country in Africa, some 33% of the land area is under 'natural vegetation', over and above the national parks and game reserves (11%), forest reserves (9%), agriculture (36%) and urban developments (11%). Except on a local basis, such figures suggest that Africa is not facing an immediate shortage of arable land. The figures also indicate a high degree of commitment by the Malawian government to wildlife conservation, and a similar pattern is found in Botswana, Zambia and Tanzania where over 10% of their land area has been allocated to wildlife sanctuaries.

The primary objectives of the World Conservation Strategy, outlined by the International Union for the Conservation of Nature and Natural Resources (IUCN) in 1980, were as follows:
1) to maintain essential ecological processes and life-support systems;
2) to preserve genetic diversity
3) to ensure the sustainable utilisation of species and ecosystems.

Bell argues that there is an inevitable conflict between short-term individual interests and long-term communal needs, and that the costs and benefits of conservation are not equally shared between the different sectors of a society. The administration of conservation programmes, in terms of management and costs, is the concern of national governments, who also enjoy the international prestige, and most of the revenue derived from wildlife resources. The benefit of recreational and aesthetic experience, Bell writes, as well as scientific opportunities are enjoyed mainly by foreigners. However, local communities who bear most of the *cost* of having wildlife sanctuaries, derive few benefits from conservation. Moreover, the World Conservation Strategy and conservation bodies tend to stress the indirect, utilitarian values that can be derived from conservation - for

181

example, the preservation of genetic diversity is justified on grounds of its potential as a source of useful products. Such stress is probably due to the fact that aesthetic and long-term ecological values are felt to carry insufficient weight with government and local communities. But, as with the 'Master Plan' for Malawian wildlife, Bell argues that the emphasis on the utilitarian justification of conservation is opportunistic and potentially counter-productive. He writes, 'If conservation is justified on the grounds of utilitarian benefits, anything that produces more of those benefits, must take precedence over conservation' (1987: 81).

The reality of the conflict between conservation and local interests is also emphasized by Bell, who notes that most conservation agencies are paramilitary organizations, with armed and uniformed game guards, and that a good deal of expenditure is devoted to law enforcement and public relations. We have noted the serious conflict that exists on the boundaries of almost all the game sanctuaries in Malawi, and Bell remarks that under existing 'game laws', normal rural existence is impossible without breaking the law. In Malawi around 500 persons a year are charged with wildlife offences, and in many African countries there are serious armed conflicts between poachers and those enforcing the wildlife legislation.

In such circumstances Bell advocates a more flexible and liberal approach to conservation, one that aims to reduce the conflict between short-term individual interests, and long-term communal needs, and which seriously takes into account the needs of local communities, and the unequal benefits and costs of wildlife conservation (1987: 90). It is this more flexible approach that is advocated by Adams and McShane (1992).

Bell recognized that many species of the larger mammals in Africa are incompatible with most forms of agricultural development, even though pastoralists and wildlife may happily co-exist if the human population is not too high. We have noted the animals that cause most of the depredations to crops and human life in Malawi: elephant, buffalo, bushpig, hippopotamus, hyena, lion, crocodile, baboons and, in some situations, the larger antelopes. Bell thus acknowledged that the integration of wildlife conservation - he suggested that the allocation of at least 5% of the land area of a country to conservation, in the form of national parks, would be sufficient to meet the objectives of the World Conservation Strategy - with other forms of land use, particularly agriculture, had always been a 'chronic problem' in Africa. Its solution entailed two strategies. The first was the *protection* of people and their cultivations from depredations through controlled hunting, the creation of 'buffer zones', and the development of electric fencing - all of which had been tried in Malawi with varying degrees of success. The second strategy aiming to reduce the conflict between local communities and wildlife was to ensure that the revenues earned by conservation areas (that is, from tourism, professional hunting or culling), should be explicitly fed back into the communities that largely bore the cost of the conservation area. Such revenue allocation schemes have been tried in Zimbabwe and Zambia. The funds often went, however, to district administrations rather than to the local communities near the conservation areas who carried the bulk of the costs. Moreover, such local communities did not participate in decision-making, nor did they derive any aesthetic benefits from conservation. But rather 'they are being treated as a nuisance that is being bribed to keep quiet' (1987: 93). Thus Bell advocated a more radical proposal, namely that local communities living in the vicinity of the conservation areas should be allocated concessions enabling them to use wildlife resources in certain areas, and that conservation agencies should act as marketing agents for their products. Bell noted that in 1981 poachers in Malawi were obtaining about $10 per kg for ivory, which at the time was fetching at least $50 per kg on the world market. If, in this situation, he suggests, the conservation agency purchased ivory from the hunter for, say, $30 per kg, 'all parties would benefit, while the reward would be targeted precisely to that sector of society paying the costs of lost opportunities' (93). It would be a mistake, however, to suggest that local people's interest in wildlife is only utilitarian - although this is clearly important for subsistence cultivators - and that they can thus be 'bought off' with development schemes or the allocation of revenues derived from the conservation areas.

Although, as we have seen, conservation areas tend to be the 'playgrounds' or 'recreational areas' of rich tourists, there is evidence to suggest that wildlife sanctuaries have an aesthetic appeal to local Malawians, although the costs and difficulties of transport and accommodation make visits to these sanctuaries impossible for the average Malawian. Both Bell, and Adams and McShane emphasize the fact that rural communities will only tend to support wildlife conservation when they not only derive some benefits from it - to offset the costs - but also become participants in the process of conservation. They fear that simply protecting wildlife for the benefits of rich European tourists, will, in the long term, be disastrous - quite apart from its failure to meet the needs of the local communities. Unless local people support conservation projects and areas, by participating in their management, and receiving some material benefits from them, then it is felt that the African national parks will not long survive. Bell cites the Campfire Project in Zimbabwe (Communal Areas Management

Programme for Indigenous Resources) and the Luangwa Integrated Resource Development Project (LIRDP), as two projects combining conservation and local community development that are worthy of consideration in terms of future wildlife conservation in Africa (for these projects see Martin 1986, Adams and McShane 1992: 105-107, 178-183; for earlier discussion on the conservation of mammals in Africa see Eltringham 1979: 207-46, Delany and Happold 1979: 364-95).

Long ago, Keith Eltringham remarked that in general 'wild animals and agriculture do not mix' (1979: 213). This is no doubt true, but what is surely needed in Malawi is the maintenance of wildlife sanctuaries that benefits not only visiting tourists but also local people, and which will ensure the 'co-existence' of humans and wildlife, for the mutual well being of both.

REFERENCES

Abdallah, Y.B. 1973 *The Yaos* (ed) M. Sanderson Orig. 1919 London: Cassell

Adams, J.S. and T.S. McShane 1992 *The Myth of Wild Africa* New York: Norton

Alpers, E.A. 1967 'North of the Zambezi' in R. Oliver (ed) *The Middle Age of African History* pp 78-84 London: Oxford University Press

Alpers, E.A. 1968 The Mutapa and Malawi Political Systems in T.O. Ranger (ed) *Aspects of Central African History*, pp 1-28 London: Heinemann

Alpers, E.A. 1969 'Trade, State and Society Among the Yao of the Nineteenth Century' *Journal of African History* 10, 405-420

Alpers, E.A. 1975 *Ivory and Slaves in East Central Africa* London: Heinemann

Anderson, D. and R. Grove 1987 (eds) *Conservation in Africa: People, Policies and Practice* Cambridge University Press

Ansell, W.F.H. 1960 *Mammals of Northern Rhodesia* Lusaka: Government Printers

Ansell, W.F.H. 1962 'Notes on some Mammals of Nyasaland and Adjacent Areas' *Nyasaland Journal* 15; 38-54

Ansell, W.F.H. and R.j. Dowsett 1988 *Mammals of Malawi an Annotated Check List and Atlas*, St Ives: Trendrine Press

Baker, C.A. 1970 *Johnston's Administration 189197* Zomba: Government Press

Baker, C.A. 1971 'Malawi's Exports: an Economic History' in B. Pachai (ed) *Malawi: Past and Present* pp 88-113 Blantyre: Claim

Balestra, F.A. 1962 'The Man-eating Hyenas of Mulanje' *African Wildlife* 16; 25-27

Barbier, E.B. et al 1990 *Elephants, Economics and Ivory* London: Earthscan Publishers

Barnard, A. 1992 *Hunters and Herders of Southern Africa* Cambridge University Press

Beachey, R.W 1962 'The Arms Trade in East Africa in the Late 19th Century' *Journal of African History* 3/3; 45167

Beachey, R.W 1967 'The East African Ivory Trade in the 19th Century' *Journal of African History* 8/2; 269-90

Beeson M. 1989 'The Origins of Barkstripping by Blue Monkeys (Cercopithecus mitis)' *Journal of Linnean Society* 91; 265-91

Beeson M. 1989 'Seasonal Dietary Stress in a Forest Monkey (Cercopithecus mitis)' *Oecologia* 78; 565-70

Bell, R.H.V. 1981 Notes on the Nyala Situation in Lengwe National Park WRU 1/50/6 Kasungu

Bell, R.H.V. 1983 Information Handbook: Kasungu National Park Lilongwe: Department of National Parks and Wildlife (DNPW)

Bell, R.H.V. 1987 'Conservation with a Human Face' in D. Anderson and R. Grove (ed) (1987) *Conservation in Africa*, Cambridge University Press; 79-101

Bell, R.H.V. and H. Jachmann 1984 'The Influence of Fire and the Use of *Brachystegia* Woodland by Elephant' *African Journal of Ecology* 22, 157-163

Benson, C.W. 1968 'The Alleged Record of Chimpanzee Pan satyrus in Malawi' *Society of Malawi Journal* 1. 21/1; 7-12

Boeder, R.B. 1982 ,Malawi, Land and Legend' *Society of Malawi Journal* 1. 35/2; 52-65

Bosman, P. and A. Hall-Martin 1986 *Elephants of Africa* Cape Town Struik

Brown, D. 1971 *Bury my Heart at Wounded Knee* London: Pan

Bruwer, J. 1950 'Note on Maravi Origin and Migration' *African Studies* 9; 32-34

Buchanan, J. 1885 *The Shire Highlands* Blantyre Printing and Publications (1982 edition)

Bulala, A. 1991 European Agriculture in the Namwera Area of Mangochi 1918, University of Malawi, Chancellor College: History Seminar Paper

Cambridge Mulanje Expedition 1957 Gerteral Report Cambridge University

Campbell, W.Y. n.d *Travellers' Records of Portuguese Nyasaland* London: King

Carr, N. 1969 *The White Impala* London: Collins

Carter, J. 1987 *Malawi: Wildlife Parks and Reserves* London: Macmillan

Cater, J.C. 1954 *The Nyika Plateau, Nyasaland Oryx* 2/5. Reprinted in F. & R. Dorward 1993 *The Nyika Experience* pp 5-9 Blantyre Wildlife Soc. Malawi

Chabal, P. *1992 Power in Africa* London: MacMillan

Chapman, J.D. 1995 *The Mulanje Cedar* Blantyre: The Society of Malawi

Chibambo, Y.M. 1942 *My Ngoni of Nyasaland* (Trans. C. Stuart) London: Lutterworth

Chimimba, C. 1980 Notes on Mbewa, personal communication

Chiwona, E.A. 1990 An Investigation of Western Uplands Potential for Ranching (Lengwe) Kasungu: WRU 1/50/6

Clark, J.D. 1959 'Rock Art in Nyasaland' in R. Summers (ed) *The Rock Art of the Federation of Rhodesia and Nyasaland* pp 163-221 Salisbury; National Publications Trust

Clark, J.D. 1972 'Prehistoric Origins' in B. Pachai (ed) *The Early History of Malawi*, London: Longman; 17-27

Clark, J.D. and C.V. Haynes 1970 'An Elephant Butchery Site at Mwanganda's Village, Karonga and its Relevance for Palaeolithic Archaeology' *World Archaeology* 1; 390-411

Clarke, J.E. 1983 Principal Master Plan for National Parks and Wildlife Management, Lilongwe: DNPW

Cole-King, P.A. 1972 *Mangochi - the Mountain, the People, the Fort*, Zomba: Department of Antiquities, Publication No. 12

Collett, D. 1987 'Pastoralists and Wildlife: Image and Reality in Kenya Maasiland' in D. Anderson and R. Grove (ed) *Conservation in Africa*; 129-148 Cambridge University Press

Colville, A. 1911 *1000 Miles in a Machila* London: Scott

Coudenhove, H. 1925 *My African Neighbours: Man, Bird and Beast in Nyasaland* London: Cape

Crader, D.C. 1984 *Hunters in Iron Age Malawi* Lilongwe: Department of Antiquities Publication No. 21

Crawshay, R 1890 'On the Antelopes of Nyasaland' *Proc. Zool. Soc.* London; 648-663

Curtin, P. 1978 *African History* London: Longman

Darwin T.M. 1982 'Bark Stripping Damage by Baboons on Dedza Mt., Zomba: Forestry Research Institutte of Malawi (FRIM) Report 82031

'1984 Blue Monkeys on Zomba Mountain' *Nyala* 10; 25-28

Dasgupta, K.K. 1990 *In Search of the Central African Past* Ndola: Prinpak

Debenham, F 1955 *Nyasaland: the Land of the Lake* London: HMSO

Delany, M.J. 1975 *The Rodents of Uganda* London: British Museum of Natural History

Delany, M.J and D.C.D. Happold 1979 *Ecology of African Mammals* London: Longman

Deodatus, F.D. and A. Lipiya 1990 Wildlife Pest Impact around Kasungu National Park, Lilongwe DNPW/FAO Field Doc. No. 10

Deodatus, F.D. and A. Lipiya 1991 Public Relations and Crop Protection Lilongwe DNPW/FAO Field Doc. No. 19

Department of Antiquities 1971 Oral Records, Zomba: National Archives

Dewar, R.J. 1993 The Nyika Plateau: Some Reminiscences and Observations in_F. and R. Dorward (ed) 1993 *The Nyika Experience* pp 10-13 Blantyre: Wildlife Society of Malawi

Dorward, F. and R. 1993 *The Nyika Experience* Blantyre: Wildlife Society Malawi

Dowsett, R.J. and N.D. Hunter 1980 'Birds and Mammals of Mangochi Mt.' *Nyala* 6; 518

Drummond, H. 1889 *Tropical Africa*, London: Hodder and Stoughton

Dudley, C.O. 1979 'History of the Declines of the Larger Mammals of the Lake Chilwa Basin' *Soc. Mal. J.* 32/2; 27-41

Dudley, C.O. and P. Osborne 1980 The Lengwe National Park Game Count 1979 *Nyala* 6; 39-46

Dudley, C.O. and D. Stead 1976 'Liwonde National Park: Part 1 Introduction' *Nyala* 2; 17-31, Part 2 The Mammals Nyala 31; 29-40

Duff H. 1903 *Nyasaland under the Foreign Office* London: Bell

Duff H. 1932 *African Small Chop* London: Hodder and Stoughton

Dyer, M. 1986 Seasonal Distribution and Abundance of Large Mammals on the High Central Plateau of Nyika National Park, Lilongwe: Report DNPW

Ebner, E. 1987 *The History of the Wangoni* Peramiho: Benedictine Publications

Elmslie, W.A. 1901 *Among the Wild Angoni* Edinburgh: Oliphant Anderson

Eltringham, S.K. 1979 *The Ecology and Conservation of Large African Mammals* London: Macmillan

Evans, P.G.H. 1979 'Habitat Preferences of Ungulates in Closed Savanna of Central Africa' *Mammal Review* 1; 19-32

Fagan, B. 1965 *Southern Africa during the Iron Age* London: Thames and Hudson

Faulkner, H. 1868 *Elephant Haunts* London: Hurst & Blackett (1984 Reprint Society of Malawi)

Fitter, R. and P. Scott 1978 *The Penitent Butchers* London: Collins

Fraser, D. 1923 *African Idylls*, London: Seeley

Gamitto, A.C.P. 1960 *King Kasembe and the Marave, Cheva, Bisa Bemba Lunda and Other Peoples of Southern Africa (Expedition 1831-32)* 2 vols (ed I. Cunnison) Lisbon: Estudios de Clencias Politicas e Sociais

Graham, A.D. 1973 *The Gardeners of Eden*, London: Allen and Unwin

Gray, R. and D. Birmingham (ed) 1970 *Pre-Colonial African Trade* Oxford University Press

Guerirt, J. 1985 *A Concise English-Chichewa Dictionary* 2 vols Lilongwe: White Fathers

Hall, M. 1987 *The Changing Past: Farmers, Kings and Traders in Southern Africa, 200-1860*, Cape Town: David Philip

Hall-Martin, A.J. 1977 'The Influence of Man and Wildlife on Rift Valley Communities of Malawi' *Nyala* 3; 3-32

Hamilton, R.A. 1955 (ed) *History and Archaeology in Africa*, London: School of Oriental and African Studies

Hanney, P. 1962 Observations upon the Food of the Barn Owl in Southern Nyasaland *Annals and Magazine of Natural History* 6; 305-313

Hanney, P. 1965 The Muridae of Malawi *Journal of Zoological Society* 146; 577-633

Happold, D.C. and M. Happold 1985 'The Natural History of Bats in Malawi' *Nyala* 11; 57-62

Happold, D.C. and M. Happold 1986 'Small Mammals of Zomba Plateau, Malawi' *African Journal of Ecology* 24; 77-87

Happold, D.C. 1987 Small Mammals in Pine Plantations and Natural Habitats on Zomba Plateau, *Malawi Journal of Applied Ecology* 24; 253-67

Happold, D.C. 1989 'The Mammals of Zomba' *Nyala* 14/l; 5-20

Happold, D.C. 1991 Ecological Study of Small Rodents in Thicket-clump Savanna of Lengwe National Park *Journal of Zoological Society* 223; 527-47

Happold, D.C., M. Happold and J.E. Hill 1987 'The Bats of Malawi' *Mammalia* 51; 357-414

Hargreaves, B.J. 1984 The Ten (or Fifty) Primates of Malawi *Soc. Mal J.* 37/2; 24-38

Hawkins, E.L 1930 Notes on Game Distribution in Nyasaland, Kasungu WRU 55/9/0

Hayes, G.D. 1948 'The Nyala in Nyasaland' *Nyasaland Journal* 1/l; 37-38

Hayes, G.D. 1954 'The Mijeti' *Oryx* 2/5; 294-98

Hayes, G.D. 1967 'How Independence saved an African Reserve' *Oryx* 91; 24-27

Hayes, G.D. 1972 'Wildlife Conservation in Malawi' *The Society of Malawi Journal* 25/2; 22-31

Hayes, G.D. 1974 'Conservation in Malawi - Old and New' *Oryx* 12; 334-340

Hayes, G.D. 1978 *A Guide to Malawi's National Parks and Game Reserves* Limbe: Montford Press

Hetherwick, A. 1902 *A Handbook of the Yao Language* London: SPCK

Hough, J. 1989 *Malawi's National Parks and Game Reserves* Blantyre: Wildlife Society of Malawi

Hunter, N. 1978 'G.D. Hayes and the NFPS' *Nyala* 4/2; 67-75

Hutson, J.A. 1977 'The Lengwe Game Counts 1967-1977' *Nyala* 3; 14-28

Jachmann, H. 1984 'Assessment of Elephant Numbers in Nkhotakota Reserve' *Nyala* 10; 33-38

Jachmann, H. 1984 'Status of the Mwabvi Rhino' *Nyala* 10; 77-90

Jachmann, H. 1986 'Notes on the Population Dynamics of Kasungu Elephants' *African Journal of Ecology* 24; 215-226

Johnson, S.A. 1995 *A Visitor's Guide to Nyika National Park, Malawi* Blantyre: Mbabzi Book Trust

Johnston, H.H. 1897 *British Central Africa* New York: Methuen

Kandawire J.A.K. 1980 'Mwabvi Game Reserve and Land Use' Lilongwe: Report DNPW

Kandawire J.A.K. 1982 'The Political Economy of Game Reserves in Southern Malawi' *Journal of Social Science* (Zomba) 9: 51-66

Kalinga, O.J.M. 1984 'The Balowoka and the Established States West of Lake Malawi' in A.I. Salim 1984 (ed) *State Formation in Eastern Africa* pp 36-52 Nairobi: Heinemann

Kelly, D. et al 1993 'Aah but those Elephants David Kelley Paints at Liwonde' Blantyre: Wildlife Society of Malawi

Kershaw, P.S. 1922 'On a Collection of Mammals from Vhiromo and Cholo, Nyasaland', *Annals and Magazine of Natural History* 10; 177-192

King, M. and E. 1992 *The Story of Medicine and Disease in Malawi* Blantyre: Montford Press

Kitchen R.W.F and A. 1978 'Some Observations on the Dwarf Mongoose in the Central Region' *Nyala* 4; 101-2

Kjekshus, H. 1977 *Ecological Control and Economic Development in East African History* London: Heinemann

Kombe, A. 1983 'Governmental and Public Reactions to Culling in Conservation Areas in Malawi' in R.N. Owen-Smith (ed) *Management of Large Mammals in African Conservation Areas* Pretoria: Heinemann Educational Publications

Lambrecht, F.L. 1970 'Aspects of Evolution and Ecology of Tsetse Flies and Trypanosomiasis in Prehistoric African Environment' in J.D. Fage and R.A. Oliver (ed) *Papers in African Prehistory*, Cambridge University Press; 87-96

Langworthy, H. 1972 'Chewa or Malawl Political Organisation in the Precolonial Era' in B.Pachai (ed) *The.Early History of Malawi*, London: Longman; 104-122

Langworthy, H. 1975 'Central Malawi in the 19th Century in R.J. MacDonald (ed) *From Nyasaland to Malawi*, Nairobi: E. African Publishing House; 1-43

Lemon, P.C. 1968 'Biology of Zebra on Nyika Plateau' *Society of Malawi Journal* 21 /l; 13-19

Liggit, B. 1979 'In Quest of Rhino' *Nyala* 5; 97-103

Linden, I. 1974 *Catholics, Peasants and Chewa Resistance in Nyasaland 1889-1939* London: Heinemann

Livingstone, D. and C. 1865 *Narrative of an Expedition to the Zambezi and its Tributaries 1858-1864* (Popular edition 1887) London: J. Murray

Long, R.C. 1973 'A List with Notes of the Mammals of Nsanje District' *Society of Malawi Journal* 26/1; 60-77

Loveridge, A. and B. Lawrence 1953 'Zological Results of a Fifth Expedition to East Africa, 1: Mammals from Nyasaland and Tete' *Bulletin of Museum of Comparative Zoology* (Harvard University) 110; 1-80

Loveridge, A. 1954 *I drank the Zambezi* London: Lutterworth

Lyell, D.D. 1912 *Nyasaland for the Hunter and Settler* London: Cox

Lyons, M. 1992 *The Colonial Disease: a Social History of Sleeping Sickness in Northern Zaire 1890-1940* Cambridge University Press

McCracken, J. 1968 'The Nineteenth Century in Malawi' in T.O. Ranger (ed) *Aspects of Central African History* pp 97-111 London, Heinemann

McCracken, J. 1982 'Peasants, Planters and the Colonial State: The Case of Malawi 1905-1940' *Journal of East African Research and Development* 12; 21-35

McCracken, J. 1987 'Colonialism, Capitalism and Ecological Crisis in Malawi: a Reassessment' in D. Anderson and R. Grove (ed) *Conservation in Africa* pp 63-78 Cambridge University Press

MacDonald, D. 1882 *Africana; or the Heart of Heathern Africa* 2 Vols Edinburgh: J. Menzies

MacDonald, R.J. 1975 (ed) *From Nyasaland to Malawi* Nairobi: E. African Publishing House

McKelvey, J.J. 1973 *Man against Tsetse: Struggle for Africa* Ithaca: Cornell University Press

MacKenzie, J.M. 1988 *The Empire of Nature: Hanting, Conservation and British Imperialism* Manchester University Press

McKibben, B. 1990 *The End of Nature* Harmondsworth: Penguin

MacMillan, H. 1975 'The African Lakes Company and the Makololo 1878-1884' in R.J. MacDonald (ed) *From Nyasaland to Malawi* pp 65-85 Nairobi: E. African Publishing House

MacPherson, D.W.K. 1973 'Wild Life of the Central Regions' *Society of Malawi Journal* 26/2; 48-55

McShane, T.O, 1985 Vwaza Marsh Game Reserve: a Baseline Ecological Survey, Lilongwe: DNPW

McShane, T.O. and E. McShane-Caluzi 1988 The Habitats, Birds and Mammals of Vwaza Marsh Game Reserve *Nyala* 12; 3966

Mandala, E.C. 1990 *Work and Control in a Peasant Economy* Madison: University of Wisconsin Press

Mann, M. 1986 *The Sources of Social Power* Cambridge University Press

Martin, R.B. 1986 'Communal Area Management Plan for Indicenous Resources (Project Campfire)' in R.H.V. Bell and E. McShane-Caluzi (ed) *Conservation and Wildlife Management in Africa* Washington: U.S. Peace Corps

Martin, V. and M. Inglis 1984 *Wilderness the Way Forward* Forres: Findhorn Press

Maugham, R.C.F. 1910 *Zambezia: General Description of the Valley of the Zambezi River* London: Murray

Muagham, R.C.F.1914 *Wild Game in Zambezia* London: Murray

Metcalf, M. 1956 'Some Rock Paintings in Nyasaland' *Nyasaland Journal* 9/l.; 58-70

Mgomezulu, G. 1983 'The Animal Community and Man's Changing Hunting Habits in the Linthipe Area' *Nyala* 9; 39-56

Mitchell, B.L. 1946 'A Naturalist in Nyasaland' *Nyasaland Agricultural Quarterly Journal* 6; 123, 25-47

Mitchell, B.L. 1950 'Some Reptiles and Amphibians of Malawi' *Nyasaland Journal* 3/2; 46-57

Mitchell, B.L. 1953 'Game Preservation in Nyasaland' *Nyasaland Journal* 6/2; 37-51

Mitchell, B.L. and C.S. Holliday 1960 'A New Primate from Nyasaland' *Southern African Journal of Science* 56; 215-222

Mitchell, B.L. and B Steele 1956 *A Report on the Distribution of Tsetse Flies in Nyasaland* Zomba: Government Printers

Mkanda, F.X. and H.S. Jamusana 1990 'People Participation in Wildlife Management: Report of a Tour of Zimbabwe', Lilongwe: DNPW

Mkandawire, J.M. 1983 'Reason for Establishment and Principal Objectives: Nyika National Park and Vwaza Game Reserve', Liwonde: DNPW

Moir, F.L.M. 1923 *After Livingstone: An African Trade Romance* London: Hodder & Stoughton

Morris, B. 1962 'A Denizen of the Evergreen Forest' *African Wildlife* 16; 121

Morris, B. 1963 'Notes on the Giant Rat in Nyasaland' *African Wildlife* 17; 103-8

Morris, B. 1964 'Mammals of Zoa Estate, Cholo' *Nyasaland Journal* 17; 71-78

Morris, B. 1970 'The Nature and Origin of *Brachystegia* Woodland' *Commonwealth Forestry Review* 49; 155-58

Morris, B. 1970 *Epiphytic Orchids of Malawi* Blantyre: The Society of Malawi

Morris, B. 1982 *Forest Traders* London: Athlone Press

Morris, B. 1993 'Mbewa: Ethnozoological Notes on the Rats and Mice of Malawi' *Nyala* 17/1; 7-16

Morris, B. 1993 'The End of Nature and the Bioregional Vision' *Antichrist Studies* 1: 59-65

Morris, B. 1995a 'Woodland and Village: Reflections on the Animal Estate in Rural Malawi' *Journal of the Royal Anthrological Institute* 1/2; 301-15

Morris, B. 1995b 'Wildlife Depredation in Malawi: The Historical Dimension' *Nyala* 18; 17-24

Morris, B. 1998 *The Power of Animals* Oxford: Berg

Morris, B. 2000 *Animals and Ancestors* Oxford: Berg

Morris, B. 2002 'Nyau and Rock Art in Malawi' *Society of Malawi Journal* SS: 31-41

Mossman, A.S. 1969 'Wildlife outside the Nature Reserves: Wildlife Survey of Malawi', Lilongwe: DNPW

Msiska, A.W.C. 1995 'The Spread of Islam in Malawi and its Impact on Yao Rites of Passage 1870-1960' *Society of Malawi Journal* 9-86

Muldoon, G. 1955 *Leopards in the Night* London: Hart-Davis

Muldoon, G. 1957 *The Trumpeting Herd* London: Hart-Davis

Munthali, S.M. 1990 'MalawI Report on Wildlife-based Tourism in the SADCC Region', Kafue Zambia: SADCC/GTZ Workshop Proceedings

Munthali, S.M. and H.M. Banda 1985 'Public Attitudes towards Culling of Nyala and Warthog in Lengwe National Park' *Nyala* 11; 73-82

Murray, S.S. 1922 *A Handbook of Nyasaland* (Also 1932) London: Crown Agents

Mutwira, R. 1989 'Southern Rhodesia Wildlife Policy 1890-1953', *Journal of Southern African Studies* 15/2; 25162

Newitt, M.D.D. 1973 *Portuguese Settlement on the Zambezi* London: Longmans

Newitt, M.D.D. 1982 'The Early History of the Maravi' *Journal of African History* 23; 145-162

Newitt, M.D.D. 1995 *A History of Mozambique* London: Hurst

Ntara, S.J. 1973 *The History of the Chewa* (ed) B. Heintze Weisbaden, F. Steiner

Nurse, G.D. 1967 'The Name Akafula' *Society of Malawi Journal* 20/2; 17-22

Nurse, G.D. 1968 'Bush Roots and Nyanja Ideophones' *Soc. Mal. J.* 21/1- 50-57

Nurse, G.D. 1972 The People of Bororo in B. Pachal (ed) *The Early History of Malawi* pp 123-135 London: Longman

Nyirenda, S. 1931 History of the Tumbuka-Henga People (trans T.C. Young) *Bantu Studies* 5; 1-77

Oliver R. 1957 *Sir Harry Johnston and the Scramble for Africa* London: Chatto & Windus

Oliver R. 1991 *The African Experience* London: Pimlico

Pachai, B. 1972 (ed) *The Early History of Malawi* London: Longman

Pachai B. 1973 *Malawi: The History of the Nation* London: Longman

Pachai B. 1978 *Land and Politics in Malawi 1875-1975* Kingston, Ontario: Limestone Press

Parker, I.S.C. 1976 *Black Rhinocerus and Other Large Mammals in Mwabvi Game Reserve* Nairobi: Wildlife Service

Pfeiffer, J.E. 1982 *The Creative Explosion* New York: Harper & Son

Phillips, E. 1980 'The Price of Development' *Society of Malawi Journal* 33/-l; 19-25

Phillipson, D.W. 1976 The Prehistory of Eastern Zambia, Nairobi: *British Institute of East African Memoir* No. 6

Phiri, D.D. 1982 *From Nguni to Ngoni* Umbe: Popular Publications

Phiri, K.M. 1973 'Early "Malawi" Kinship and Dynamics of Pre-colonial Chewa Society' *Journal of Social Studies* (Zomba) 2; 21-30

Phiri, K.M. 1975 'Chewa History in Central Malawi and the Use of Oral Tradition 1600-1920' PhD Thesis, Madison: University Wisconsin

Phiri, K.M. 1976 'Pre-colonial Economic Exchange in Central Malawi' *Journal of Social Studies* (Zomba) 5; 15-27

Phiri, K.M. 1979 'Northern Zambezia 1500-1800' *Society of Malawi Journal* 32/1; 6-22

Phiri, K.M. 1982 'Traditions of Power and Politics in Early Malawi Kasungu District 1750-1933' *Soc. Mal. J.* 35/2; 24-40

Phiri, K.M. 1984 'Political Change among the Chewa and Yao of Lake Malawi Region 1750-1900 in A.I. Salim (ed) *State Formation in Eastern Africa* pp 53-69 Nairobi: Heinemann

Phiri, K.M. 1988 'Pre-colonial States of Central Malawi' *Society of Malawi Journal* 41/1; 1-29

Phiri, K.M. et al 1977 *Amachinga Yao Traditions II* Chancellor College, University Malawi: Dept History

Pike, J.G. and G.T. Rimmington 1965 *Malawi - a Geographical Study* Oxford University Press

Pollock, N. 1969 *Struggle against Sleeping Sickness in Nyasaland and Northern Rhodesia 1900-1922* Centre International Studies, Ohio University

Potous, P.L. 1956 *No Tears for the Crocodile* London: Hutchnson

Price, T 1952 'More about the Maravi' *African Studies* 11; 75-79

Rangeley, W.H.J. 1954 'Bocarro's Journey' *Nyasaland Journal* 7/2; 15-23

Rangeley, W.H.J. 1959 'The Makololo of Dr Livingstone' *Nyasaland Journal* 12/1; 59-98

Rangeley, W.H.J. 1963 'The Earliest Inhabitants of Nyasaland' *Nyasaland Journal* 16/2; 35-42

Rangeley, W.H.J. 1966 'The Angoni' *Society of Malawi Journal* 19/2; 62-86

Rangeley, W.H.J. nd Papers and Correspondence, Limbe: Society of Malawi Library

Ransford, O. 1966 *Livingstone's Lake* London: Murray

195

Rashid, P.R. 1978 'Originally Lomwe, Culturally Maravi, and Linguistically Yao: the Rise of the Mbewe c 1760-1840', Chancellor College, University Malawi: history seminar paper

Read, M. 1956 *The Ngoni of Nyasaland* Oxford University Press

Rendall, P. 1898 'Field Notes on the Antelopes of Nyasaland' *Novitates Zoologicae* 5; 207-215

Riddell, J. 1956 *African Wonderland* London: Hale

Ridding, C. 1975 Report on Mwabvi Game Reserve, MSS unpublished, Kasungu: WRU

Roberts, A.D. 1970 Pre-colonial Trade in Zambia *Afr. Soc. Research* 10; 715-46

Robinson, K.R. 1982 *Ironage in Northern Malawi* Lilongwe: Department of Antiquities Publication No. 20

Rogers, P.M. and H.S. Jamusana 1989 *Wildlife Pest Impacts and Wildlife Management in Malawi* Lilongwe FAO/DNPW Field Document No. 2

Rood, J.P. 1975 Population Dynamics and Food Habits of the Banded Mongoose *East African Wildlife Journal* 13; 89-111

Sandelowsky, B.H. and K.R. Robinson 1968 'Fingira: a Preliminary Report', Zomba: Department of Antiquities Publication No.3

Sanderson, G.M. 1954 *A Dictionary of the Yao Language* Zomba: Government Printers

Schoffeleers, J.M. 1968 'Symbolic and Social Aspects of Spirit Worship among the Mang'anja', PhD Thesis Oxford University

Schoffeleers, J.M. 1971 'The Religious Significance of Bush Fires in Malawi' *Cashiers des Religions Africaines* 10; 271-287

Schoffeleers, J.M. 1972 The Meaning and Use of the Name Malawi in Oral Traditions and Pre-colonial Documents in B. Pachai (ed) *The Early History of Malawi*, London: Longman; 91-103

Schoffeleers, J.M. 1980 Trade, Warfare and Social Inequality in the Lower Shire Valley 1590-1622 *Soc. Mal. J.* 33/2; 6-24

Schoffeleers, J.M. 1987 The Zimba and the Lundu State in the Late 16th and Early 17th Century *Journal of African History* 28; 337-355

Schoffeleers, J.M. 1992 *River of Blood* Madison: University Wisconsin Press

Schwarz, A. 1982 'Obituary: George Dudley Hayes (1904-1981)' *Society of Malawi Journal* 35/1; 6-7

Scott, D.C. 1929 *Dictionary of the Nyanja Language* London: Lutterworth

Selous, F.C. 1881 *A Hunter's Wanderings in Africa* London: Macmillan

Selous, F.C. 1908 *African Nature Notes and Reminiscences* London: Macmillan

Shaxson, T.F. 1977 A Map of the Distribution of Major Biotic Communities in Malawi *Society of Malawi Journal* 30/1; 36-48

Shepperson, G. 1966 'The Jumbe of Kota Kota and Some Aspects of Islam in British Central Africa' in I.M. Lewis (ed) *Islam in Tropical Africa*, London: Hutchinson; 253-65

Sherry, B. 1989 Some Aspects of the Ecology of the Elephants of the Middle Shire Valley, Msc Thesis: University Malawi

Sherry, B and A.J. Ridgeway 1984 *A Field Guide to Lengwe National Park* Blantyre: NFPS

Sidney, J. 1965 'The Past and Present Distribution of some African Ungulates' *Transaction of Zoological Society of London* 30; 5-397

Simons, H. 1989 Wildlife Inventory, Lilongwe: FAO/DNPW Field Document No. 9

Simons, H. 1990 'Liwonde National Park: a Pilot Area for Wildlife Management in Malawi', Kasungu: DNPW, WRU

Simons, H. and P. Chirambo 1991 'Wildlife Pest Impact around Liwonde National Park', Liwonde: FAO/ DNPW Field Document No. 11

Smithers, R.H.N. 1966 *The Mammals of Rhodesia Zambia and Malawi* London: Collins

Stannus, H.S. 1922 'The Wayao of Nyasaland' *Harvard African Studies* 3; 229-372

Steinhart, E.I. 1989 'Hunters, Poachers and Gamekeepers: Towards a Social History of Hunting in Colonial Kenya' *Journal of African History* 30; 247-64

Stevenson-Hanülton, J. 1947 *Wild Life in South Africa* London: Cassell

Swann, A.J. 1969 *Fighting the Slave Hunters in Central Africa* (Orig 1910) London: Cassell

Sweeney, R.C.H. 1959 *A Check List of the Mammals of Nyasaland* Blantyre: Nyasaland Society

Sweeney, R.C.H. 1970 *Animal Life in Malawi* 2 vols Belgrade: Yugoslavia

Tembo. M.I. 1980 A Sociological Study of the Mbenje Area in Relation to Mwabvi Game Reserve, Kasungu: WRU 50/7/0

Tew (Douglas), M. 1950 *Peoples of the Lake Nyasa Region* Oxford University Press

Theal, G.M. 1899d) *Records of South-Eastern Africa* 9 vols, Cape Town: Government Press

Thomas, O. 1892-1898 'On Mammals from Nyasaland' *Proceedings Zoological Society* London

Thomson, R. 1986 *On Wildlife 'Conservation'* Cape Town: United Publishing Institute

Thorold, A. 1995 Yao Musmims PhD Thesis, University of Cambridge

Timberlake, L. 1985 *Africa in Crisis* London: Earthscan

Tobias, P.U. 1972 'The men who came before Malawian history' in Pachai (ed) *The Early History of Malawi*, London: Longman; 1-16

Turner, W.Y. 1952 *Tumbuka-Tonga-English Dictionary* Blantyre: Hetherwick Press

Vail, H.L. 1972 'Religion, Language and the Tribal Myth: the Tumbuka and Chewa of Malawi' in M. Schoffeleers 1979 (ed) *Guardians of the Land* Gwelo: Mambo Press, 209-233

Vail, H.L. 1977 Ecology and History: the Case of Eastern Zambia *Journal of Southern African Studies* 3/2; 129-156

Vail, H.L. 1983 'The Political Economy of East-Central Africa' in D. Birmingham and P.M. Martin (Eds) *History of Central Africa*, vol II, London: Longman; 200-250

Van Breugel, J. 1976 'Some Traditional Chewa Religious Beliefs and Practices', unpublished thesis, Lilongwe: White Fathers

Van der Merwe, N.J and D.H. Avery 1987 'Science and Magic in African Technology Traditional Iron Smelting in Malawi' *Africa* 57; 143-172

Van der Post, L. 1952 *Venture to the Interior* London: Hogarth

Van Onselen C. 1972 Reactions to Rinderpest in Southern Africa 1896-97 *Journal of African History* 13; 473-88

Van Strien, N.J. 1989 'Notable Vertebrates of Mulanje Mt.' *Nyala* 14/2; 75-80

Vansina, J. 1985 *Oral Tradition as History*, London: J. Currey

Vaughan, M. 1978 Uncontrolled Animals and Aliens: Colonial Conservation Mania in Malawi, Chancellor College, University Malawi: history seminar paper

Walker, C. 1981 *Signs of the Wild*, Cape Town: C. Struik

Westrop, A. 1968 *Green Gold*, Bulawayo: Cauldwell

Wiese, C. 1983 *Expedition to East Central Africa 1888-91* (ed) H.W. Langworthy, London: Collings

Willan, R.G.M.1961 'Ufiti - Nyasaland's Mystery Animal - is an Ordinary Chimp' *Wildlife (Nairobi)* 3; 21-24

Wood, R.C. 1922 Notes in Kershaw (1922)

Wood, R.C. 1932 'Nyasaland, Nyala-Hunting' in H.C. Maydon et al (ed) *Big Game Shooting in Africa* London: Seeley

Wye College 1972 Report on Nyika, University London: Wye College

Young, T.C. 1932 *Notes on the History of the Tumbuka-Kamanga Peoples of Nyasaland* London: Religious Tract Society

Zambezi Mission 1972 *The Students English/Chichewa Dictionary* Blantyre: Claim

Note:

DNPW: Department of National Parks and Wildlife
FAO: Food and Agricultural Organisation
WRU: Wildlife Research Unit

Archives

1. Wildlife Research Unit (WRU), Kasungu\National Park, Department of National Parks anzd Wildlife (DNPW)
2. Society of Malawi Library, Limbe
3. Wildlife Society of Malawi Archives, Centre for Environmental Education, Lilongwe
4. Nationa Archives of Malawl (MNA), Zomba

www.ingramcontent.com/pod-product-compliance
Lightning Source LLC
Chambersburg PA
CBHW021904020426
42334CB00013B/473